CW01456704

DRINKING THE WORLD

Pavilion
An imprint of HarperCollins*Publishers* Ltd
1 London Bridge Street
London
SE1 9GF

www.harpercollins.co.uk

HarperCollins*Publishers*
Macken House
39/40 Mayor Street Upper
Dublin 1
D01 C9W8
Ireland

10 9 8 7 6 5 4 3 2 1

First published in Great Britain by Pavilion
An imprint of HarperCollins*Publishers* 2025

Copyright © Pavilion 2025
Text © Bert Blaize and Victoria Brzezinski 2025

Bert Blaize and Victoria Brzezinski assert the
moral right to be identified as the authors of this
work. A catalogue record of this book is available
from the British Library.

ISBN 978-0-00-862626-6

Publishing Director: Laura Russell
Commissioning Editor: Lucy Smith
Copyeditors: Clare Double and Lisa Pendreigh
Editorial Assistants: Shamar Gunning and
    Daisy Gudmunsen
Design Manager: Alice Kennedy-Owen
Layout Designer: maru studio G.K.
Cover Design: Luke Bird
Illustrator: Sophie Winder
Production Controller: Grace O'Byrne
Proofreader: Corinne Colvin
Indexer: Ruth Ellis

Printed and bound by Papercraft in Malaysia

All rights reserved. No part of this publication
may be reproduced, stored in a retrieval
system or transmitted, in any form or by any
means, electronic, mechanical, photocopying,
recording or otherwise, without the prior written
permission of the publishers.

Without limiting the author's and publisher's
exclusive rights, any unauthorized use of this
publication to train generative artificial intelligence
(AI) technologies is expressly prohibited.
HarperCollins also exercise their rights under
Article 4(3) of the Digital Single Market Directive
2019/790 and expressly reserve this publication
from the text and data mining exception.

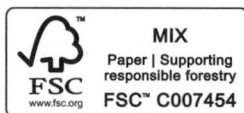

MIX
Paper | Supporting
responsible forestry
FSC
www.fsc.org
FSC™ C007454

For more information visit: www.harpercollins.
co.uk/green

DRINKING THE WORLD

A WINE ODYSSEY

VICTORIA BRZEZINSKI BERT BLAIZE

PAVILION

Wine is a volatile business. Big risk. Uncertainty. Experimentation, blind alchemy and good fortune are required. So many variables impact the final product, and ultimately, the winemakers' fate is in Mother Nature's hands.

Hail, frost or pests can have a devastating effect, meaning in blockbuster wine regions like Burgundy, Champagne and Piedmont, millions of euros worth of wine can be lost in a single storm.

It takes a special kind of person to live by the rhythm of the vines, the cellar and the seasons, dealing with day-to-day unpredictability– and there are no shortcuts to making good wine.

Where there's good wine, there's almost always great food, beautiful landscapes, a rich history and fascinating characters who can speak to our complex and evolving relationship with our planet – because few people have a closer relationship with the earth than those who make wine from it.

The winemakers we spoke to for this book are among the most interesting individuals we've ever encountered. The thing that really resonates with us about the producers we've selected is the pure craft that they pour into each bottle. Innumerable people come together to create something that is a true expression of the terroir. We can't help but compare them to rockstars.

We remain in awe of everything they do; even more so having spent this time with them, and that's something we've tried to capture in this book.

Some of the winemakers are old friends. Others came recommended via other producers, like Jan Klein from Staffelter Hof in Germany, who suggested we should meet his Portuguese pal Pedro, founder of Vale da Capucha. There are so many stories we wanted to – but couldn't – include. Vitalii Shmulevych from Bolgrad Wines in Ukraine told us of a vigneron neighbour with cameras in the vineyard. He spotted a group of Russian soldiers among his vines and gave the coordinates to the government to destroy his livelihood with an air strike.

All the best sommeliers are storytellers. Rather than just presenting the bottle and naming the grapes ensconced inside, a proper somm should inspire you to get lost in a bottle via the winemaker's story. For drinkers out for dinner, this tale is not just the gateway to a new taste but instant transportation to the producer's ethos and culture.

This is not a comprehensive guide to drinking the world. Do not expect a snooty and inaccessible encyclopaedia of winemaking. Rather, we have put together a motley collection of tales and tips from producers we love across 20 countries, woven together with experiences amassed during our travels; the people we met and our evenings on restaurant floors recommending bottles of wine.

Above all, we want this book to be a celebration of the winemakers around the globe that we should be talking about now.

We skipped the hallowed French region of Bordeaux; instead choosing to interview winemakers going against the grain in the less-travelled likes of Wales, Belgium and Armenia. In Burgundy, with its epic wines written about ad infinitum, we spoke only to a single winemaker, an outsider who's come to call the region home, for his fresh perspective on this vaunted spot.

This book is best enjoyed with a delicious glass of wine in hand. We hope these stories and our travels will encourage you to source a bottle of wine from one of these incredible winemakers while learning about their story, or even better – seek out these countries and regions in person for full-on immersion.

There's a lack of diversity in the wine industry and these are the producers doing things differently that need shouting about. If you're inspired to get into wine, it doesn't matter if you're based in the middle of nowhere or a metropolis – there are winemaking opportunities nearer than you think.

IT TAKES A
SPECIAL KIND
OF PERSON
TO LIVE BY
THE RHYTHM
OF THE
VINES

ABOUT THE AUTHORS

Bert and Victoria met through their love of wine, food and travel.

Sommelier BERT BLAIZE used to be based in London, UK, one of the wine-tasting capitals of the world. After working in some of the best restaurants in the city, Bert co-wrote his first book *Which Wine When* – what to drink with the food you love. He now lives in Norfolk, where he runs North Norfolk Cellars, an independent wine merchants. His favourite wine destination is Northern Italy.

VICTORIA BRZEZINSKI first met Bert while he was the head sommelier at the Clove Club. The wine pairing was brilliant – at least the first few glasses from what she can remember. A multi-award winning feature writer, columnist and restaurant critic, she has written for *The Times* and *The Sunday Times* since 2018 on myriad topics from design to food and farming. Victoria started out in hospitality, working for some of London's liveliest restaurants, and wine tastings were always the best part of the job. Her favourite wine destination is Georgia.

ARMENIA

As far as wine origin stories go, the Armenians have a pretty legendary claim to fame. Fittingly, we're kicking off with a tale from Genesis – the opening book in the Old Testament – which follows the great flood and recounts Noah crashing his biblical ark into Ararat, the dormant volcano dominating much of Armenia's skyline. After disembarking said shipwreck on the mountainside, Noah whipped out some vines and planted them, thus becoming the world's first vigneron.

We're calling Armenia the newest old winemaking country. Neighbouring Georgia currently holds the record for the most ancient bit of winemaking kit – an 8,000-year-old terracotta amphora which once held wine – but Armenia, meanwhile, possesses the world's oldest winery – a 6,100-year-old setup discovered in the mountainous Vayots Dzor. Who knows what further archaeological treasures still lie buried? What's more certain is that the South Caucasus – a transcontinental chunk flanked by the Black and Caspian Seas comprising modern-day Armenia, Azerbaijan, Georgia and a bit of Southern Russia – is rightly called the cradle of wine; where the modern-day *Vitis vinifera* wine grapes were first domesticated. There's ongoing research to figure out the number of Armenian indigenous varieties; some estimate it hovers around the 400 mark.

Today, Armenia is nestled between Georgia to its north and Iran to its south, while borders with Turkey and Azerbaijan remain closed, and over the past 200 years swathes of land have been annexed. This includes Mount Ararat, a holy mountain for Christians and Muslims alike, which has long been a potent symbol for Armenians but now lies in eastern Turkey since the Soviets rejigged the borders.

This landlocked country (smaller than Belgium) has a multi-layered story of triumph and tumult – one reason its ancient winemaking culture has only just in the past decade or so begun its revival and renaissance. It lies on the Silk Road, a network of trading routes that connected the Far East to the western world for more than 1,500 years, and over the centuries Arabs, Greeks, Mongols, Persians and Romans have all left their mark.

11

ARAGATSOTN

YEREVAN

ARMAVIR

ARARAT

TAVUSH

VAYOTS
DZOR

ZORAH

Ottoman occupation turned to oppression, then a genocide in 1915: as many as
1.5 million Armenians were left dead and many more fled. For a country of fewer
than 2.8 million people it numbers one of the largest and oldest diasporas,
estimated to be between 5 and 9 million dotted across the globe – counting
everyone from Cher to Kim Kardashian and Andre Agassi. Now, increasing
numbers of 'repats' are returning to their homeland. During the era of Soviet rule,
between 1922 and 1991, it was decided that Armenia would produce brandy via
collectivized farms (apparently Winston Churchill was a fan), while neighbouring
Georgia would be responsible for wine. Gorbachev's Soviet sobriety programme
in the 1980s saw countless more vines grubbed up, a further hammer blow.

Armenian cuisine reflects its rich and multifaceted past. Lavash – papery bread
made in clay ovens called *tonirs* – is a national obsession and served on every
table. Expect endless rounds of plates piled high with splendid cheeses such
brined *lori* and stringy *chechil*, and charcuterie (*basterma* is air-cured spiced
beef). Handfuls of wild greens make up the backbone of many of the dishes
– seek out *jingalov hats*, a type of flatbread stuffed with finely chopped native
herbs, originally from the Republic of Artsakh, part of the Nagorno-Karabakh
region. You will encounter borscht – a Soviet hangover – while the food of
Western Armenia sees the influence of Lebanon, Greece and Turkey, with
dishes like *manti* (teeny lamb-stuffed dumplings), *dolma* (stuffed vine leaves)
and *kharpert kufta*, a bulgur meatball dish. *Khorovats* is Armenia's answer to
barbecue: fire-licked chunks of pork or lamb. And the country's seasonal fruits
are fat and fragrant: cherries, green plums, white mulberries and the country's
national symbol, apricots (*Prunus armeniaca*). Wood from apricot trees is used
to make the *duduk*, an Armenian oboe with a haunting timbre.

Its ancient capital, Yerevan, is actually a few decades older than Rome but
with all the modern construction here, you wouldn't necessarily arrive at that
conclusion. The 'pink city' is built from coral-hued volcanic stone, with wide
and walkable tree-lined boulevards and striking Soviet-era Brutalist architecture.
Coffee culture is big in Armenia – the elaborate painted walls and inlaid
ceiling make Lumen 1936, housed in an old tobacconist, perhaps Yerevan's
most gorgeous café. After touring the usual sites (including the rose-flanked
Republic Square and the History Museum of Armenia, housing a 5,500-year-
old leather shoe unearthed in Vayots Dzor) take a stroll down to vibey Saryan
Street, nicknamed Wine Street as it's a hotbed of hip wine bars – the first, In
Vino, opened at the end of 2012. At the end of the road is Kond, Yerevan's oldest
neighbourhood, which makes quite the foil to the rest of the cosmopolitan city
with its ramshackle buildings, labyrinthine streets and bright murals.

The country's landscape is mostly mountainous; a jumble of semidesert, grassy plains, forest, alpine meadow and high-elevation tundra, and full of wonders – manmade and natural. Enjoy the crisp mountain air and cool waters of Lake Sevan, an enormous high-altitude body of water in the east, while dippable hot mineral springs spew from the earth at the likes of Jermuk or Hankavan. There's the Ancient Roman temple of Garni, and Etchmiadzin, the world's oldest cathedral (the Armenians were the OG converts to Christianity) built about 300 CE.

About 90 per cent of Armenian wine comes from four regions.

In the northwest, the vineyards of **Aragatsotn,** meaning 'foot of Aragats', sit at the base of a hulking snow-tipped mountain massif reaching 4,090m (vineyards are planted at altitudes of 1,100-1,400m/ 3,600–4,590 feet above sea level). The province is home to family-run producers such as Van Ardi; good Voskehat – a golden grape nicknamed the 'Queen of Armenian Grapes' – grows here. To its south lies **Armavir**, a large region focused mostly on white grapes and the distillation of brandy (900–1,100m/2,950–3,600 feet) which, along with the sunny plateau of **Ararat,** makes up the Ararat Valley (with vineyards at 800–1,000m/2,600–3,280 feet) near Yerevan. Here, the volcanic soils are stony, black and red. The old red Khaket grape is popular here. The most prestigious region is **Vayots Dzor**, in southeastern Armenia, which lies about a two-hour drive from Yerevan. In springtime, the mountains are blanketed with an explosion of wildflowers and herbs and the countryside is dotted with blossoming fruit and nut trees. Vines grow at the same altitude as on Ararat. By comparison, vines in the Boca region of Piedmont, Italy, sit at the foothills of the Alps between 450–500m (1,480–1,640 feet). Our favourite winery in Vayots Dzor is Zorah (see pages 14–21) which, for the moment, is not yet open for tastings.

Look out for Areni Noir, a red grape with a perfumed nose and plenty of character. Some of the best examples are compared to Pinot Noir and Nebbiolo. When Bert hosted a blind tasting in 2023 he served lesser-known grapes from a range of countries and regions. The 2017 Zorah, 'Karasì' Areni Noir made in Vayots Dzor, was by far the star of the show, with a completely unique profile that many fellow sommeliers had never tasted. Think warming aromatic spice with tart but ripe blackberries; firm tannins broken up by a long mineral finish. Crazy delicious.

Zorik Gharibian
Zorah Wines

'I'm a very proud Armenian guy,' says Zorik Gharibian, a diasporan born in Iran who grew up in Milan, Italy. He was 33 when he first returned to his ancestral home in 1998 after his family had fled the Turkish genocide of 1915. 'It was love at first sight. Back then I was in fashion; wine was just my passion. The situation in Armenia was very troubled and I started to think of doing something to help my motherland.'

Zorik and his wife, Yeraz, had been dreaming of owning a winery and vineyards, but instead of making yet another Chianti in Tuscany, decided to build something from scratch out of the ashes of post-Soviet Armenia. The plan? 'To make a contemporary wine with local grapes and traditional ageing methods that would reflect my roots,' Zorik says. People scoffed at his idea and routinely denounced it. 'At that time, nobody was thinking about making a wine that could stand shoulder to shoulder with international wine.'

Years of Soviet rule had changed the habits of the locals, erasing thousands of years of wine-drinking past. Armenia had become a nation of vodka and cognac lovers. But every architectural site you visit in the country will be adorned with grapevine motifs – old churches, monasteries and so on. 'All our folkloric songs are about wine, getting drunk, having fun dancing, but I couldn't see the reflection of these signs in the population,' says Zorik.

Things kicked off around the millennium. After much questing, Zorik eventually decided to plant on a sloping plateau 1,400m (4,593 feet) above sea level near the village of Rind, on virgin land in the south of the mountainous Vayots Dzor province. The winery was christened Zorah, a nod to Zorik's nickname, but he insists that wasn't his idea. 'My mother has always called me Zorah; my wife decided on the name of the winery and the labels. I am an egocentric guy, but not that much,' he jokes, quick to laugh. Perhaps you have to be, given Armenia's history of repeated occupation and geopolitical conflict.

A little later he bought a boulder-strewn 'vineyard' further up the mountain – well, more of a forgotten jumble of gnarled vines growing over the rocks – furnishing a pair of locals in a clapped-out Lada with envelopes stuffed with cash to do the deal for him, a 'foreigner' in their eyes. The vines are at least a hundred years old (no one knows for sure) and at 1,600m (5,249 feet), the plot is so high that you may struggle to catch your breath in the thinning air. He named it after his wife, Yeraz, which means 'dream' in Armenian. Zorik produces his top wine from these centenarian grapes – a field blend that was the first Armenian wine Bert ever tried in early 2023. He had no idea what to expect but the 2015 'Yeraz' was vibrant and generous on the nose, jumping out of the glass like fine Italian wine such as Barbaresco. The complex palate was all velvety tannins and a long finish developing into something savoury and herbal. It's very hard (and unfair) to compare it to anything else. You'll have to try it yourself.

This is a land of deep gorges and spectacular cliffs at the foothills of the beautiful Mount Ararat on the old Silk Road. It's like something out of an Indiana Jones movie and what's even more impressive is that from the Yeraz vineyard, you can see a gaping opening cut into a karst cliffside. This is the Areni-1 cave complex, a 6,100-year-old winery – thought to be the world's oldest – which was discovered in 2007. Excavations yielded a wine press for stomping grapes, fermentation and storage vessels, drinking cups and withered grape vines, skins and seeds.

Vayots Dzor's remoteness and elevation spared this dramatic highland from the same brandy-producing Soviet fate as much of Armenia. It's also mercifully free of phylloxera, the invasive aphid-like pest from North America that destroyed most European vineyards in the nineteenth century. 'Here we have a terroir that has never seen grafting of its native grape varieties,' Zorik says. However, that also meant there was no precedent; no nurseries to ring up for some vine cuttings; no one he could get advice from. Working with Stefano Bartolomei, a consultant agronomist, he spent a decade isolating and developing his initial vineyard, including creating his own selection of Areni, a red grape sourced from old vines from an abandoned monastery. The thick skin gives the wine structure and balance. It's so old that it is called an orphan grape as it has no identified parentage, but is perfectly adapted to the extreme climate of Vayots Dzor. 'I called it Areni Noir to give a name to my selection. It has nothing to do with Pinot Noir,' Zorik says.

In the winery, he ferments most wines in a combination of concrete tanks and clay amphoras or *karasi* ('both porous materials so you have micro-oxygenation, which helps in the development of those complex aromas and flavours'). 'I owe the decision to age my wine in amphoras to my next-door neighbour [at Areni-1]. Amphora for us is not a fashion – it's my culture,' he says. Unlike in Georgia, where wine made in clay vessels, *qvevri*, has enjoyed a renaissance, the Armenian's firing techniques have been forgotten. 'We have lost the craftsmanship of making amphoras,' says Zorik, so instead he digs unwanted ones out of people's basements. Each handmade *karas* is a different volume and thickness, so after fermenting in a *karas*, some wines will spend time in large untoasted wooden casks (*botti*) to standardize.

He buries two-thirds of the vessel underground, a decision he landed on after much experimentation and as a consequence of seeing photos of an archaeological site at Teishebaini, near Yerevan, where hundreds of intact amphoras dating from 700 BCE had been buried in this fashion. 'Back then, my forefathers were using this technique. Almost 500 large amphoras were discovered at this location, meaning Armenia was the centre of a huge winemaking process.' The wine held in the one-third above ground will be a different temperature, which, Zorik explains, 'creates a continuous natural rotation of the liquid during the whole period of ageing, without pumps or technology. I'm promoting this to my other Armenian colleagues – this is the copyright of Armenia.'

The first batch of Zorah's Areni Noir wine, Karasì 2010, was released to the international market in 2012 and soon after scooped a place on Bloomberg's list of top ten wines of the year. Quality is always the focus and Zorik lavishes TLC on each vine. 'I respect every millimetre of my soil,' he says.

You may spot the odd lone shepherd or glimpse a rare bezoar goat in the distance, but Vayots Dzor is the country's least populous region, flanked by Shahumyan, Nagorno-Karabakh to the east, and abutting the border of the Azerbaijan-controlled Nakhchivan exclave to the west (historically a part of Armenia and where Zorik's family originally hail from), and bordering Armenia's southernmost province, Syunik. Conflict remains pervasive. During 2023's harvest, cars heaving with people and their possessions rumbled past Zorah HQ, after Azerbaijan's large-scale military offensive in the disputed region of Nagorno-Karabakh. 'We witnessed ethnic cleansing. The road that connects Nagorno-Karabakh to Yerevan passes very close to our vineyard.' Imagine, a population of 150,000 had just three days to run away.'

Zorah's heritage project aims to revive grapes on the verge of extinction. The first wine, Chilar, is a skin-contact white made in amphoras, with a delicious texture and a citrussy finish. 'It has amazing potential and low yields,' Zorik says. The second heritage is a blend of Arati (a late-ripening white named after Mount Ararat) and Sireni – also called Khndoghni – a deeply coloured red variety indigenous to Artsakh, Nagorno-Karabakh. 'We cannot go back to the vineyards where we were getting Sireni,' Zorik says.

Despite the peaks and troughs of his homeland's tumultuous history, Zorik is relentlessly upbeat: 'Viticulturally talking it is highs and highs, the opportunities we have here.' His son Oshin was two years old in 1998 but is now an intrinsic part of the winery, splitting his time between Armenia and Italy. 'It's a team-working effort,' Oshin says. 'Growing up, my father explained that wine isn't just about drinking something; it is a kind of ambassador through which you discover culture and terroir.' He has since completed WSET exams and a Master's degree in agronomy and oenology at Università Cattolica del Sacro Cuore in Milan. 'There's been a huge rebirth in the understanding of wine in Armenia; there's such a generational difference. If you were born after the collapse of the Soviet Union, you're completely different. Even culturally – you don't drink vodka, you drink wine. Today in Yerevan there are entire streets dedicated to wine bars. It's an incredibly dynamic environment. We have everything: the terroir, the grape varieties and the quality, so it's just a matter of time. I love working here in the vineyards; it feels like the Wild West sometimes, on the frontier of winemaking. You're really pushing the envelope.'

WORD FROM THE WINEMAKER

What's the name of the domaine you make wine at?

Zorah Winery. The project began in 1999/2000 and we produced our first vintage after 10 years of research, in 2010. We have no phylloxera in our region and therefore no nurseries; we had to create our own nurseries and spent 10 years conducting intensive massal selection [propagating by cuttings] to make sure we worked with the best vines from the Areni varietal in order to maintain the vineyard's distinctive traits and its relation with the terroir intact.

What local produce do you enjoy pairing with your wines?

We connect with local farmers and cheese makers who supply us with meats and cheeses, which make for good pairings with our wines. Our region is very rural, and thus everything is done on a very local scale.

Do you have any insider tips on what to see in your region?

Noravank Monastery, a thirteenth-century monastery in Vayots Dzor. Areni-1 cave, a 6,000-year-old archaeological site, where the world's oldest winemaking facility was discovered in 2007.

Which foods remind you of home?

Dolma, different meats rolled in grape leaves or stuffed in local vegetables. A classic.

Your favourite restaurants in the region?

Our region is very rural and still under development; it is just opening up to tourism and the outside world. There are a lot of roadside local restaurants and bed and breakfasts. I suggest Gohar's Guest House, a small family-owned business where locally grown produce is used to cook traditional meals by the wonderful Madame Gohar.

What do you hope for the future of the Armenian wine industry?

After the collapse of the Soviet Union, Armenia lived through a period of rediscovering its ancient, but lost, winemaking traditions. The USSR had designated Armenia as a brandy-producing region and thus it became almost impossible to reliably produce wines in Armenia. Prior to the Soviet takeover, the genocide of 1915 had depopulated historical Armenian lands, leaving nobody to farm vineyards and produce wines. Due to the Soviet legacy and the genocide, Armenian winemaking had been largely put on hold. Wine-producing regions which once had vibrant Armenian communities were lost during the genocide, and during the early Soviet period family plots were nationalized. Moreover, the art of making amphoras (the traditional wine-ageing vessel in Armenia) was neglected. As amphora makers would often sell their amphoras to wineries, this was considered business by the Soviets and outlawed. Our hope at Zorah is that Armenia can rediscover the incredible diversity that exists in the country's grape varieties, and slowly rebuild the knowledge and craftsmanship to build large 2,000-litre (528-gallon) amphoras. A further hope is that a new, young generation of Armenian winemakers, who can now travel the world and study abroad, will come back, set roots in their homeland and propel Armenia into a new chapter in its winemaking history. In so doing, they will give a distinct character to the Armenian wine-producing landscape.

Name three of your favourite restaurants in Yerevan.

Wine Republic, Dolmama and Vostan. Wine Republic has a great atmosphere and is a good hangout to try all sorts of wines from Armenia and beyond (even though the cuisine is not Armenian). Dolmama was the first to give a modern twist to traditional Armenian cuisine and introduce an all-Armenian wine list. Vostan offers traditional Armenian food in a beautiful setting.

Name five of your favourite wine bars in Yerevan.

On Saryan Street in central Yerevan you can find an entire street dedicated to wine bars: a testament to the rebirth of wine in Armenia. The street is also home to the annual Armenian wine festival.

What is the best thing about making wine in Armenia?

The wine world is divided between the New and Old World wines, but when working in Armenia one gets the impression that here we are introducing a whole new category: wines from the ancient world. Working in the Armenian wine industry is all about rediscovering something ancient but giving it a modern twist. Witnessing entire communities now start to see winemaking as a sector with great potential for economic development also gives us an incredible sense of satisfaction.

What are your favourite facts about Armenia?

Armenia was the first nation to adopt Christianity as its state religion, which is also an important event in relation to wine, as it reinforced the role of wine in society for ceremonial and cultural reasons. There are about 10 million Armenians – 3 million in Armenia and 7 million in diaspora communities around the world – creating incredible diversity in what it means to be Armenian.

AUSTRALIA

Beyond the sharks circling its shores, Australia is a country of great whites. You can expect excellent Rieslings and Chardonnays, but it is Semillon, a Bordeaux grape, that is the country's gift to wine drinkers. Australia makes the world's best examples of single-variety Semillon; it's not blended, as in France, and it is treated with the respect it deserves. Red-wise, Oz is synonymous with Shiraz (an inky, dark-fruited grape known as Syrah elsewhere), and there's much more beyond the jammy, powerfully oaked supermarket versions with kangaroos or emus on the label. Cabernet Sauvignon and Merlot are Australia's second and third most planted reds respectively.

Calling Australia a 'New World' region is jarring: some of its living vines are 180 years old. The country includes 65 wine regions producing more than a billion litres each year, and it can be hard to get your head around the scale of things until you visit. For the most part Aussie wines are accessible, and creative winemakers take an unfettered approach. The friendly winery vibe has much in common with South Africa, where cellar doors are a respected part of the business (in France, many winemakers see them as a distraction).

Flick through any 'best of' wine list in the Australian section and the lion's share of listings will likely come from two of its six states: South Australia and Victoria. We like to look beyond the obvious spots, so we haven't included either of the big dogs in this book, but here's a rundown of these territories.

Before we crack on, we have to talk about screw caps, the arch-nemesis of any aspiring wine snob, but widely embraced by Aussie producers. Screw caps, or 'Stelvins' as they're referred to in the industry, are the perfect closure. Sure, they lack the romance of popping a bottle (or smashing it against a tree with a shoe) but they're easy to open, carry no risk of cork taint and are much cheaper than a quality cork so, in theory, more of your money goes towards the juice. So why aren't these used throughout the wine world? There's a misconception that the wine doesn't age well with a screw cap, but after trying hundreds of brilliant wines under Stelvin, we can confirm they age gracefully without any worry that the cork is going to damage your bottle. Long live the Stelvin. Don't be put off spending money on a screw-top bottle.

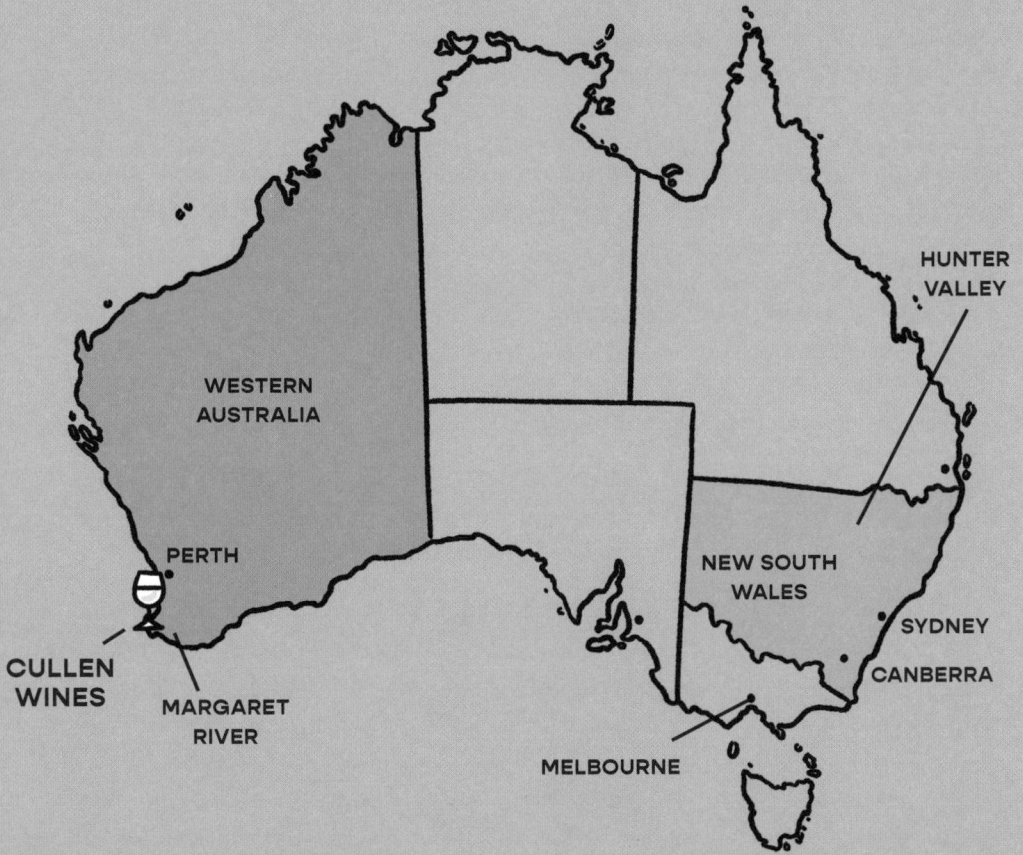

WESTERN
AUSTRALIA

PERTH

CULLEN
WINES

MARGARET
RIVER

HUNTER
VALLEY

NEW SOUTH
WALES

SYDNEY

CANBERRA

MELBOURNE

SOUTH AUSTRALIA

The south and central parts of Australia, with Adelaide as its capital, churn out almost half of the country's wines. For context, it's about four times the size of the United Kingdom, and economies of scale really kick in: compared with, say, a typically sized European winery, a winery in South Australia would tend to cover a much greater number of hectares. There's good diversity here, from the bold reds of the McLaren Vale to cool-climate pockets for Riesling in the Eden Valley.

Favourite South Australia regions and producers
Barossa:
Torbreck, Penfolds, Yalumba, Cirillo, John Duval, Powell and Son
McLaren Vale:
d'Arenberg, Clarendon Hills, Thistledown, S.C. Pannell
Clare Valley:
Grosset, Mount Horrocks, Jim Barry, Wendouree, Koerner
Adelaide Hills:
Ochota Barrels, Shaw + Smith
Eden Valley:
Henschke, Dandelion Vineyards

VICTORIA

This south-eastern chunk of Australia, nestled below New South Wales (NSW), capital Melbourne, is home to more regions, climates and innovative wineries than any other state in Australia. It's all about elite Chardonnay and Pinot Noir here (and a cracking food scene – Attica by Ben Shewry is a fave restaurant).

Favourite Victoria regions and producers
Geelong:
Bannockburn, By Farr Gippsland, William Downie, Patrick Sullivan
Mornington Peninsula:
Yabby Lake, Jane Eyre
Yarra Valley:
Bobar, Luke Lambert, Timo Mayer, Giant Steps, Jamsheed

TASMANIA

The 'Apple Isle' has a cool maritime climate, meaning long, slow ripening and some big-hitting cool-climate Pinot Noir and Chardonnay. Look out for lean, mineral-rich Rieslings too. Top Tassie producers include Tolpuddle, Chatto, Dr. Edge and Pooley. The island is also home to some top-notch whisky distilleries like Sullivans Cove, which nabbed an award for best single malt in the world in 2019.

NEW SOUTH WALES

NSW is super-diverse, with 16 different wine regions making up a melting pot of climates and terroirs. Flat, hot and dry **Riverina** and **Murray Darling** produce a lot of NSW's supermarket plonk, but there are pockets of quality such as De Bortoli's sweet wines, which you'll spot on the lists of top restaurants like the Ledbury or Chez Bruce.

If NSW is the birthplace of Australian wine, then the **Hunter** is the birthplace of NSW. Wide-scale winemaking dates back to the early nineteenth century, the genesis of vine cultivation in Oz.

The Hunter's most important grapes are Semillon and Shiraz, both of which make fine wines that are unique to the region. Attitudes can be traditional in some estates (let's compare the vibe to Bordeaux), but a new wave of winemakers like Usher Tinkler, Angus Vinden and Andrew Thomas are bringing spice and dynamism to the wines – sometimes to the disdain of the old guard.

After landing in Sydney, we suggest kicking off a NSW wine journey in **Orange**, the region three and a half hours' drive west that takes its name from the largest town. Commercial winemaking only found its feet here in the 1980s. Producers tend to be on the boutique side, and the food scene, replete with farm-to-table, artisanal restaurants, is much the same. Orange's relatively cool, sun-soaked hillside wineries (600–1,000m/2,000–3,280 feet) are the country's highest, clambering up the slopes of the extinct volcano Mount Canobolas. Less than 1 per cent of vineyards in Australia sit above 600m (2,000 feet), so this altitude gives serious freshness to the wine. Pinot Noirs, Rieslings and Chardonnays from Orange are the bomb. The crème de la crème producers include Philip Shaw Wines, Mayfield, Ross Hill and Printhie. Gilbert makes our favourite fizz in Oz – the Gilbert Méthode Traditionelle, a zero-dosage sparkling which comes alive in the glass. And Jilly Wine Co's Lone Ranger skin-contact Sauvignon Blanc – an orange wine from Orange! – matches like magic with some pizza-flavoured Shapes (Aussie savoury biscuits).

Tim Kirk is the chief winemaker behind the legendary estate Clonakilla, made in the **Canberra** region of NSW. His wines have a cult following, none more so than his Shiraz with a dash of Viognier, which takes its cue from the classic Côte Rôtie blend from Northern Rhône.

THE HUNTER VALLEY

Welcome to wine country! Oz's OG viticultural region is split into three subregions. First we have **Pokolbin**, home to many of the best-known, most established names in Hunter – Tyrrell's, Brokenwood, Mount Pleasant (together this trio is known as the big three) as well as Andrew Thomas Wines, Briar Ridge and Vinden Wines. The **Upper Hunter Valley** is perhaps more famous for its stunning scenery and nature reserves than its wines, but those made by producers such as Hollydene Estate are certainly worth a look. Family-run wineries like Margan have put the drier and less-travelled **Broke Fordwich** subregion in the lower Hunter Valley on the map. Look out for Oli Margan's side project for some of the most exciting wines coming out of Australia right now.

Pokolbin's big three producers set the benchmark for great Hunter wine. We'll kick off at Tyrrell's. The old part of their cellar housing maturing barrels looks like little has changed since it was founded in 1858, complete with its red earth floor. Meanwhile, Mount Pleasant is home to Oz's oldest Pinot Noir vineyard, planted in 1921, and the estate's founder Maurice O'Shea is well known as a standard-setter for elegance and quality in Hunter. At Brokenwood, Bert's guide was the CEO Geoff Krieger, a hilarious music nut, who put a side of lamb on the barbie to accompany a flight of his best wares. This included the ILR reserve Semillon, a wine named after their iconic former head winemaker (Iain Leslie Riggs). Bert used to pair it with langoustines at The Clove Club.

Hunter's two most important grape varieties are Semillon and Shiraz. The subtropical region can be hot, wet and without massive diurnal temperature swings – not the usual recipe for making quality white wines – but cloud cover mitigates the fierce sun. Hunter's single variety Semillons are the best in the world, with lower alcohol and an age-worthiness making them completely unlike any version produced elsewhere. The region's Shiraz also expresses a more delicate, fresh style than is the norm in Australia, with plenty of high-tone, tart red fruit.

WESTERN AUSTRALIA

Calling Western Australia (WA) a wine region is a bit of a misnomer, given that vines only grow in a tiny coastal corner in the southwest. A massive state that covers almost a third of the country, WA represents less than 10 per cent of Oz's grape crush but a much larger proportion of her finest bottles. A significant chunk of Western Australia is uninhabited arid semi-desert, but the serene, ancient region has an abundance of curious natural wonders, from Shark Bay (home to dugongs drifting along the seagrass beds and also the oldest living fossils on earth, stromatolites) to Ningaloo Reef, where you can swim with whale sharks, and the remote Purnululu National Park with its 350-million-year-old, stripey sandstone mountain range, the Bungle Bungles, which was little known to anyone besides indigenous people and local farmers until 1983.

About three-quarters of the state's population live in the sunny state capital, Perth, considered the most isolated big city in the world. Three wine regions lie within an hour's drive of the city: the most northerly (and generally the hottest) **Swan Valley**, a wine region almost as old as the Hunter Valley; the **Perth Hills** to the east of the Swan District; and **Peel**. The following regions follow the coastline in a southeasterly scoop – **Geographe, Blackwood Valley, Manjimup,** (famous for its black truffles blooming during June and July in the jarrah and karri forests) and **Pemberton**. The **Great Southern**, tucked into the bottom of WA, is a vast chunk including some exciting up-and-coming spots like Frankland River (where Rieslings are particularly good). By far the state's most famous wine region, **Margaret River**, abuts Geographe and runs along a 60-mile (97-km) stretch of coast, from Cape Naturaliste in the north to the Cape Leeuwin promontory.

MARGARET RIVER

One of the most geographically isolated wine regions in the world, Margaret River is a gorgeous place producing wines in the upper echelon of Aussie Cabernet Sauvignon and Chardonnay. The eucalyptus-flecked Cabs are beautifully balanced with a floral nose, and often blended with Merlot with great potential for ageing. If you're a Bordeaux lover, then this is the place for you. Grassy SSB blends of Sauvignon Blanc and Semillon are also classics of the region.

Margaret River is a three-hour drive south via the Kwinana Freeway and Forrest Highway from Perth. Expect white sand beaches lapped by azure waters, cliffs and caves ideal for whale and dolphin spotting, as well as forests home to flora and fauna found nowhere else. Vines grow on a medley of gravelly loam layered upon ancient granite and gneiss, cooled by maritime breezes from the Indian and Southern Oceans. Helpfully, these heat-relieving winds are strongest during the summer months (December, January and February), when they are nicknamed the 'Fremantle Doctor'.

A research paper published in the 1960s by Dr John Gladstones catalyzed viticulture in the region. He is widely credited as the first to recognize the potential of the region. In 1999 another of his papers suggested Margaret River could be further divided into six subregions based on distinct climate and soil type: Yallingup, Carbunup, Wilyabrup, Treeton, Wallcliffe and Karridale. We're stopping off at one of our absolute favourite Australian producers, Cullen; other excellent Margaret River producers include Leeuwin Estate, Cloudburst and Vasse Felix.

Vanya Cullen
Cullen Wines

'The Wadandi people say that before white people came the Earth was soft, and there was a connection from the sky. That's what the land feels like now with biodynamics – it's very soft and silky and open and healthy,' says Vanya. Head winemaker at Cullen Wines since 1989, she is describing the indigenous people's 50,000 years of sustainable land care – a 'very sophisticated agricultural life'.

Work in the Cullen vineyard and winery is carried out in accordance with the Wadandi six-season calendar – Birak, Bunuru, Djeran, Makuru, Djilba and Kambarang – which represent the seasonal changes in land and sea, acknowledging what plants and animals are doing. Conserving biodiversity has always been linked to the health of the Wadandi people, both spiritually and physically. 'What is a problem in society is that disconnect from nature. The Wadandi people's values and how they looked after the land are very much where we need to look now,' she says, noting growing interest in traditional indigenous practices such as fire management, which had long maintained Australia's delicate ecosystems.

The Cullens are a special bunch. Vanya is the youngest of six children born to Dr Kevin and Diana – among the first pioneers to plant vines in Margaret River in 1966, on the advice of Dr Gladstones (see page 29). His 1960s research uncovered the potential of the terroir (and its similarity to Bordeaux), at a point when Wilyabrup and its surrounds were a sleepy surfing community on a sparsely populated stretch of coastline. Vanya's late mother, Diana, recalled Dr Gladstones' reaction on seeing their land: 'Oh, you're mad growing cattle and sheep, why don't you grow grapes?'

Her parents set up Cullen Wines in 1971. 'Dad's work [as a paediatrician] paid for all the winery things. Mum used to work on the farm every day. Both of them were very intuitive. Because of the energy of my parents, it was a childhood that was very rich in culture, even though we were isolated. Mum always used to say quality, not quantity. Nothing has really changed in that aspect of it,' says Vanya.

'My parents fought hard and were successful with a group of friends in stopping the mining of bauxite on the Margaret River coastline from Cape to Cape in 1969, which was extraordinary given that Margaret River now is one of the great wine regions and holiday destinations.

A lot of winemakers talk the talk, but Vanya walks the walk. Certified organic since 1998, she steered the winery to biodynamics in 2003, the year Diana died. 'At the time, [the attitude to biodynamics] was very different outside Australia, where they understood the principles of working around the moon, but in Australia and in Margaret River there was a lot of hostility and aggression.'

The Cullen winery has been carbon neutral since 2006 – at times carbon positive – with Vanya overseeing the creation of a biodiversity corridor in the Yarra Yarra. A whole host of awards include the Order of Australia on King Charles III's 2023 Birthday Honours list for her services to viticulture and oenology. Next on her agenda? She's lobbying for official subregional status to give Wilyabrup its own Geographical Indication (GI). 'I love the land. Wilyabrup is home,' she says.

Vanya's top-end wines include a Cabernet Sauvignon 'Diana Madeline', and Chardonnay, 'Kevin John', made in honour of her parents (which will set you back around £100 a bottle) but her quaffable oranges are a nice (and more affordable) introduction to the world of skin-contact wine (£30ish). Her Amber wine is one that Bert will almost always add 'by the glass' when he's putting wine lists together for restaurants. The blend of Semillon and Sauvignon Blanc (same as Bordeaux's whites) spends time in an amphora, lined with beeswax from the farm, and is packed full of dried stone fruits and honeysuckle, an excellent companion to a pork chop, charcuterie or semi-hard goat's cheese.

WORD FROM THE WINEMAKER

Which wineries and locations have you previously made wine at?

Robert Mondavi in Napa Valley in 1985 and Joseph Drouhin in Burgundy in 1987.

Do you have a winery mascot?

A dingo red heeler cross called Solstice.

Which local restaurants represent your region?

Alberta's Kitchen: they work sustainably and source local ingredients. Lamont's: Kate Lamont is a friend and I love what she does refreshing her menu and making it relevant and matching to wine.

Your favourite view from a restaurant/bar locally?

View of the creek and peppermint trees at Blue Manna.

Name your favourite family recipe using local ingredients.

King George whiting with salad and Kevin John Chardonnay.

What foods do you enjoy pairing with wines from your local region?

Crayfish and Chardonnay. Blue Manna crab with Sav Blanc. Venison with Cabernet.

Do you have any other insider tips for the city or region you're based in?

Smith's beach, the most beautiful aqua water and a long beach to walk along. Spectacular views up the coast to Cape Naturaliste. Cowaramup Bay is lovely for swimming, snorkelling or surfing. Several beautiful beaches, one dog-friendly. Lots of fish, and in season you can sit and watch whales go by. A peaceful place for all ages to enjoy.

Your favourite restaurants in Western Australia that list your wine?

Wildflower is elegance, seasonality and class all in one, with excellent cityline views. Lamont's wine bar in Margaret River [there are also outposts in Swan Valley, Perth City and Cottesloe]: their signature dish is tempura whiting, and the wine list is sensational. Balthazar, a more romantic and cosy option, has a great wine list and fresh oysters on the menu.

Are there any artists or genres of music that are on repeat in the winery during harvest?

Mozart's Symphony No. 40. Handel's *Messiah*. Glenn Gould, Bach's Goldberg Variations.

What are your favourite red and white vintages and why?

2017 Diana Madeline has the savoury-sweet nervous energy of Cabernet with a sweet fruit lift and gorgeous length. 2023 Kevin John Chardonnay. 2020 Legacy Sauvignon Blanc: skin-contact Sauvignon Blanc harvested during its best biodynamic days. 2019 Vanya: still has years to go but is perfumed, elegant and bright.

Any other insider tips?

The best surf school is with Josh Parmenteer. Cowaramup Bay is a good place to start (go to White Elephant for café food).

Who is your favourite Western Australia chef?

My friend, Kate Lamont (of Lamont's). Aron Carr has a generous spirit and serves seasonal sustainable produce.

What's the best thing about making wine in your region?

The quality of the grapes every year, Wilyabrup biodynamic ancient soils and maritime climate trees. Cabernet Sauvignon is the crowning glory of the region, so it's beautiful every year.

AUSTRIA

Ask any sommelier or restaurant bod about Austrian wine and they'll wax lyrical. The country is quietly producing some of the best wines in the world, but they haven't yet found mass-market appeal – this may be down to competition from its German and Italian neighbours, or distant memories of a scandal back in the 1980s (when a few bad eggs were caught illicitly sweetening wines with diethylene glycol, a solvent used in antifreeze). Generous and characterful, Austria's white wines pair brilliantly with so many dishes and can stand up to spice and strongly flavoured Asian cuisine, thanks to their aromatic characteristics and tropical complexity.

Austria is also at the vanguard of organic viticulture. Dr Rudolf Steiner, the controversial Austrian philosopher, developed the theories of biodynamic agriculture in 1924; a form of organic farming, biodynamics emphasizes the interconnectedness between earth, plants, man and cosmic forces. Although some of the ideas seem completely woo woo, both winemakers we've chosen for this chapter farm in this manner.

Red tape can be an issue in Austria, with perhaps the most strictly regulated wine industry in the world. The letters DAC ('Districtus Austriae Controllatus') on a label indicate that the wine is an area-typical and origin-controlled Qualitätswein (quality wine). Some producers, however, believe they can make even better wine if they don't follow the rule book.

The Alps cover more than 60 per cent of the land and Austria's main wine-growing regions cluster the east of the country. Niederösterreich, or Lower Austria, in the north-east, is Austria's largest wine region. It is split into eight specific wine-growing regions running along the Danube and its tributaries. Wachau is one of them, famed for prestigious producers such as Knoll, Nikolaihof, F. X. Pichler and Prager and Kamptal. Bordering Hungary is the region of Burgenland and to the south is Steiermark (Styria), producing aromatic white wines and a locally famous pink, *Schilcher*.

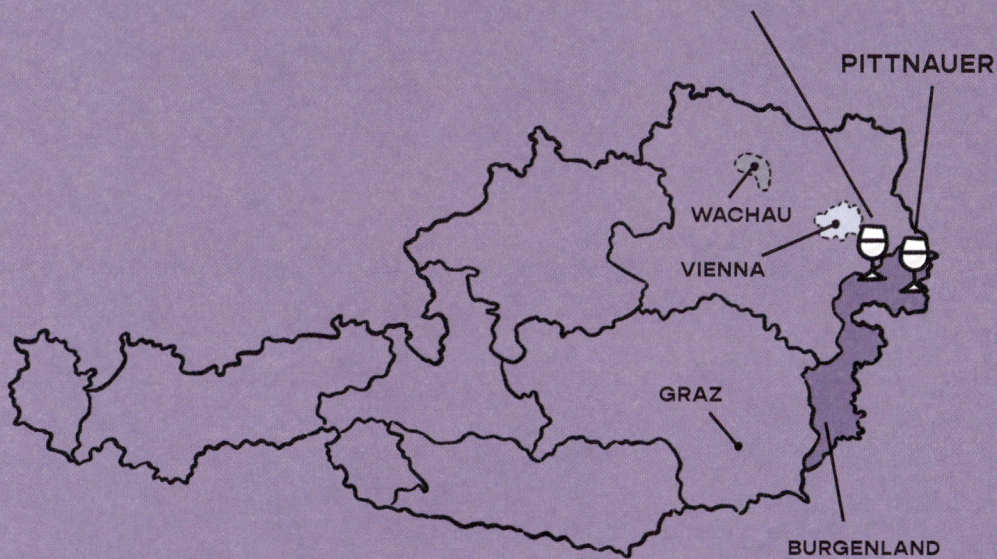

WEINGUT
BIRGIT
BRAUNSTEIN

PITTNAUER

WACHAU

VIENNA

GRAZ

BURGENLAND

MARVELLOUS RED WINES

&

AROMATIC WHITES

BURGENLAND

Austria's easternmost state was part of Hungary until 1921. With Slovakia to the north and Slovenia to the south, this is an agricultural borderland with a complicated history. Centuries of successive wars and waves of invaders meant its people never took stability for granted and economic hardship was the norm. Its viticultural history is one of Europe's most ancient: its sweet Ruster Ausbruch wines were adored by kings and tsars of old. The traditional cuisine here has a palpable influence from Hungary: you'll find little in the way of dairy besides quark (curd cheese) and wholesome dishes seasoned with paprika and caraway.

Burgenland is on the western fringe of the Pannonian Basin, named after the Roman province of Pannonia, and in the region's north (which we're focusing on here) the low-lying landscape is dominated by the Neusiedlersee (Lake Neusiedl), the largest steppe lake in Central Europe and a hub for biking, hiking and birdwatching. The climate is the warmest in Austria: summers are hot, dry and bright, with 300 days of sun per year – coupled with cold but snow-free winters, it has ideal conditions for producing marvellous red wines and aromatic whites.

The region has five DAC areas: from north to south these are Neusiedlersee, Leithaberg, Rosalia, Mittelburgenland and Eisenberg. Austrian wine rules are strict: some vintners embrace the regulations, and some rebel, craving creative freedom.

Birgit Braunstein
Weingut Birgit Braunstein

The Braunsteins have been making wine in Leithaberg since 1632, but the region's viticultural history stretches back much further. 'The Celts brought us the vine,' says Birgit, who took over the family estate in 1995 aged 25 after learning the ropes in Bordeaux. Grape pips were discovered in a Celtic burial mound dating back 2,700 years and these early ancestors of Grüner Sylvaner, Welschriesling and Chardonnay show that the area is among the oldest wine-growing regions in the world.

Birgit pays homage to the forces of nature within her 9-hectare (22-acre) vineyard, just as the ancient Celts did. 'We have a wonderful terroir,' she says, describing the situation as an 'alchemy of place and time'. Balance is the byword here: the vines grow on a medley of heat-retaining schist, limestone and crystalline quartz. Temperate, humid breezes from Lake Neusiedl's north-west shores are tempered by the cooling night winds from the surrounding forests and Leitha Hills, an offshoot of the Alps forming a connection to the Carpathian Mountains. There's a freshness and purity to all the wines: they're generous and fruity on the palate, but Birgit manages to find savoury and mineral notes that balance them out perfectly.

Weingut Braunstein was certified organic in 2006 and Birgit joined Demeter, the international biodynamic association, in 2009. The bucolic vineyards are bursting with life, fringed with cherry, almond and plum trees amid bee hives and perches for birds of prey. Compost comes predominantly from Birgit's clutch of chickens, rare breed goats and sheep. 'We try to support nature, the soil and the plants with the teas, preparations and compost to get an elasticity in the vineyards,' she says. The wines are naturally fermented and bottled unfined, and minimal sulphur is added.

You can feel Birgit's harmonious philosophy everywhere: her land and its vines thrum with energy. Another of her passions is teaching qigong, a Chinese form of movement and meditation that

aims to sharpen the powers of observation and perception, and she practises Kriya yoga, a breathwork-based meditation.

Braunstein HQ is in Purbach, a medieval town surrounded by historic walls constructed from the same chalky limestone that underlies the vineyards. Here, you'll find a hotel and restaurant founded in 1979 by her parents (now run by Birgit's brother Paul and his wife Alexandra). It's an area popular for picnics, hiking and biking: come springtime, cyclists zip by along the cherry blossom cycling trail (*Kirschblütenradweg*), one of 40 bike routes around the lake. We visited Birgit's vineyards during Lake Neusiedl's 'blue hour' – the period before sunset when the water shifts from steely grey to indigo – to sip on a glass of her blushing 2023 Pet Nat. All of the bottles feature Birgit's initials intertwined as an ancient Celtic symbol of luck – but this hibiscus-hued release named *Rosenquarz* (rose quartz) shows her signature BB surrounded by illustrations of the sun, moon and constellations. 'I wanted the label to express our biodynamic, holistic approach: that we are born on earth, we are rooted on earth but we are longing for light and heaven, and that we are influenced by stars,' Birgit tells us.

She grows a selection of both indigenous and international varieties across 35 parcels: a split of 70 per cent red wine varieties and 30 per cent white. Monks brought Chardonnay to the area 900 years ago and we taste an incredible bottle (the Chardonnay Ried Thenau Leithaberg DAC) with a complexity that we've not experienced in the grape before, with an almost spicy edge to it.

In the naturally cool stone-walled winery, you'll spot protective black cat statues among the tanks, amphoras and barrels bearing chalked-on words like 'joy', 'abundance', 'muse' and 'respect'. Felix and Max, Birgit's identical twin sons, are following in their mother's footsteps. The duo have undertaken winemaking training in Germany and New Zealand, bottling their first experimental wines from the 2020 vintage under their own label: Braunstein Brothers.

There's more than just wine at Weingut Braunstein: visitors can get on board with Birgit's sidelines by joining events such as Kriya yoga seminars.

WORD FROM THE WINEMAKER

Which local restaurant would you visit if you were celebrating?

Restaurant Braunstein Pauli's Stuben, my brother's place in Purbach. My sister-in-law is the cook.

Your favourite bar for a late-night drink?

Selektion Vinothek Burgenland in Eisenstadt offers more than 800 wines from 140 Burgenland winegrowers in the former court stables of Schloss Esterházy, plus live jazz and Pannonian cuisine.

Favourite foods to pair with your wines?

Fogos (zander fish) with Chardonnay. Purbacher Bohnenstrudel (white bean strudel) with Pinot Blanc. Geschmortes Lamm (braised lamb) with Blaufränkisch. Backhuhn (baked chicken) with Zweigelt. Topfennockerl (curd cheese dumplings) with Pet Nat Rosenquarz.

Insider tips for your region?

Visit Schloss Esterházy, a seventeenth-century palace in Eisenstadt, the capital of the Burgenland (Haydn composed many of his symphonies here).

Do you have a winery mascot?

Zorro the cat is the boss.

A book that inspires you?

The Book of Joy by Dalai Lama and Desmond Tutu.

Gerhard Pittnauer
Pittnauer

Tragedy struck when Gerhard was 18. The sudden death of his
father meant that instead of following his dream of becoming a
painter or writer, he had to skip college to take over the family
winery in the mid-1980s, amid the chaos and uncertainty of the
Austrian antifreeze scandal.

At that point the wine world was embracing industrial technology
and international grape varieties like Chardonnay and Sauvignon
Blanc. Gerhard decided to continue to make wines the way his
father traditionally did: focusing on Austrian varietals, harvesting
by hand, using spontaneous fermentation and ageing in large
wooden barrels. Since then he's put his creative nature to good
use: experimenting, improvising and making bold decisions that
don't follow fashion. He was among the first wave of producers
who saw the potential of obstreperous St Laurent, a local grape
reminiscent of a morello-flavoured Pinot Noir, and by 1992 his
St Laurent was rated the best in Austria.

Today, he runs his 6-hectare (15-acre) estate with his wife Brigitte.
'We really are a team: she is totally involved in the winemaking
process,' says Gerhard. Their chic winery in Gols, near Weiden on
the north-east side of Lake Neusiedl, is a steel, concrete and glass
construction built in 2001, filled with low-slung leather sofas and
an extensive vinyl collection. Pittnauer's playful labels, designed
collaboratively with artist Tobias Hermeling, look like something
that could easily adorn a record sleeve.

Gerhard describes Weingut Pittnauer's principles as elegance,
finesse and drinkability. Biodynamic since 2006, the winemaking
style here is low intervention, which is the art of making a big
impact by doing as little as possible in the winery to allow the
quality of the fruit to shine through. Tasting dictates the perfect
timing for picking, rather than chemical analysis, and everything
from composting to pruning is done by hand. The Pittis – as the
couple is nicknamed – do embrace some hi-tech kit in the winery,

including a pneumatic press, pumps and temperature-controlled steel tanks, but everything they do is to express the purity and freshness of the fruit. They have carved out their own way without adhering to the strict rules defining Austrian Qualitätswein.

Despite the domestic palate favouring full-bodied reds, the couple shifted their production style towards light, low-extraction reds. 'The most popular red wines in Austria are still the New World styles – lots of oaky notes and vanilla – so not really wines of origin,' Gerhard says. 'I decided to quit chaptalization [adding sugar] with the 2009 vintage. This was our first biodynamic certified vintage and it felt somehow wrong to add sugar (even if it was organic) just to raise the alcohol,' he explains. Chaptalization is often used in cooler climates where it's hard to achieve ripeness: lots of wineries do it and aren't honest about it, including in Burgundy.

'I want to express my freedom as a winemaker.'

When we stop by for a lunch of cabbage and pasta squares in bacon and cream followed by local lake-caught pikeperch, we taste a perfect example of the work of the estate with a domaine-aged bottle of Blaufränkisch from 2008. This isn't a grape renowned for its long ageing potential, but here Gerhard shows what it can do: the wine remains so fresh and alive. It's a real testament to the quality of fruit and the winemaking.

The all-vinyl lunchtime soundtrack meanders from Okou (a French-German musical duo) to Italian chamber music and Gerhard's all-time favourite musician, Townes Van Zandt, a country singer-songwriter whose compositions were recorded by the likes of Willie Nelson and Merle Haggard, Emmylou Harris and Don Williams. 'He's probably not the best singer. He's probably not the best guitar player. But to me, he's one of the greatest songwriters ever.'

The Pittis employ some playful ways to circumnavigate the naming conventions of Austrian Qualitätswein. For instance, Pittnauer's Blaufränkisch (often shortened to BF among trade pals) is labelled Best Friend. 'I'm not a big fan of regulations. And to be honest, I don't care anymore – our export rate is 70 to 80 per cent – so if the bottle says 'wine from Austria', it's okay,' says Gerhard. 'For wines

with names like Mash Pitt or Perfect Day [both are white blends]
or Rosé by Nature we don't necessarily need a single vineyard site.
In other words, I want to express my freedom as a winemaker and
not be regulated by specific expectations.'

Pittnauer has become a celebrated name among natural wine
enthusiasts, but the term is not one that Gerhard loves. 'The
problem with 'natural wine' is that there's no definition of it.
We call our wine a natural wine when there are no additives at all
or a maximum of 10 milligrammes of sulphur per litre.' The Pittis
are part of Pannobile in Gols (a well-known group of winegrowers
around Lake Neusiedl) and in 2007 were one of the founding
members of Respekt, an international group of biodynamic
wineries, along with their next-door neighbour, Claus Preisinger.
'We are strong together, not against each other,' Gerhard says.

WORD FROM THE WINEMAKER

A local restaurant you'd visit if you were celebrating?

Heimlichwirt in Gols, a cool, creative bistro run by the German sommelier Peter H. Müller. It's open for lunch and dinner with a tiptop wine list.

What's the most authentic local restaurant?

Gasthaus zur Dankbarkeit in Podersdorf, Markus Lentsch's beautiful restaurant specializing in a rotation of locally produced, seasonally changing dishes.

Your favourite bar for a late-night glass?

Neu Neusiedler in Neusiedl for quality burgers and a cool ambience.

Which dishes do you enjoy making to pair with wines from your local region?

Pannonian fish soup; pasta squares with white cabbage; beef goulash.

Insider tips for your region?

Follow the Gols 'WeinWeg' (a 10-km wine trail) with two great viewing platforms over Lake Neusiedl.

BELGIUM

When Victoria's partner, Rafi, relocated from London to Brussels for work, friends were sceptical: the Belgian capital has a rep as technocrat HQ, known for a heavy rotation of beers, chips and chocolate, and little else. Trust us, having spent a lot of time in the city and in Belgium more widely, this image problem is entirely unfounded. Scratch the surface and you'll find a cool, creative vibe with a heady gastronomic scene – so much more than moules frites – as well as sumptuous architecture and galleries; uncrowded, unspoiled countryside; brilliant bars (Rebel, Nightshop, Grabuge, Le bain des dames, for wines and grazing), music (tons of jazz) and clubbing (shoutout to Kiosk Radio, Horst and C12 for the best nights).

Wine-wise, viticulture in Belgium is in the throes of a renaissance, though it has a long way to go to match up to its heyday in the ninth century, when grapes were cultivated on the exposed hillsides straddling either side of the Meuse River in present-day Wallonia (the country's French-speaking southern region). Wine production dwindled post-1700s, usurped by large-scale brewing.

The Belgians have some stiff competition from their neighbours, sharing borders with two of the chunkiest wine-producing countries in the world, France and Germany. As a cool-climate region at the northern limits of winemaking, much of what's made here is geared towards white wines and fizz, which together account for around 90 per cent of production. Most of the wines you'll see will be fizz or still wines made from Chardonnay, in a Burgundy-lite style, but others include Pinot Gris, Riesling, Müller-Thurgau and, increasingly, disease-resistant hybrids.

We are side-stepping the sparkling wine crew to focus on a little pocket of West Flanders called Otegem, just outside the city of Kortrijk, roughly 40 minutes' drive from Ghent or Lille. Nestled between the rivers Leie and Scheldt, the small town sits at one of the higher points of this mostly flat region and is home to one of the most compelling and forward-thinking winemakers we met while writing this book.

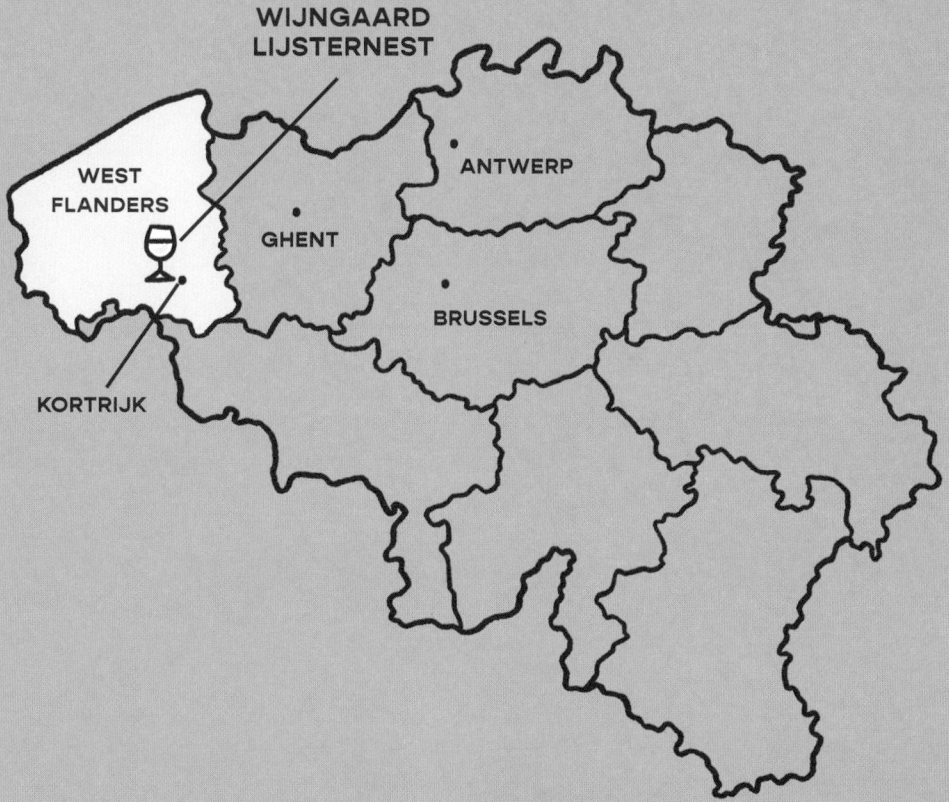

47

WIJNGAARD
LIJSTERNEST

WEST
FLANDERS

ANTWERP

GHENT

BRUSSELS

KORTRIJK

Servaas Blockeel
Wijngaard Lijsternest

Big agri-business, watch out. Servaas is a winemaker determined to demonstrate that the trappings of large-scale farming are redundant. On his four hectares (10 acres) of vineyards in the green environs of Otegem he produces beautiful low-intervention wines, showing that nature can work perfectly on its own, with (almost) no input whatsoever. We soon discover that his philosophy of 'functional laziness' turns out to be a lot of work.

His Wijngaard (vineyard) is called Lijsternest, which means thrush's nest in Flemish and is also the name of the house built by Stijn Streuvels (1871–1969), a local baker turned writer whose works are considered some of the masterpieces of Flemish prose. 'Streuvels made keen naturalistic descriptions of the landscape, the local farmers (mostly flax at the time, for the linen industry), popular festivities and so on,' says the eloquent winemaker.

Our chats veer from history to botany and anthropology. We discuss the difference between the cereal-based arable farming developed in the Middle East and the sustainable indigenous systems in the Amazon rainforest, which focused on a range of crops grown together under a forest canopy. 'Grasses such as wheat are pioneer plants, which tend to grow more aggressively on demolished soil,' Servaas says. 'So in order to be successful in this agricultural system, you need to destroy your soil every year – we call it tilling, or working the soil. After thousands of years of this, eventually you end up with a desert.'

Wijngaard Lijsternest's first vines were planted by hand next to Streuvels' house in 2013. Servaas has never sprayed his vines with copper or copper sulphate (approved fungicides in both organic and biodynamically certified farming). He adheres to a no-till approach inspired by Masanobu Fukuoka (the late Japanese farmer, philosopher and advocate of 'do-nothing farming') to foster a healthy, rich soil microbiome. The diversity among his

16,000 vines is palpable. Insects hum. Birds chatter. A pair of hawks nesting on the side of the elegant straw-and-timber winery raise an annual brood of 'deputy mousers' that keep the field mice in check in his Fatima vineyard, named after a nearby chapel. 'We have a stock of nitrogen in the soil here for the next decade,' Servaas says.

Many winegrowers (even those who describe themselves as natural) will apply copper sulphate to their vines to prevent and fight downy mildew. However, the compound does not degrade in the soil, and spraying can become a vicious cycle, as Servaas explains: 'When you use sulphur to treat downy mildew, you kill the downy mildew but you also kill all the insects, all the bacteria and all the fungi on the plant. There is (at least) one species of fungus and bacterium that competes with it, and a little beetle that grazes on downy mildew like a cow. So, you spray your sulphur and everybody's dead. What will come back first? The downy mildew. But before the others redevelop, you need to have enough downy mildew. By then for the farmer, it's too late, and the farmer has to spray again.'

Servaas produces beautiful low-intervention wines, showing that nature can work perfectly on its own, with (almost) no input whatsoever.

Things do get out of balance at Wijngaard Lijsternest. Slugs were a problem during the very wet summer of 2023. Many grapes were gobbled up by pigeons (a large bird of prey was brought in as a deterrent) and other bunches were damaged by *Drosophila suzukii*, an invasive fruit fly from Asia. Servaas remains sanguine about these losses. 'I know that nature will always take her part,' he says.

Each plot is planted with four to nine disease-resistant hybrid grape varieties, such as Muscat Bleu, Cabaret Noir and Sauvignon Soyhières, which can flourish in Belgium's cool climes. '[A vineyard] is quite self-regulating if everything is there. When the equilibrium is gone, that is when you tend to be in trouble,' Servaas says. 'The use of pesticides is a consequence of soil destruction but if you plant the wrong DNA in a vineyard, you've messed up from the beginning, because you will use pesticides. There's no choice.'

Hybrid grapes have been around since the 1860s, originally cultivated in response to the ravages of phylloxera, but the wine-growing community has been slow to accept them. These crossings of classical European *Vitis vinifera* vines (such as Chardonnay or Pinot Noir) with American *Vitis labrusca* or *Vitis riparia* grapes are resistant to downy mildew, a disease of the foliage caused by a fungus-like organism which is one of the wine world's biggest problems right now.

In each of Wijngaard Lijsternest's parcels, every row is planted with a different variety. Servas points to a row of Solaris: 'This variety is a little more sensitive to downy mildew, but the two rows next to it are not so it gives a bit of a buffer.' After harvest, the mixed grapes from each plot are co-fermented in a field blend: 'black and white, all together'.

Winemaking is as low intervention as possible, relying on indigenous yeasts and a lot of whole bunches 'to get the same effect as in *macération carbonique*, as in Beaujolais, which gives us a little more fruit in a fermentation'. Every bit of kit in his naturally temperature-regulated cellar is simple but ingenious. Servaas

makes the wine in manoeuvrable eggs made from high-density polyethylene (HDPE). The resulting wines are deliciously refined, complex and fruit-forward. No sulphur dioxide is added at bottling and oakiness is certainly not what he's aiming for. 'You work your ass off all year to have beautiful fruits. Who wants to drink vanilla and cigar boxes?' he says.

Meeting Servaas, it is plain to see how his warmth, sense of purpose and strict ideology resonate with others. At harvest, everyone from his Belgian distributor, Jan, to the guy that wrote a 300-page report on his soil, and a professor who Servaas uses as a sounding board were all mucking in. Lab results show that the 2019 vintage of Mag Da (meaning 'is it allowed?' in Flemish) was made with less than 20 litres of fuel per hectare and a positive carbon footprint. The blend of Solaris, Rondo, Bronner and Muscat Bleu also had zero residual sugar and, unusually, zero sulphites – generally thought to be a natural by-product of yeast during the fermentation process.

Wijngaard Lijsternest's wines have a cult following, selling like hotcakes all over the world. 'At the beginning, I thought, I don't want to spray, so I need disease-resistant hybrids, but in the end, I created a new style of wine.'

WORD FROM THE WINEMAKER

Name a restaurant that represents your region.

My favourite is Rebelle in Marke (south-west Kortrijk). The talented young chef Martijn Defauw and his wife Tessa D'haene are all about quality and have made a beautiful restaurant. He's got a Michelin star already and is on his way to another for sure.

Where else would you recommend dining in West Flanders?

For fine and lush cuisine that's a little more casual than Rebelle, Va et Vient ('Comes and Goes') on the banks of the river Leie in Kortrijk. Chef Matthias Speybrouck describes his style as 'rough and refined' [it's really quite refined].

Het vliegend tapijt ('The Flying Carpet') in south Kortrijk for high-end cuisine from my dear friends chef Felix François and his wife Nel Desmet.

A little more classic but worth the detour to the countryside south-east of Kortrijk: L'Envie in Sint Denijs, with chef David Grosdent and his wife Ines.

What do you like pairing with your wines?

I like Mag Da with sushi, but the best pairing I ever had with it was at Rebelle with an amazing tomato dish – a sort of consommé made with semi-dried tomatoes. Generally, I like them at any moment. I sometimes drink them slightly chilled (about 16°C); a little warmer with food.

What are your favourite childhood dishes?

We often had sausages with apple sauce and potato mash, and on Sundays, roast beef with green beans. These days the most typical local dish is Stoofvlees (meat stew) with chips; others include chicory rolls in cream sauce and white asparagus.

Local delicacies to look out for?	In Kortrijk we have a typical apple cake with Calvados and almonds called Kalletaart (and of course, a lot of beer and chocolate). I can recommend either Patisserie Courcelles or Ridder & Hove for Kalletaart.
Best breweries near you?	Brouwerij Bockor aka Brouwerij Omer Vander Ghinste (in Bellegem, just south of Kortrijk), Brouwerij Verhaeghe (close to Vichte station, east of Kortrijk) and Brouwerij 't Verzet (in Anzegem). Flanders red, or Flemish red-brown, is an old style of sour ale from West Flanders.
Do you have any insider tips?	A bike ride along the river Leie or the Scheldt is beautiful. Kortrijk for its history; a vibrant city with well-preserved medieval architecture. Tournai is another historic town that was famous in medieval times for its hand-woven wall tapestries.
What's your favourite Flemish phrase?	*Voortdoen*, meaning 'to keep on going'. In the same context as Churchill's enduring quote: If you are going through hell, keep going.

BOLIVIA

Latin America's wine industry shares a common denominator: the Spanish, who brought vines over with them from Europe in the 1500s. But unlike the continent's better-known winemaking behemoths such as Chile and Argentina, the story that unfolded in Bolivia later that century was shaped by an almighty discovery: the world's biggest silver deposit, in Potosí.

This turned the remote Incan settlement in southern Bolivia into what the author Jack Weatherford described as 'the first city of capitalism'. To put it into context, at its early seventeenth-century peak, Potosí had a population larger and richer than that of London or Milan. The rapid rise of silver mining and a swelling population was accompanied by a new and growing thirst for wine, from everyone from enslaved people to the freshly minted business elite. A Bolivian wine boom followed, with grape-growing regions springing up in Mizque, Cinti, Tarija and Santa Cruz. Besides wine, these grapes made their way into the country's beloved spirit, *singani*, which is distilled exclusively from the white grape called Muscat of Alexandria (known as Moscatel). It's a different beast to pisco, the grape brandy made in Chile and Peru.

The country's winemaking industry never really recovered from its first big blow, courtesy of the Bolivian War of Independence (1809–1825), a rebellion that started after centuries of Spanish colonial rule. A succession of conflicts, revolutions and dictatorship has kept Bolivia's wines out of the spotlight until the last couple of decades. The volumes are tiny compared with its more established neighbours, but both wine and *singani* production are now on the up.

It's painfully difficult to get your hands on Bolivian wine beyond its borders. The country ranks as the poorest in South America and a lack of sea access has hampered its economic growth. Bolivia lost its Pacific coastline in 1879 in the war it fought alongside Peru against Chile, and it is still a sore point. And it means that if you're a winemaker trying to build up an international rep, unless you can produce wine on a huge scale, it's going to be very difficult to export bottles at a competitive price. This is another reason to seek them out on a visit.

The biggest thing that separates Bolivia's wines from many other nations is altitude: the average vineyard starts at 1,500m (4,920 feet) above sea level.

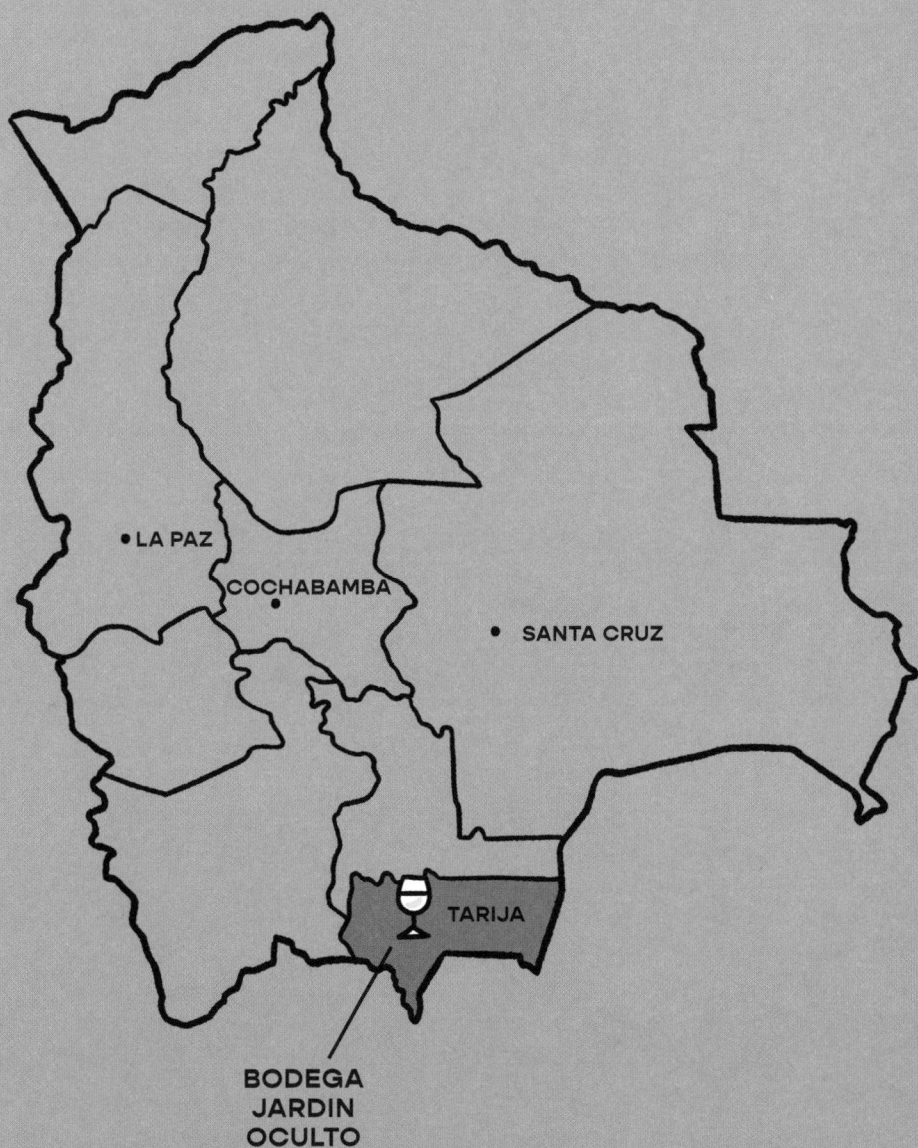

LA PAZ

COCHABAMBA

SANTA CRUZ

TARIJA

BODEGA
JARDIN
OCULTO

By comparison, those on Burgundy's prestigious Côte d'Or are all way lower than 400m (1,130 feet). Nestled between Brazil, Paraguay, Argentina, Chile and Peru, the country's landscape is raw, beautiful and supremely varied. About twice the size of France, it is also one of Earth's most biodiverse, with more than 20,000 documented species of plants, including 2,000 types of potatoes in a rainbow of funky shades.

'Bolivia really is unlike anywhere else in the world. The country itself, from its breathtaking altiplano lakes and salt flats to the dense Amazon rainforest, is extreme. And the wine is no less extreme,' explains Amanda Barnes, an authority on the continent's wines and the author of the excellent *South America Wine Guide*. 'All of the wine regions are high altitude, some of the highest in the world, and the wines reflect the landscape – wild, rugged and memorable. Production is relatively small and due to the remoteness of Bolivia, landlocked in the centre of the continent, it can be quite a challenge to taste the wines outside of Bolivia. However, I believe it is a true gem in South American viticulture, and well worth the adventure to get to taste the wines!'

The three main wine regions are all clustered towards the south of the country. 'Pockets of vines are spread far and wide, planted along the original footpaths used by the Spanish colonizers 500 years ago. These regions have the advantage of seasonality rarely experienced at these tropical latitudes, influenced by their proximity to the Chaco plain and moderated by altitude,' says Amanda.

Tarija (3,300 hectares/8,154 acres). More than 70 per cent of Bolivia's commercial grape-growing centres around the city of Tarija, a semi-arid zone not far from the Argentinian border. The wines made here tend to be typically New World in style: full-bodied, with big aromas and higher alcohol levels. Muscat of Alexandria (for *singani*) is the most-planted grape, followed by a slew of international varieties like Cab Sav, Syrah, Sauv B and Merlot. Some of the French grapes don't show their best selves in this climate, where altitude means the intense UV is double what they'd get in their native Bordeaux. Some big producers based here include Campos de Solana, Casa Grande and Aranjuez. Tannat is a robust red growing in popularity throughout South America, first planted in 1999 by the owners of Aranjuez. It is originally from Madiran, southwest France, where it is often used in blends.

Santa Cruz valleys (600 hectares/1,483 acres). Northeast of Tarija, this subtropical region sits at a latitude of 18 degrees south of the equator, between the Andes and the Amazon River Basin. It is a land of agricultural bounty (producing everything from exotic fruits to coffee and tobacco) and breathtaking scenery – with caves, waterfalls and the UNESCO World Heritage Site El Fuerte de Samaipata, Bolivia's biggest pre-Inca site. Vineyards are kept cool by cold winds (*surazos*) blowing up via Patagonia, through the Argentine pampas and into the valleys. There's some great Syrah, Tannat and Torrontes made here. Samaipata – today a low-key mountain town about three miles from Santa Cruz city – has become a bit of a hub for travellers. Expect lots of chilled-out cafés, craft beers and a generally hippyish vibe.

Cinti Valley (350 hectares/865 acres). Four centuries ago, the Cinti Valley was the biggest producer of grapes; these days Amanda Barnes calls it 'the wild west of Bolivian wine production – a diamond in the rough'. Los Cintis (as you might see it called) is a lush, otherworldly oasis; a 80km (50 mile) long stretch surrounded by cactus-filled scrublands and desert plains. Here you'll find vines that are hundreds of years old, planted by Spanish missionaries, growing unchecked up tree trunks. It's about a three-hour, gorgeous but very windy, drive from either Tarija or Potosí. Production is tiny and centres around Criolla varieties.

Criolla is a confusing term – the literal meaning is 'of Spanish descent'. Here, it refers to the varieties that are descendants of the original grapes planted across South America by the Spanish. Some were existing grapes and others were crosses. The wines of the Cinti Valley are one of Bolivia's four DOs – *denominación de origen*. The others are *singani*, quinoa and chilli peppers. Besides Jardín Oculto, our pick on pages 58–61, Amanda's recommendations include Cepa de Oro, San Francisco de la Horca, San Pedro (in the northern Cinti) and, in the south, Cepas de Fuego and Tierra Roja.

Nayan Gowda
Jardín Oculto

One of the most exciting – and intrepid – winemakers we spoke to for this book is Nayan Gowda, a British–Indian ex-chef from Glossop, Derbyshire, who makes wines in the Cinti Valley for a tiny label called Jardín Oculto, or 'hidden garden' in Spanish. Take one look at the vineyards and you'll see why: the gnarly 200-year-old vines cling to pink peppercorn (*Schinus molle*) and wild quince trees as living stakes, intercropped as part of a wider polyculture of chillies, corn and other crops – a cultivation method from centuries past.

It's a magical situation, and vertical farming in the truest sense. Ladders reign supreme over machines. Everything in the vineyards is manual out of necessity. 'It's nuts, and difficult to manage because modern vineyards are set up for modern equipment,' explains Nayan, Jardín Oculto's consultant winemaker, who has worked everywhere from Ukraine to South Africa, Kazakhstan and even Norway.

The Cinti Valley lies close to the Argentinian border; a coral-coloured canyon created by an ancient fault line nestled between steep cliffs, nicknamed El Cañon Colorado ('the colourful canyon') due to the multi-hued iron-rich soils. 'The region where our vineyards are is one of the most stunning places I've ever been,' he says. 'You've got waterfalls, you've got rock pools, you've got petroglyphs [cave carvings] dating back thousands of years, you've got dinosaur fossils that you can just pick up off the ground.'

Nayan is all about championing underdog grapes. He admits that seeking out new varieties has become a bit of an addiction. The son of doctor parents who don't drink, smoke or eat meat, he was introduced to wine while cheffing at the Ivy in London in the 1990s. 'I've done lots of things over the years. Winemaking is something I fell into; like a lot of people, it's something you tend to come to later in your life unless you have a wine family heritage,' he says. 'I'd never really been interested in wine before.

I mean, it was just a drink. Working as a chef suddenly put it into context with the thing I loved the most, which at the time was food. It was a slippery slope from there.'

Several WSET (Wine and Spirit Education Trust) courses and a stint as a project manager for JP Morgan later, Nayan got to a point where he thought, 'If I can work as a chef, I can probably make wine.' So aged 31 he enrolled on a four-year oenology undergraduate degree at Adelaide University, South Australia. That was in 2002. 'One of the reasons I went into winemaking is that I love travelling, immersing myself in cultures, learning about people and food. Being a winemaker for harvest allowed me to go to a country for three to four months and really dive in.' He's worked as a flying winemaker and globetrotting consultant for his Vinosity biz ever since.

Jardín Oculto was set up by María José Granier in 2019, who comes from one of the oldest winemaking families in Bolivia. The more conventional Granier enterprises include Singani Casa Real and Viñedos y Bodegas Campos de Solana. The latter is one of Bolivia's biggest producers of *singani*, but María decided to create something quite different with her own venture. She began working with a handful of growers in the Cinti Valley on the advice of a Dutch master of wine, Cees van Casteren. Within five minutes of her posting an ad for a winemaker on a Facebook forum for viticulturalists, vineyards and wineries that December, Nayan had replied. He flew out to Bolivia four weeks later, in early 2020. Their first 2021 vintage was tiny, about 700 bottles, made more challenging through pandemic-related delays, difficulties and a dislocated shoulder (Nayan's). Each wine celebrates a single varietal.

Their roster of grapes includes the old white, fragrant Muscat of Alexandria; Vischoqueña, a red grape exclusively found in Bolivia (which Amanda Barnes calls 'the unsung hero in Bolivian Criolla wines'); and Negra Criolla (called País in Chile and Mission in California), which yields a Pinot Noir-like wine with lots of peppery, strawberry vibes. Each vintage is another step into the unknown. 'I had in my mind what [these varieties] could do here, but the Negra Criolla we have in Bolivia is quite a different biotype to the País in Chile. The berries are much smaller, with

more concentration and a lot more oomph, which is absolutely
fascinating.' Experimentation remains the name of the game. Nayan
is making Tannat in *macération carbonique* style – lower-extraction à
la Beaujolais – which is a rogue move for a bold grape known for its
deep notes of black fruits, cassis and chocolate.

In Bolivia, Nayan has found something particularly special; a reason
to park his passport in the drawer. The Cinti Valley vineyards
planted in the nineteenth century by Franciscan and Jesuit
missionaries grow at 2,330m (7,644 feet) above sea level – twice
the height as the tallest Alpine vineyards in mainland Europe –
and 22 degrees south of the equator. This is past the usual limit for
the *Vitis vinifera* grape, where sun and UV are fierce (and which is
thought to result in much higher levels of resveratrol, the potent
antioxidant found in red grapes). And what's even more interesting
is that the winery's low-intervention practice of intercropping
with trees can result in grape yields double those from modern,
mechanical vine production.

Jardín Oculto's rented winery in Tajira lies a perilous three-hour
drive away, via two mountain ranges. Everything Nayan and María
do aims for purity. The style of their wines is also quite different
to those throughout most of Latin America. 'It's much lighter,
fresher, lower alcohol, crunchy and crispy. Generally speaking, it's
what the modern palate is after. We don't use oak. It's all stainless-
steel ferments. We're kind of modern, insofar as we do have
cooling tech and a pneumatic press. But we're also very traditional
because it is very hands off. We don't use yeast. We don't use
enzymes. We're quite trad. So, best of both worlds really.'

'The heritage varieties that we have in Bolivia and throughout
South America have generally not been taken seriously. A lot of
them were blended into table wine. There has been a movement
in Chile, especially with Roberto Henríquez and a few others, who
are doing really interesting things in Bío Bío and Itata, but not
through the rest of Latin America. And definitely not in Bolivia.'

'Part of the self-appointed brief of Jardín Oculto is that we are
slowly trying to take a register of similar vineyards and plantings
throughout Bolivia when we have spare time – which is not often,

unfortunately. It appears that this kind of training is actively being carried out. We went to a really remote area and saw that somebody was planting young vines against saplings. So it's still happening.'

Bolivian wines are not competitive overseas. 'There isn't necessarily the impetus for export. There's no support from the government; everybody relies upon their own initiative. The domestic market soaks up pretty much all of the production.' The biggest market is one of the country's two capitals, La Paz, where Noma co-founder Claus Meyer's Gustu restaurant helped to kick off the country's bubbling gastronomic revolution when it opened in 2012. 'Bolivia has a lot of potential, not just for wine: the food is amazing. There are so many Amazonian products that are completely unknown anywhere else. We keep discovering them as well. They recently have commercialized Amazonian vanilla, for example, which nobody had seen before. Bolivia is also the last vestige of wild cacao vines that grow on trees.'

Tarija is not a wealthy place, and the restaurant scene reflects that. 'One of the gems here is *pensiones*, which are little restaurants that can be set up in somebody's lounge. You'll pay 10–15 bolivianos [less than £2] for two courses and a drink – it's basically whatever they feel like cooking or whatever they've got fresh that day.' The food scene has evolved a lot in La Paz and Santa Cruz. 'La Paz in particular,' Nayan says. 'Why Bolivia? Why not? It's a country I've always wanted to visit. There's a sort of fairly wealthy, young middle class here, who have come back from studying overseas, they have money and they want to put it into Bolivia to create something. I want to ride that wave and see what happens.'

WORD FROM THE WINEMAKER

What's the best way to get to Bolivia from Europe?

The easiest way to get to Bolivia is to come through to Santa Cruz. You can arrive at La Paz, but I would not recommend landing at such high altitude. The airport is 4,100m (13,451 feet) above sea level – it's an absolute killer. Generally what I do is fly to São Paulo, and then get a connection. It tends to be a bit more comfortable.

Can you get by with just English?

It's a Spanish-speaking country. I think there are 37 languages recognized here. Very few people speak English, so you need to at least have a smattering of Spanish. Bolivian people are a bit shy, but they're also incredibly friendly. So if you make an effort, they will love it.

What are the local specialities in the Tarija department?

We are on the border with Argentina, so there's a lot of Argentinian influence in the food. We have our own version of empanadas: *salteñas*, a sweet pastry with a soupy filling. You've got to be Bolivian to be able to eat one without it falling all over your front. *Saice de Tarija* is probably my favourite thing: a spicy meat stew that often is served with a triple threat of carbs – pasta, potatoes and rice. *Asado* is a big thing here: steaks and meat cooked on an outdoor grill. In Tarija, there's a street called Belgrano, which is where all the butchers are. Every Sunday, you go down there from about 9:30, and everybody's got their barbecues out, barbecuing away.

Can you share some of your favourite walks?

There are lots of great hikes around here. It's stunning.

Can you book a tasting with Jardín Oculto?

We don't have a formal cellar door but anybody can give us a call and we can try and arrange something if we have any wine left.

CANADA

Icewine is the first thing that springs to mind when most people think about Canadian wine. Like *Eiswein* in Germany (see page 133) and Austria, this complex yet refreshing sweet wine is made in the depths of winter from grapes that have frozen on the vine and are harvested in subzero temperatures, often during the middle of the night. The resultant wines taste like they are pumped full of honey, stone fruits and candied citrus – the optimum after-meal digestif or dessert pairing. Icewine is usually made from grapes like Vidal, a hardy hybrid, or Riesling, our favourite. Be warned, though, it is pricey, but that's a reflection of all the effort it takes to make.

Canada's first commercial winery opened in the mid-1800s but, as in the USA, Prohibition put paid to the country's wine industry for over 40 years. In 1975, a winery called Inniskillin in Ontario's Niagara-on-the-Lake was granted the first winery licence in Canada since the nation's alcohol ban. Its trailblazing wines helped to pave the way for a swathe of exciting producers and over the past couple of decades winemakers have been chasing the elegance and finesse of Burgundian wines made from Pinot Noir and Chardonnay. The effects of climate change have played their part too; the country has warmed at roughly twice the global average rate.

Two provinces are responsible for producing the vast majority of Canada's wines. The largest and most diverse is Ontario, with about 6880 hectares (17,000 acres) under vine, roughly on the same latitude as Piedmont in Italy, on glacial soils and tempered by the moderating effect of the Great Lakes. Ontario's major wine-producing region is the Niagara Peninsula (see page 67), churning out most of the country's icewine as well as quality bottles of Chardonnay, Riesling, Pinot Noir and Cabernet Franc. Top producers to look out for are Bachelder (see pages 68–70), Inniskillin, Konzelmann Estate, Peller Estates, Pillitteri Estates and Wayne Gretzky Estates. The provinces of Quebec and Nova Scotia produce wines in much smaller quantities. Nova Scotia has some tiptop traditional method fizz – we like Benjamin Bridge's stuff.

65

VANCOUVER

REGINA

ONTARIO

QUEBEC
CITY

WINNIPEG

NOVA
SCOTIA

TORONTO

BACHELDER
WINE

Western Canada's winemaking stronghold is in southern British Columbia, close to the US border with Washington State. Here, the major winemaking HQ is the super-scenic Okanagan Valley – a long, dry wine region set around two big, slender lakes. The northern part is cooler, resulting in elegant Pinot Gris and Pinot Noir, while weightier reds like Merlot and Cabernet Sauvignon are made in the semi-desert-like south. If you're here drop by the Nk'Mip Cellars in the southern Okanagan Valley, the first indigenous owned and operated winery in North America, or sip on cool, low-intervention glasses at Anthony Buchanan.

It can be hard to get your mitts on the country's wines; Canadians tend to keep it for themselves. We can't blame them. Little even makes its way over the US border – all the more reason to seek it out on a trip. Most wineries have a cellar door, so fill up on each stop if you're travelling for a while.

If you see VQA (Vintners Quality Alliance) on a bottle, this means that all the grapes that went into the wine were grown in Canada, within the appellation named on the label.

NIAGARA

About 90 minutes' drive from downtown Toronto, Niagara Peninsula is Ontario's major wine-producing region, just west of the Niagara Falls – the roaring curtain of water (2.8 million litres per second!) marking the US-Canada border – between the Lakes Ontario and Erie. This narrow strip of land is mild and lush – with its undulating landscape enjoying a moderate climate and longer growing season, lending itself to pick-your-own peach farms, strawberries and of course, grapes.

There are two main VQA appellations – Niagara Escarpment and Niagara-on-the-Lake – and ten sub-appellations.

The Niagara Escarpment is named after the 1,000-km (650-mile) long rocky spine with UNESCO World Biosphere Reserve status spanning North America and Canada, covering forest, wetlands, rolling farmland and dramatic cliffs with vertiginous drops down to the water. The drive from Niagara Falls to Niagara-on-the-Lake runs along the Niagara Parkway, a tree-lined road hugging the Niagara River, which Sir Winston Churchill once described as the "prettiest Sunday afternoon drive in the world".

After taking in the almightiness of the Niagara Falls, avoid the surfeit of tourist traps, casinos and chain restaurants in the city that surrounds them and head further afield to discover picture-postcard towns, phenomenal scenery and a lively gastronomic scene (farm-to-table restaurants are very much the vibe).

Besides wines, there are superb breweries making craft beers (such as the Bench Brewing Company in Beamsville) and farms growing some of the country's most delicious grapes, cherries and apples – for some excellent cider. Lovers of all things fishy should look out for Lake Erie pickerel (a member of the perch family) or the fantastic East Coast salmon.

Thomas Bachelder
Bachelder

A true force in the Canadian wine industry, Montreal-born Thomas has pioneered cool-climate Pinot Noir and Chardonnay (and more recently Gamay) in Ontario's Niagara Peninsula region, having spent years mastering the craft in France and the US.

'Growing up Quebecois, we have a fascination with France. The Quebecers don't want to be French but they love to be descended from the French,' explains Thomas, sharp-witted and energetic, with a shock of white hair.

'What has happened in Canada is very similar to England's explosion – a theme that's repeated around the world,' he says. The beautifully executed wines made by Thomas and his wife Mary Delaney under the Bachelder label sing of the place they come from: the limestone-laced Niagara Peninsula. 'Niagara Falls happens to fall from a dolomitic limestone bench. But that bench is actually a glacial escarpment that continues for hundreds of kilometres. That part of the limestone bench that faces Lake Ontario is the best place to grow vines because of the winter warmth of the lake, which protects us from the cold weather.'

It all started in 1985. Thomas's first foray into winemaking was courtesy of a Christmas present from his brother: an at-home DIY Beaujolais-style kit. After fermenting his first five litres, Thomas was hooked. The initial home-made barrels were followed by a career in wine writing, but that still hadn't scratched the itch. 'I told Mary, I can't stop at being a wine journalist; can't stop at being a home winemaker; I think I should go to wine school.' So the pair relocated to France and Thomas began studying at the Burgundian wine school in Beaune, then spent the early 1990s working for prestigious names including Domaine de la Créa in Bligny-lès-Beaune and Domaine Marius Delarche of Pernand-Vergelesses. 'I only ever wanted to live in Burgundy,' he muses. 'It's still my favourite place on the planet for making and drinking

The beautifully executed wines sing of the place they come from.

wine. I was at the school with Luisa Ponzi [the daughter of Oregon wine pioneers Dick and Nancy Ponzi], but she dragged us back to Oregon.'

After working in Burgundy thrice and Oregon twice for Ponzi and Lemelson, Thomas moved back to Canada as Le Clos Jordanne's founding winemaker in 2003. The aim was to create a 'domaine' in the Niagara region to produce top-quality, low-intervention Chardonnay and Pinot Noir within the magical terroir of the Jordan Bench. The results? Spectacular. Thomas left to set up his own label; between 2009 and 2015 it was a crazy three-country project from vintages in Niagara, Oregon and Burgundy, acting as a micro-négociant (i.e. buying grapes in each region and renting winery space). 'Mary was a great help. Greta Thunberg made it all less cool, being a flying winemaker.' The couple now focus exclusively on Niagara, tending to vines, and live 'on the edge of the country in a little town', close to the cellars in Beamsville, which are lovingly nicknamed the 'Bat Cave'.

'I want to keep focused; keep the muscle tone for understanding the terroir.'

They're big on dinner parties, hosting a regular rotation of friends and fellow winemakers: 'all of us relate to being foodies. Our life does centre around wine and food,' he says, but Thomas hasn't lost any love for his favourite wine region. 'I drink a Burgundy every week; I want to keep focused; keep the muscle tone for understanding the terroir. Wild yeasts are as much of a part of terroir as humans are. When you're making terroir wines, it behoves you to use the yeasts that grew on the skins in that vineyard in that particular season.'

We think one of Thomas's best wines is 'Les Villages' Bench Niagara Chardonnay. At a 2024 tasting, we sampled the 2020 vintage: this wine is a love letter to the icons of Meursault. Here, Thomas combines Burgundy philosophy with some of his top fruit from the Niagara Peninsula's sub-appellations of Short Hills Bench, Twenty Mile Bench and Beamsville Bench. It's treated with respect, with hand harvesting, gentle pressing and slow, spontaneous fermentation. Malolactic conversion – where sharp malic acid is converted to softer-tasting lactic acid – takes place in the French oak barrels that Thomas sources with his connections in Burgundy, to create a rounder, fuller mouthfeel. The nose is fresh, pure and aromatic, and the palate generous with flavours of fleshy pears and lemon tart. This wine showcases the great potential of the region and what is achievable if you're absolutely dedicated like Thomas.

WORD FROM THE WINEMAKER

Favourite local restaurants?	Garrison House, a gastropub in Niagara-on-the-Lake; BarBea and Ruffino's, also in Niagara-on-the-Lake; in the city of St Catharines I like Solaia (Italian), Oddbird, Wellington Court, and Bolete; Just Cooking, rustic Italian in Vineland; Rizzo's House of Parm, near Fort Erie.
And the most authentic local restaurants?	Treadwell (farm-to-table) in Niagara-on-the-Lake and Root and Bone (locally sourced veg, cheese and meat) in Fonthill.
What's your favourite wine spot in Toronto?	Chez Nous wine bar – the first all-Ontario wine list!
Which local produce do you enjoy pairing with your wines?	Organic meats from Churchill Natural Meats in Fonthill.
Best-loved family dishes?	Slow-roasted seven-hour leg of lamb. Local free-range chicken slow grilled over a charcoal fire, with Pinot Noir.
What is the best thing about making wine in Niagara Peninsula?	It is a beautiful place, nestled in a peninsula between two Great Lakes (Ontario and Erie), and the dolomitic limestone makes the wine sing.
Insider tips for your region?	Niagara Falls – of course – and the Parkway between the Falls and Niagara-on-the-Lake along the Niagara River. At the edge of the Escarpment, there is a jaw-dropping, sweeping view of the Niagara River.

ENGLAND

In some aspects, not being an established wine-producing nation has meant that England is more open to wines from many countries, while its classical counterparts in France, Italy and Spain tend to favour their own locally made tipples. England is also one of the biggest markets for fine wine in the world (think Champagne, Burgundy and Bordeaux).

The overwhelming majority of English wine is made in the warmer and drier south and south-east, from Cornwall, Devon and Dorset, through Hampshire, Surrey and Sussex, to Kent, with around 4,000 hectares (10,000 acres) of land under vine in England, the area has nearly doubled in ten years, in large part due to climate change. Warming temperatures have also extended the possibility of wine-growing further north, from the Chilterns to the Midlands, and as far as Yorkshire.

Roughly 70 per cent of production is sparkling, but volumes remain minuscule when compared with established players in the game. To get an idea of scale, Britain produced 8.3 million bottles of sparkling wine in 2022 whereas the Champagne house Moët et Chandon makes 30 million bottles every year.

English growers keen to mimic Champagne-style wines and price points have led to a focus on planting grapes such as Chardonnay, Pinot Noir and Pinot Meunier. Achieving the full ripeness required for still wines can be a challenge. It's only really since 2018 (the perfect conditions for wine in England) that the first good still examples emerged. Will Davenport makes an excellent example of still Pinot Noir from his vineyards in Kent and Sussex.

While growers are still working out the intricacies of the best land to use for each grape, English wines are becoming ever more impressive. The winemakers representing England in this chapter are brilliant creatives, relishing the lack of restrictions hanging over them. Unlike many countries, winemakers in England can pretty much make wine any way they like, and many say that experimenting is one of the most fun parts of the job – sometimes these can go horribly wrong, but that's part of the journey.

73

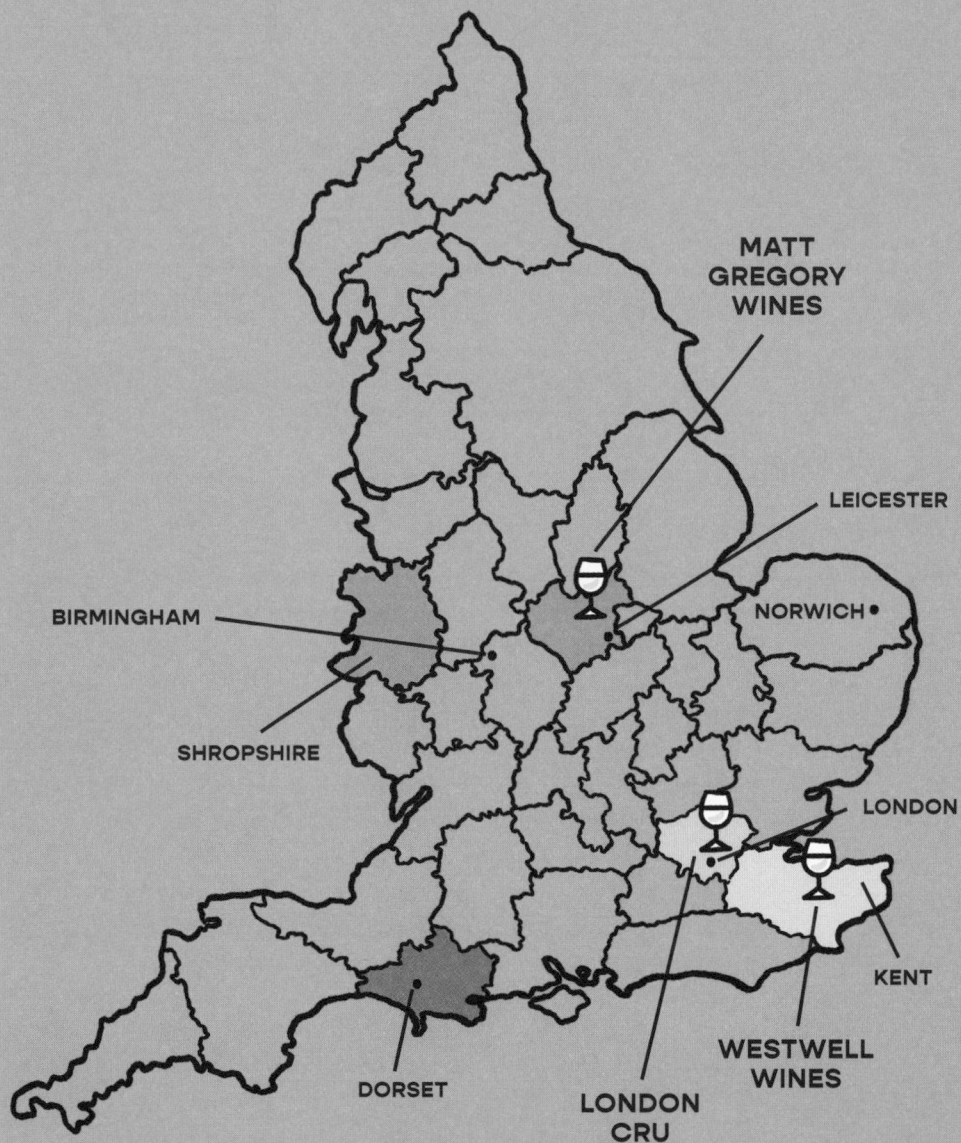

MATT
GREGORY
WINES

LEICESTER

NORWICH

BIRMINGHAM

SHROPSHIRE

LONDON

KENT

DORSET

LONDON
CRU

WESTWELL
WINES

LONDON

So you've found your passion in life – winemaking – but you're a city slicker who loves gigs, galleries and a thronging gastronomic scene. Once you're making wine in a certain spot you're tied to that location; however, the majority of winemaking regions are remote, and much like other agricultural professions, it can be a lonely job. Plumping for traffic-choked London as your winemaking HQ may seem a challenging choice given the eye-watering prices for square footage here.

We're both Midlanders by birth, but it wasn't long until our paths led to London. It's here where we cemented our longstanding love of the city's food and drink scene, and though we might be biased, we'd argue that the Big Smoke is the wine epicentre of Europe.

Any trip to the UK should include a visit to London to sample its stellar eating establishments and bars. And we'd also advocate popping into one of its urban wineries – they often open their doors to the public for tastings and tours, and these are important not just for restaurateurs and sommeliers but for everyday enthusiasts looking to connect with the vinification process and understand how much dedication goes into making a bottle of wine.

Winemakers choosing to base themselves from London demonstrate that it's perfectly possible to make killer wine to a soundtrack of wailing sirens in one of the most crowded cities in the world.

Alex Hurley
London Cru

Bert first met Alex – the head winemaker at London Cru, the UK's first urban winery – during 2018's harvest at Le Grappin in Burgundy, a négociant project from Emma and Andrew Nielson. 'Fond memories!' says the easygoing Aussie. 'That period at Le Grappin changed the way I make light red.' A geologist by training, Alex spent much of his twenties traversing Australia and Asia, working for oil companies. He threw in the corporate towel in 2012, U-turning after an 'early midlife crisis' and joining his wife Steph on a posting to East Timor. Soon after, Alex was living in a caravan, obsessively learning how to make 'biodynamic, inspirational and very creative' wine with Ray Nadeson and Maree Collis at the much-respected Lethbridge Wines in Victoria, Australia.

In 2016 he embarked on a Master's at L'Institut Agro in Montpellier and in Piedmont: a full-on immersion in viticulture and oenology, followed by a thesis on yeast in a research lab. One thing Alex didn't anticipate was falling head-first for English sparkling wine after a couple of friends snuck some into Champagne tastings at Le Grappin. He ended up in England working at Gusbourne Estate in Kent and by the end of 2018 started at London Cru, a West Brompton winery set up in 2013 by Cliff Roberson, a fine wine importer since the 1960s, once working for the iconic Sherry-Lehmann in uptown Manhattan, where regular customers included Rockefeller, Andy Warhol and Salvador Dalí.

Alex takes great pride in taking London Cru to new heights. Still wines make up three-quarters of their output and a quarter sparkling, the reverse of most English winemakers. 'Sparkling is like making soufflé. If you change the recipe, the chemistry won't work. A lot of the time, English sparkling is so consistent that it doesn't have a personality. We've been working hard to hone reds here. The style we're making is light, low extraction, carbonic maceration and pressed off early, deliberately. It's a style I saw in Tasmania – halfway between a rosé and a red – at cult winemaker Sinapius.'

WORD FROM THE WINEMAKER

A London restaurant you'd visit if you were celebrating?

10 Cases in Covent Garden. Their private dining room is a wine wonderland. I love throwing the keys to the sommelier.

Which restaurant represents your region?

St John [the OG is in Smithfield].

Your favourite bar for a late-night drink?

The Mulwray in Soho.

Which foods pair well with London Cru wines?

Maldon rock oysters are an absolutely perfect pairing for most English wines. Bacchus and sparkling wines love seafood! Or they can stand up to the power of a Pad Thai.

What's on the winery playlist?

A lot of Australian 1990s hip-hop which, for some reason, always offends everyone.

Your winery mascot?

Ned the dog.

Any insider tips for London?

We love a picnic at Richmond Park as it feels like a nice escape from London. Great for dogs, deer and a bottle of vino.

KENT

When you mention English wine, the south-east will likely be the first place that springs to mind. Kent and Sussex in particular battle it out for medals and draw constant comparison with the Champagne region in north-east France.

The French term 'terroir' can be roughly translated as a sense of place, which encompasses the natural environs where a particular wine is produced – the soil, elevation and climate – which shape the finished product. So it's perhaps unsurprising that companies like the French Champagne house Taittinger and the Californian giant Jackson Family Wines are investing in grape-growing in Kent, given it shares the same chalky geological layer (fossils, minerals and all) that runs through Sussex, Kent, Champagne and Chablis.

There's a core of excellent producers in Kent, such as Gusbourne, who have done much to put the region on the winemaking map. However, one producer stood out for us. His creativity in the winery is infectious, and on tasting the wines from tank and amphora for the first time, we were hooked.

Adrian Pike
Westwell Wines

There are heaps of super-cool winemakers out there and we've
interviewed a bunch of them for this book. Tbh, anyone who
makes wine for a living is cool in our eyes but Adrian, managing
director and winemaker of Westwell Wines, is on another level.
He started out in the music industry, co-founding the record label
Moshi Moshi in 1998. Sometimes he'd be scooting between seven
gigs in a single night and every summer he'd make a pilgrimage
to Midem, a music conference in Cannes, in a decrepit Citroen
2CV, stopping off in the French wine-producing behemoths of
Champagne, Burgundy and the Rhône Valley.

But when Adrian found that he'd stopped listening to music,
instead craving green and pleasant hills, he set his sights on wine.
The plan was to swap Tottenham in north London for France.
Then Adrian tried one of Will Davenport's Sussex wines and it
changed everything. 'I was really blown away that you could make
something like that in England,' Adrian says. We agree; Will's
wines have long been some of our all-time favourites. Will has
been pioneering organic viticulture in England since the early
1990s and has influenced a whole generation of winemakers in
the UK.

'An average day in the music industry is a bit like working in wine.
There isn't ever an average day,' he says. After a stint working at
Davenport Vineyards and a viticulture course at Plumpton College
in Sussex [the only institution in the UK to offer such a course],
when the opportunity arose in 2017 to take over the 'perfect site'
in Kent, 'it was a no-brainer. There's a reason why fruit has been
grown in Kent for centuries. We're on a chalk bedrock, but we've
got this lovely rich loamy soil – sand in some places, and clay in
others. We are protected by the North Downs, so the site hasn't
been frosted since it was planted, which is one of the biggest
problems for English vineyards.'

Now Adrian focuses on making experimental low-intervention still and sparkling wines that nod to the low-intervention practices of central and eastern Europe: fermenting with wild

'I absolutely love pouring skin-contact wine.'

yeasts, ageing in handmade amphoras, producing pét-nats, skin-contact and orange wines. On 16 hectares (40 acres) Adrian grows Ortega (a German varietal first grown on the Mosel) and French clones (Pinot Meunier, Pinot Noir, Chardonnay), adhering to the philosophy: 'plant well, respect the soil, and make great, honest wines from brilliant fruit'.

Pelegrim is among our favourite English bubblies, a characterful and authentic wine that has a sense of place which tells a story. Pelegrim is named after the Middle English for pilgrim, a reference to the Pilgrims' Way, a centuries-old walking route that runs along the North Downs above the vineyard on its final leg to Canterbury.

The labels, designed by Adrian's partner, Galia Pike, a composer for film and television, have an indie vibe that wouldn't look out of place on an album cover. But they're all related to the wine: one illustrates a close-up of the soil featuring a coccolith, another a zoomed-in piece of Westwell vinewood viewed under a microscope.

'We're members of the Wine Garden of England. The remit of the group is to try and drive more traffic to wineries with cellar doors (the customer-facing part of the winery, normally a shop or bar) – it's something Kent's really got right,' says Adrian. 'One of my favourite things is pouring skin-contact wine for people, because I absolutely love it. It has a reputation as a Marmite thing, but I have been amazed by the reaction. The more we can do tours and tastings, the better.'

WORD FROM THE WINEMAKER

A Kent restaurant
you'd visit if you were
celebrating?

The Fordwich Arms, a Michelin-starred gastropub near Canterbury.

Which restaurant best
represents your region?

Angela's in Margate.

What's your favourite bar
for a late-night drink?

Old Neptune in Whitstable.

Which foods pair well with
your wines?

Simple seafood, from oysters to mackerel pan-fried with garlic.

List any songs that are on
repeat in the winery during
harvest.

Generally just the sound of the ferments bubbling. Otherwise Moondog and dodgy old techno.

Your winery mascots?

Inky, our miniature Dachshund, and Izzy, a red Labrador pup.

Any insider tips for Kent?

The Pilgrims' Way, after which our signature cuvée Pelegrim is named, runs above the vineyard and all the way from Winchester to Canterbury – so many beautiful parts of it to walk along.

MIDLANDS

Those making wine this far north are few and far between, but as OG Midlanders we thought it imperative to include this region to demonstrate the viticultural diversity of England. Some notable producers in the region include Grove Estate and Halfpenny Green Wines in Staffordshire, Rothley Wine in Leicestershire and Rowton Vineyard in Shropshire, whose undulating landscapes are the 'blue remembered hills' in *A Shropshire Lad* by A. E. Housman and the inspiration for the Shire in J. R. R. Tolkien's *The Lord of the Rings*.

Famous for its balti houses, the British behemoths Walkers Crisps, David Attenborough and Melton Mowbray pork pies (from the market town where Victoria's dad grew up), Leicestershire also churns out some spectacular cheeses: sunset-hued Sparkenhoe Red Leicester, for example, is made using milk from a herd of pedigree Holstein-Friesians. Tynt Meadow is the UK's only Trappist ale, brewed by monks in an Augustus Pugin-designed abbey in Coalville. We've included rural Rutland in this section, the UK's smallest county (which for a while during the 1970s and 80s was deemed to be part of Leicestershire), known for its lush, fertile soils and rich agricultural history.

Matt Gregory
Matt Gregory Wines

It takes gumption to grow grapes in Leicestershire, yet Matt
Gregory has precisely the right blend of vision and talent (and
perhaps foolhardiness) to set up shop within this nascent
community of wine producers. Going by the alias of The English
Winemaker, the bespectacled renegade appears every inch the
Edwardian explorer, with a wardrobe chock-full of excellent
knitwear, tweed and silk neckerchiefs. His wines are an explosion
of wholesome English countryside and after tasting his Ancestral
Pink 2021, a hedgerow-heavy, cherry blossom-coloured pét-nat
made from Pinot Noir, Pinot Gris and Bacchus, it's abundantly
clear he's putting Leicestershire on the wine map.

A wine merchant for 20 years, Matt started working at Oddbins
Wine during his first year as an impoverished geography student at
the University of North London. In 1993, his final-year dissertation
on the growing popularity of winemaking in England interrogated
whether it was a sensible thing to do or not. 'Obviously, it's not,
but it seems slightly less quixotic these days,' he quips.

On an unassuming Monday in September 2017 Matt decided he
wanted to make wine. You could call his subsequent 12 months
– three harvests at three different vineyards – a baptism of fire.
After a sesh in Sussex at one of England's biggest producers,
Matt soon found that large-scale winemaking was not for him. 'I
made a phone call to my old mate Theo Coles, at The Hermit Ram
[vineyard] in New Zealand, and asked him for a job. So I biffed
it over there for the 2018 vintage.' Harvest with Theo – who is
known for his delicious, low-intervention wines made in the north
of New Zealand's South Island – was followed by another at Villa
Giada, on a friend's family estate in northern Italy. Indeed, Matt
continues to produce his own range of Italian wines from this
vineyard in Piedmont.

Originally from Guildford, Surrey, home for Matt is now Oakham, a market town in Rutland. In 2020 he took on the lease for Walton Brook Vineyard in the Leicestershire Wolds. Planted in 2009, the conventionally farmed vines on a two-hectare (five-acre) site rolling down a south-facing slope were 'in total disarray' but in a few short years, Matt has converted to organic methods and nursed the vineyard back to health and equilibrium. It is back-breaking work requiring gargantuan dedication: Matt prunes every one of his 8,500 vines himself.

'Rule number one: it's got to be delicious. The secret is hard work because you can't work hands-off,' Matt says. His mantra? 'Head down, bum up and get on with it.' Grown on a combination of Jurassic soil and glacial deposits, the resulting wines are the essence of England in a glass – zippy and fun, with a raw edge that shows best when paired with local delicacies such as Stilton or Lincolnshire Poacher cheese.

'We've got two artisan bakers in Oakham: Hambleton and a tiny one called Lily and Honey,' Matt says. 'I can stop off to buy a litre of milk from a vending machine from two dairies on the way to the winery. Local meat and game is exceptional. In the winter, we eat a lot of pheasant and partridge as it is plentiful and good. We buy lamb, pork and beef at the farm gate, directly from the farms that produce it. There is so much food and drink stuff going on here. It's all in plain sight if you start looking for it.' His friend, Matt Wright, set up the Great Food Club as a directory of the best East Midlands producers and restaurants, from small brewers to bakers and farms producing outstanding quality meat, charcuterie and cheeses. It's a good place to start a gastronomic tour of the region.

WORD FROM THE WINEMAKER

A local restaurant you'd visit if you were celebrating?

The Olive Branch in Clipsham, near the Lincolnshire border, is a country pub with a sure-footed kitchen cooking to a high standard, with lovely people and a pretty decent wine list.

Which restaurants best represent your region?

The King's Arms in Wing, Rutland, for game and charcuterie. Sarpech is a brilliant curry house in Oakham.

What do you like to pair with your wine?

Melton Mowbray pork pies. The hand-raised pork pie at Leeson's on Oakham High Street is outstanding. Dickinson and Morris at Ye Olde Pork Pie Shoppe in Melton Mowbray do a good one which goes out nationally.

Who's your winery mascot?

An idiot Irish Terrier, Teddy.

What's on the winery playlist?

P.I.M.P by 50 Cent; Cheater, Cheater by Joey + Rory; Stayed Til Two by Gord Bampford.

Any insider tips for Leicestershire or Rutland?

Rutland Water dominates the landscape in Rutland. With 42km (26 miles) of walkable track around it and over 1,400 hectares (3,500 acres) of surface water to play on it's a beautiful spot that belies the fact that it is manmade. It offers some of the best reservoir trout fly fishing in the country.

FRANCE

We don't really need to say how big the French imprint on the global wine stage has been and while France is not the country that invented wine, it is certainly one that has finessed the craft of winemaking. Whichever route you take training to be a sommelier – experience on the floor through a mentor, Wine and Spirit Education Trust (WSET) qualifications, Court Master Sommeliers (CMS) or a combo – French wine will dominate. The same is true for those learning the techniques of *la cuisine* at chef school, even down to the French names of the knife skills, from julienne to jardinière and chiffonade.

Ground zero for fine wine starts with Champagne, Bordeaux, Burgundy and Rhône. But the complexities of the climate and layers of tradition can be mind-boggling. Terroir is hallowed here – an Old-World word which translates as 'earth'; a good definition is 'a sense of place'. If a winemaker has done their job right, all the environmental factors including climate, soil, altitude and aspect can be identified in the glass. A party trick for a sommelier is to give them a blind tasting and they'll try to tell you which specific vineyard it's from. This is what great wines will do, they'll transport you to another place. And French vignerons are among the very best at this.

As a junior sommelier, Bert worked as a stagiaire at Raymond Blanc's Le Manoir aux Quat'Saisons. It's a heavy-hitting wine list and hard to put a foot wrong. And he learned just as much from French somms, fervent obsessives keen to dish out knowledge about their country's wares.

Granted, France has a long, long list of some of the most esteemed winemakers in winedom, but all those appellations and French grape names and crus, clos and chateaux are sometimes the reason why wine can feel so intimidating and incomprehensible in the first place. If you don't know where to start, see it simply as a challenge and list of epic terroirs to taste and explore. There are some obvious regions that haven't been included in this chapter that get airtime already, but here's a whistlestop tour of some of our favourite alternatives.

MAISON
JÉRÔME
LEFÈVRE

REIMS

DOMAINE
BARMÈS-
BUECHER

PARIS

NANTES

DIJON

MARK
HAISMA

LYON

CHÂTEAU
PESQUIÉ

BORDEAUX

TOULOUSE

NICE

MARSEILLE

MONTPELLIER

Bordeaux makes some of the most revered red, white and sweet wines out there. Blends are king here, and reds make up about nine in ten of the bottles (generally referred to as Claret) made in this enormous chunk of southwest France. The classics like Château Lynch-Bages, Haut-Brion, Margaux, Pontet-Canet and Cos d'Estournel are all names inaccessible to the majority of wine lovers just starting out. They're expensive and need to be aged to be enjoyed properly. Nor are they what's cool and sexy right now (which would be the other B: Burgundy). The progressive, contemporary Bordeaux makers we love include Le Puy, Ormiale, Château Raymond-Tapon and Frédéric Mallier. These are great smaller houses for any curious Bordeaux drinkers, with more affordable prices and stock released with the aim to be drunk young(er).

You can increasingly find pét-nats and skin-contact wines made in lesser-known parts of the region such as the Côtes de Bordeaux, on the right bank of the Gironde estuary. The 1855 Bordeaux classification is where it all started for wine classification systems. The five first growth estates – Latour, Lafite Rothschild, Mouton Rothschild, Margaux and Haut Brion – are a major part of Bordeaux history and the reason why the region has long been seen as the crème de la crème.

Following the Loire River northwest, the region is a benchmark for fine white wines, where you'll struggle to find better examples of Chenin Blanc and Sauvignon Blanc. Loire's laser-focused wines are a dream to pair with seafood and goat's cheese, with their mineral edge, electricity and energy bringing so much fun to the dinner table. A couple of names you need to know here include Didier Dagueneau, an influential iconoclast in the Pouilly-Fumé appellation who met an untimely death in a tragic aircraft accident in 2008, and Nicolas Joly, based in the Savennières appellation, an outspoken champion of the controversial biodynamic approach. Skip the fashionable Sancerre region and seek out some much more rewarding Loire producers like Richard Leroy, Guiberteau, Thomas Batardière and Belargus.

When it comes to red, Clos Rougeard are up there, showing what Cabernet Franc can do in Samur Champigny (a finer, silkier alternative than that of Bordeaux). These primo wines are mega expensive (let's call them 'collectible'), so to get a taste of the finest crus check out the likes of Antoine Sanzay, Domaine des Sables Verts or Le P'tit Domaine – all of these winemakers work in the same top vineyards, Les Poyeux and Le Bourg, that Clos Rougeard do. Richard Desouche makes wine under the Le P'tit Domaine label. He used to be the vineyard manager of Clos Rougeard and you can buy the wines at retail for under £30.

Finally, Jura. A bit of a sore subject. It's hard to get an appointment at a domaine in this small, subalpine region nestled amid Switzerland and Burgundy. Growers have to be hands-on in these steep vineyards, coupled with the fact that Jura's wares are like crack to sommeliers and the wine of choice for hipster wine collectors – most are sold on allocation, so more attention is simply not required (or desired). After lots of research, we decided to visit Laura Bourdy of Domaine Bourdy and booked ourselves into a couple of restaurants (Hostellerie Saint Germain les Arlay and La Parenthèse on her recommendation), with a few tips from Wink Lorch, a passionate Jura advocate who has written two brilliant books, *Jura Wine* and *Wines of the French Alps*. We'd crashed at a hotel in Colmar, Alsace, and went to bed dreaming of comté and vin jaune, only to meet up in the hotel car park the next morning to discover a comically flat tire. In terms of Jura producers, our favourite stars include Domaine Macle, Lucien Aviet, Domaine Labet, Jacques Puffeney, Domaine Overnoy, Les Marnes Blanches, Domaine de la Tournelle, Domaine Pignier, Peggy et Jean-Pascal Buronfosse and Rolet P&F. There are some very obvious names that have been intentionally left out in this list – the hype and price have exceeded the quality of wine at an alarming level.

CHAMPAGNE TASTING NOTES & FOOD PAIRINGS

Bert's favourite grower Champagne houses, with tasting notes and matches with street/comfort food.

CHAMPAGNE HOUSES	TASTING NOTES	FOOD
Pascal Agrapart	*Racy, saline, chalky*	Fish and chips
Bérêche & Fils	*Nutty, spice, yellow apples*	Chilli crab
Chartogne-Taillet	*Milk bread, quince, lemon confit*	Lobster roll
Ulysse Collin	*Toasted nuts, tomato skin, lime zest*	Cheese toastie
Michel Gonet	*Brioche, lemon zest, greengages*	Burger
Olivier Horiot	*Rhubarb, red cherries, hazelnuts*	Salt beef sando
Laherte Frères	*Stone fruits, floral, redcurrants*	Tacos
Larmandier-Bernier	*Bergamot, pears, flinty*	Poutine
Georges Laval	*Jasmine tea, yellow apple, chalky*	Dim sum
David Léclapart	*Gingerbread, baked apples, wild strawberries*	Pulled pork
Marie-Courtin	*Crème fraîche, raspberries, Victoria plums*	Pizza
Jacques Picard	*Apple blossom, butter biscuits, red cherries*	Fried chicken
Eric Rodez	*Red apples, honeysuckle, Earl Grey*	Hot dog
Aurélien Suenen	*Hazelnuts, Golden Delicious apples, lemon oil*	Mac 'n' cheese
Vouette & Sorbée	*Apricot skin, cranberries, lemon rind*	Banh mi

CHAMPAGNE

What is a party without fizz? In a masterful demonstration of perfect PR, the big Champagne houses, such as Moët & Chandon, Perrier-Jouet, Louis Roederer and Veuve Clicquot have become household names forever associated with clinking glasses, sparkling embraces, your most glamorous outfit. These sparkling wines are made exclusively in Champagne, a region of north-east France, roughly 90 minutes' drive from Paris.

Let's not beat around the bush: Champagne is not cheap. The reasons why are manifold. Demand is ever-growing and grape prices here are steeper than anywhere else in the world. Land is expensive and hard to come by. The region is plagued by unpredictable vintages, meaning that in bad years production volumes are teeny. And the *méthode champenoise* (traditional method) has many labour-intensive steps and stipulations, including a minimum 15 months' in-bottle ageing on lees.

This region is all about blending. You'll often see the term non-vintage (NV) on bottles – this means it is a blend from two or more years. Of the seven permitted grapes – Chardonnay, Pinot Noir, Pinot Meunier, Pinot Blanc, Pinot Gris, Petit Meslier and Arbane – the first three are the most used by quite a significant margin. It's common to blend red and white grapes together. Look out for the terms *blanc de blancs* – white wine made from white grapes (lean, cool-climate Chardonnays typified by razor-sharp acidity and citrus notes like lemon and grapefruit pith) – and *blanc de noirs* – white wine made from red grapes (tart red fruits such as cranberries and raspberries, with a softer acidity).

The majority of the region's 20,000 growers sell their fruit either to a cooperative (usually within a particular village) or to one of the big houses such as Pol Roger or Pommery, essentially brand names that produce steadfast styles in large quantities, typically blended from the grapes grown by dozens, even hundreds, of individual farmers across the region. These wines are a world away from the terroir-driven diversity of grower Champagnes: wines that are made and bottled by the same person who grew the grapes. Growers who make their own wine can be identified by the letters RM (récoltant-manipulant) on the label.

A bottle made by Jacques Selosse was the first grower Champagne that stopped Bert in his tracks, and remains the greatest sparkling wine he's ever tasted. It was like freshly toasted sourdough with a knob of butter, just-picked cobnuts and a Cox's apple, with deep, sweet flavours that you wanted to keep smacking around your mouth. Super vinous (like a wine), the fine bubbles complemented the texture of the wine perfectly rather than being intrusive.

Selosse is sometimes dubbed the godfather of grower Champagne. His approach to winemaking has much in common with the Burgundian greats – single parcels in some of the best villages, such as Le Mesnil and Ay and Ambonnay, fermented in Burgundy barrels to impart his celebrated texture and richness to the wines. Along with the likes of Pascal Agrapart, Cédric Bouchard, Larmandier-Bernier and Jacques Lassaigne, these new-wave growers focus on healthy soils and fastidious viticulture to express the vintage and the character of the land.

Myths about Champagne's origins abound. Its history owes at least some part to a Benedictine monk called Dom Pierre Pérignon, cellarmaster at the abbey of Hautvillers in the late seventeenth century. However, both the English and the Germans had a big part to play in Champagne's rise. In the 1660s it became a fashionable drink in London society – though at first the effervescence was accidental rather than intentional. During the first half of the nineteenth century, some enterprising German families emigrated to the Reims area, including the Krugs, Bollingers, Heidsiecks – incidentally our favourite house brands – helping to make a success of house Champagne. Of course, this kind of Champagne has its place, but don't forget about the tireless folk behind grower Champagne who don't have marketing teams – you're investing in one person rather than a brand.

Jérôme Lefèvre
Maison Jérôme Lefèvre

Screech! Jérôme parks up in his pick-up truck, an air freshener emblazoned with Suicidal Tendencies (the thrash band) dangling wildly from the rear-view mirror. 'I know that I drive like I stole the car,' he laughs, letting us into his compact little winery in Nogent l'Artaud, in the Vallée de la Marne – a patchwork of honeyed countryside filled with flitting chaffinches and fields of swishy-tailed milk-white cattle. 'It's a humble place, don't expect too much,' he says quickly.

Clad in an Alice Coltrane tee and Vans Half Cab skate shoes, Jérôme is not the stuffy stereotype of a grower in Champagne, a pretty conservative neck of the woods. He farms organically, adhering to Masanobu Fukuoka's principles – no tilling, no pesticides, no fertilizer, no weeding, no pruning – and work is done entirely by hand without any machines, just the way his grandfather taught him as a young boy. He does not describe his philosophy in the vineyard as punk, but it is certainly DIY. This is an approach that's far from the mainstream in Champagne but undoubtedly comes from a lifetime immersed in the underground scene.

Jérôme had his first taste of heavy metal aged seven, introduced by an uncle, and soon became captivated by Iron Maiden, Motorhead and Judas Priest. 'My father's passion was restoring motorcycles and lots of bikers would come by,' he says, recalling hours spent polishing chrome on Harley Davidsons. Around that time he was also put to work on his mother's inherited vineyard, convinced he would do 'anything to avoid working here' in the future. As a teen his music tastes expanded to punk and hardcore, and a stint singing and playing guitar in a grindcore band called Dismal Death. 'I went to lycée [high school] to escape the things my parents are. Through music I discovered contemporary art: the posters and album covers of Raymond Pettibon, the brother of the founder of [hardcore punk band] Black Flag,' he explains, cue a decade-long career of writing about art and curating exhibitions across the globe, many on the theme of music subcultures.

When Jérôme's mother, Éliane, was approaching retirement in 2007, he asked himself what he should do with the vineyards. 'My brother and I were of the opinion: this is not for us. Then I thought, why don't I try?' Jérôme continued working in the art world while beginning to make wines under his mother's surname, Delalot, converting the vineyard to organic in 2009. 'The first two Delalot cuvées were more classic exercises of style. I grew in confidence to evolve the style and labels with time,' he says.

These are wines with an intense fruit and a subtle sparkle but, as Jérôme wanted to keep his mother's parcels 'untouched', he set up Maison Jérôme Lefèvre, a boutique experimental line to create cuvées even more avant-garde than Champagne Delalot, and bottled his first vintage in 2018. And the results from his small parcels (less than 1.5 hectares/3.7 acres on the hillsides of Charly sur Marne, Saulchery and Bonneil) have been knock-out: 'A parcel of Meunier planted on sandy soil has a minerality that's not supposed to happen. The soil is amazing,' he says.

You wouldn't immediately point to Champagne when tasting these wines as there's something deeply artistic and contemporary about them. After sitting with his wine in your glass for some time, you really see Jérôme's care, devotion and the quality of his fruit. Like any good creative, he is asking questions and pushing boundaries. 'I don't want to enter into a routine. Each year I use the same grapes but vinify in a different way,' Jérôme says.

Playing with Fire is a rosé made up of around 90 per cent Pinot Meunier and the rest Pinot Noir, aged for (only) three months in barrique. The abstract label bears the reflection of a plastic bin bag in the winery and it is named after a song by the rock band Godflesh. It's so delicate: a super-soft rosé Champagne with a whisper of bitterness. Jérôme's embrace of faults within his wine has much in common with the distortion and controlled chaos in the music genres he so loves: 'I deal in imperfection.'

'I make the wines I want to drink,' Jérôme says simply. As we say our goodbyes, we spot a piece of card propped up on the windowsill. It's a quote from the Beat Generation writer William S. Burroughs: 'What do artists do? They dream for other people.'

WORD FROM THE WINEMAKER

What are your favourite restaurants?

L'Epicerie Au Bon Manger in Reims [there's an excellent selection of grower Champagne, but it's teeny, be sure to reserve]. If I'm in Paris, Caffè Stern [Italian, spenny] with my lover for special days.

Where else would you recommend in Reims for enjoying your cuvées?

Sacré Burger [a cool and casual hamburger and hotdog spot – ask for their Champagne list]. Racine, for a Japanese-inspired tasting menu.
 Domaine Les Crayères [a chichi restaurant with two Michelin stars in a mansion set in grounds that used to belong to Louise Pommery].

A local delicacy to look out for?

Abbaye de Tamié, a cheese made by the monks at the Trappist Abbey of Tamié.

ALSACE

There's no place like Alsace. Part of France since the end of the Second World War, this long and slender region bordering Germany and Switzerland has flipped between German and French control five times since 1681. Alsace's culture and cuisine are French with a distinctly Germanic flavour. Even the regional language, Alsatian, is a German dialect just like Bavarian or Swiss German, and its honeypot towns and romantic villages (credited with inspiring Disney's *Beauty and the Beast* and Hayao Miyazaki's *Howl's Moving Castle*) are filled with half-timbered houses and flower-lined canals.

Alsace is divided into two *départements*: the Bas-Rhin (Lower Rhine) and the Haut-Rhin (Upper Rhine). Somewhat confusingly, the terms 'Bas' (low) and 'Haut' (high) refer to elevation rather than geographical placement. So Bas-Rhin is located to the north, near Strasbourg. Haut-Rhin, in the south, is mainly at a higher elevation, thanks to its location in the foothills of the Vosges Mountains. It's here, in the Haut-Rhin, that you will find many of the best and most prestigious Alsace Grand Cru vineyards.

The phenomenal wines produced on these sun-baked slopes are a perennial sommelier fave but remain supremely undervalued throughout much of the wine-drinking world. This means you can discover site-specific expressive wines in Alsace and understand the meaning of terroir in a glass without bankrupting yourself (which is easily done in Burgundy).

THESE SUN-BAKED SLOPES ARE A

ARE A

PERENNIAL SOMMELIER FAVE

Geology nerds: Alsace's setting on a tectonic fault means the soil types here are a marble cake of complexity, a mosaic of sedimentary, volcanic and metamorphic origin. Alsace is also – perhaps surprisingly – one of the driest regions in France, sitting in the rain shadow of the Vosges Mountains, which act as a giant precipitation sponge. This means the vines must burrow deep to seek moisture, thoroughly exploring the fantastic patchwork of terroirs.

The 51 best sites, the Grands Crus, are dotted on the headlands and foothills of the mountains. Many are treacherously steep. The combination of hot, dry summers coupled with cool winters, and a big diurnal temperature range results in magnificent Riesling: one of the best is Trimbach's Clos Ste Hune Riesling. Alsace is also famed for its spectacular Gewurztraminer, Pinot Gris, Sylvaner, Muscat and Pinot Noir. The latter isn't as popular, but we love the light reds made here from the likes of Léon Beyer,

Albert Boxler and Bruno Sorg. Alsace Pinot Noir has to be the best value for money in France, making fleshy and vibrant easy drinkers.

The tall, tapered green glass bottles are generally labelled with the grape variety – Alsace is the only region in France that routinely does so – but there is also a tradition of blended wines, made from a mix of grape varieties grown on the same terroir. The master of this style is Domaine Marcel Deiss. One of our favourites is Engelgarten ('the garden of angels') – a medley of Riesling, Pinot Gris, Pinot Beurot, Muscat and Pinot Noir. Complex and aromatic, it is pure, refreshing, and a joy to drink. Try it alongside a hot and spicy fish dish – it would work a treat with the smoked kipper jungle curry that we were served at the Thai restaurant Kiln, the Soho-based stalwart.

Maxime and Sophie Barmès
Domaine Barmès-Buecher

Sophie Barmès is as chic as our surroundings. We're tasting on the top floor of her family's Wettolsheim winery, with its double-height ceiling, a massive gong in the corner for the occasional session of sound bath immersion and bouclé-covered furniture from BoConcept. A balcony overlooks a quaint street of half-timbered buildings surrounded by broad, vineyard-clad hills. Sophie points out a house on the other side of the road: 'My parents grew up across the street from one another,' she says.

The estate took shape in 1985 when these two neighbours – Geneviève Barmès and François Buecher – married and combined their family holdings as Barmès-Buecher, although their roots here stretch back more than 200 years. In 1998, the couple began converting their 16 hectares (40 acres) to biodynamic viticulture; the dry Alsatian climate with its long cold winters, makes it particularly well-suited to this method of working.

Sophie moved to New Zealand in her mid-twenties to figure out what to do with her life. Seeing how hard her parents worked, she wasn't sure winery life was for her. 'I wanted it to be my choice,' Sophie says. On her return to France in 2010, Sophie had *'une révélation'* and decided to join the family business. A year later, the death of her father François in a cycling accident meant her younger brother Maxime, a graduate of Burgundy's winemaking school in Beaune, would come on board too, to the production side of the business. When Maxime got the call with the tragic news, he was 21. 'I was working at a domaine in the south of France,' he says. 'My plan was to travel for ten years. Life decided another way. I always wanted to do this job, but not straight away.'

'We are lucky because nobody tells us what to do,' Sophie says. 'We are free and for me, this is a gift. We work with nature. We decide which wines we want to make. We decide the people we want to employ. We continue the work of past generations.'

The domaine has parcels in three Grands Crus: Hengst, Pfersigberg and Steingrubler. When Bert was first introduced to Barmès-Buecher by Claire Thevenot (a master sommelier and importer) in his early days as a sommelier, he was struck by how individual the plots were side by side – the same grapes, the same winemaking, just slightly further down the road. As a winemaker, this is the ultimate goal and only the elite manage to do so, but these wines seemed to do it effortlessly and were so much joy to drink too.

Many of their 80 parcels are steeply sloping and old. 'It is on the hillsides that we make the best wines,' Sophie says. One of our favourite Grands Crus in Alsace is Hengst (Alsatian for stallion) in Wintzenheim, vines planted more than half a century ago on calcareous marl-limestone soils rich in iron, where horsepower rather than machines is used for farming to avoid soil compaction. It's been a vineyard since at least the ninth century. Sophie points out the south-facing site from the balcony; it slopes down from 360m (1,180 feet) to 270m (885 feet) towards Wettolsheim. Riesling, Pinot Gris and Pinot Noir do very well on Hengst, making wines that have power and tension, but the Gewurztraminer is on another level, with a ripe acidity and aromatic intensity on the palate and nose. The expression of the terroir is so full; the mineral lick you get on the finish invites you to come back for more and makes you wonder how it is possible that a wine is so intense and aromatic yet so drinkable.

Barmès-Buecher's Hengst holds a special place in both our hearts. Other brilliant winemakers making wine from Hengst include Famille Hebinger, Josmeyer, Albert Mann and Domaine Zind-Humbrecht.

WORD FROM THE WINEMAKER

A restaurant you'd book for a special occasion?

JY's in Colmar, a two-Michelin starred restaurant in the Champ de Mars park.

Where would you go for a casual lunch of Alsatian favourites?

Winstub at Le Chambard in Kaysersberg [make sure to finish with the hand-churned ice cream].

Any other restaurant tips?

In Colmar: Bord'eau and L'Epicurien. Auberge Le Bouc Bleu in the village of Beblenheim.

What's your favourite local wine bar?

L'Un des Sens in Colmar.

Any insider tips for Alsace?

The covered market in Colmar – a nineteenth-century building with more than 20 merchants selling fruits and vegetables, charcuterie, cheeses, breads, cakes and more.

BURGUNDY

Welcome to the capital of Chardonnay and Pinot Noir. Burgundy (*Bourgogne* in French) is where things get serious, and sometimes a little overwhelming. One of the best reference guides we've come across is Jasper Morris's *Inside Burgundy*, which takes a deep dive into the region, covering all the vineyards and vignerons you need to know about, with maps defining vineyard boundaries.

There are so many intricacies, terroir-driven differences and local accents to wine here. In Bert's younger sommelier years, he really struggled with Burgundy, but everything fell into place when he went to do harvest in the Côte de Beaune. He vividly remembers taking a break from cutting Pinot Noir and pulling up a map of wine regions on his phone, with hands blistered and swollen from working in the vineyard the previous day. He could compare exactly what he could see on the map to his viewpoint, properly visualizing the places where the wines he'd tasted and talked about thousands of times come from. Here was the emblematic landmark, Colline de Corton, a heavily forested limestone hill (a favourite of Emperor Charlemagne). To the west, the vines of the beautiful Pernand-Vergelesses village. At the southern foot of the hill he could pick out the prestigious Aloxe-Corton appellation. It was all a bit like being on set with his favourite winemakers. So, if staring at maps doesn't do it for you, even with a delicious glass in hand, you need to get out to these places, feel the dirt, talk to the winemakers, listen and understand.

Unlike Bordeaux, with its grand châteaux and massive estates often managed by professionals on behalf of absentee owners (many of them international investors), Burgundy's most revered vineyards are split into tiny parcels which remain the property of the families who farm them. Land prices are crazy and even with sacks of cash, often the only way to make wine here is to be born into the tradition. To complicate things further, Burgundy's inheritance system means everything must be shared equally among heirs (hence all the small plots).

It's no exaggeration to say Burgundian wines are the most desirable in the world, and demand often pushes the prices up to record highs. Spring marks the annual *en primeur* tasting for the choicest wines from the most sought-after producers in the region – a chance for professionals to taste from tanks and barrels before the wines are ready to be bottled. They're assessing what the wine will taste like in five years or so, to make an offer on the wine, sometimes years before they'll receive the finished bottle. Madness. And experts get it wrong all the time.

Bert has – with extreme difficulty – managed to narrow down his favourite Burgundian wines. This is as small as he can make this list of white wines, but he's had the best experience with the following producers: Château de Béru, Vincent Dauvissat, De Moor, Yann Durieux, Arnaud Ente, Benoît Ente, Goisot, Maison Harbour, Domaine Leflaive, Pierre-Yves Colin-Morey, Domaine François Raveneau, Domaine Roulot, Domaine Valette.

For red wines, Bert's ultimate producers include: Jane Eyre, Domaine Jean-Marie Fourrier, Emmanuel Giboulot, Le Grappin, Henri Gouges, Marchand-Tawse, Domaine Prieuré Roch, Domaine Georges & Christophe Roumier, Domaine Armand Rousseau.

BURGUNDY'S WINE-GROWING REGIONS
From north to south, these are:

Chablis is the town at the centre of Burgundy's northernmost region. It's so far north that its nearest wine region is actually Champagne, rather than the rest of Burgundy. Chablis wines are made from 100 per cent Chardonnay grown on the same kind of limestone soils that can be found in much of Champagne, resulting in possibly the purest Chardonnay anywhere, with a flinty and fresh lemon zest character.

Côte de Nuits This northern half of the Cote d'Or region is Pinot Noir paradise, home to some of the most sought-after vineyards in the world (including 24 of Burgundy's 33 Grand Cru vineyards and over 100 Premiers Crus). Some of its starriest communes include: Gevrey-Chambertin, Morey-Saint-Denis, Chambolle-Musigny, Vougeot, Flagey-Echézeaux and Vosne-Romanée. It's all about quality over quantity here: a single bottle can set you back thousands (and will often need ageing for five years minimum) but you can still find (relative!) value in villages like Fixin.

Côte de Beaune The southern part of the Côte d'Or takes its name from Beaune, a medieval gem of a town. Larger, more diverse and prolific than its northern neighbour, Côte de Beaune includes Volnay, for lifted pretty Pinots, and highly rated white wines from communes such as Meursault, Puligny-Montrachet and Chassagne-Montrachet. Pick up more affordable, energetic whites from Saint-Aubin, a hilly village with 20 Premiers Crus.

Côte Chalonnaise The rolling landscape of Côte Chalonnaise is a medley of vineyards interspersed with other types of agriculture. There are no Grands Crus, but many of the wines punch above their weight, with some bargains to be had compared with the rest of Burgundy. Its teeny Bouzeron appellation is unique, dedicated to the Aligoté grape. The communes to note are Rully, Mercurey, Givry and Montagny. The entry-level wines labelled as Bourgogne blanc or Bourgogne rouge can be enjoyed while they're young.

Mâconnais Arguably Burgundy's most dynamic region; the wines of the Mâconnais (labelled as Mâcon-Village) can be hit or miss, but insiders like Dominique Lafon (one of Burgundy's most innovative winemakers) are snapping up land here. The undulating limestone and sandstone hills result in tiptop Chardonnay for a snip. As we're further south we get more ripeness and in warm vintages the wines can develop stone fruit notes. Look out for Pouilly-Fuissé and Pouilly-Vinzelles.

Mark Haisma
Mark Haisma

Industry legend Mark Haisma breaks easily into a smile. The amiable Aussie made his name after a decade spent at Yarra Yering in Victoria, the revered Yarra Valley winery set up by the late Dr Bailey Carrodus. What we love most about Mark (besides his cracking wines) is his hands-on approach to hosting tastings and dinners, not just to the trade but with the public too. 'It's obligatory,' he says. 'We exist for the pleasure of our customers. I can't be there all the time but I'm really into people coming to explore and discover.'

He's a salt of the earth kind of guy, light-hearted and straight-talking, but don't be fooled: he's whip-smart and his wines are serious stuff. 'I've just dragged myself through a vineyard and taken a sample ready for harvest 2023. It's all getting to the pointy end now,' he tells us cheerfully on a late August afternoon. 'Every vintage is different. We like to think we know what we're doing but at times we're flying by the seat of our pants.'

Mark grew up in rural Victoria, the son of two immigrants: 'My mum is French, a northerner from Lille. Dad's Dutch. I was born in Australia. I'm the most unpatriotic person on the planet – except for the rugby.' He swapped hemispheres in 2009, initially setting up in Burgundy as a micro-négociant (making wine sourced from small parcels of grapes grown by other people).

A combination of grit and good-naturedness has got him far. Incrementally, Mark built lasting relationships with growers. He first made wine here in rented space in a cellar tucked behind a supermarket off the D974 road near Gevrey-Chambertin. 'Modest is the term I used to begin with,' Mark explains. 'It was all out of the back pocket. You can't walk into Burgundy and say, right, I'm gonna reinvent the wheel. You can do what you like in your winery, but when it comes to the fruit and the vineyards, you've got to show a little humility and respect.'

His Gevrey-Chambertin is his calling card – it's opulent, drinkable and refreshing yet you savour every sip as there's so much complexity. However, the first Haisma wine that caught Bert's eye way back was a Côteaux Bourguignons called A Bogan in Bogandy. The label features Mark in a bucket hat out in the vineyards clutching a tinny, drawn by Guy Venables, the cartoonist for the *Metro* newspaper. 'He's a good mate. We got drunk one night and I said, I need a label, and he got his colours out,' says the twinkly-eyed winemaker.

By 2016, Mark had built a winery in Gilly-les-Citeaux, a modern HQ dubbed Le Shed by his mother. 'That gave me an opportunity to cement myself as a producer and grower in Burgundy,' he explains. In addition to the grapes he still buys, Mark now owns four hectares (10 acres): two of Pinot in Gevrey-Chambertin, super desirable plots formerly owned by a family from whom he used to buy fruit at the start of his French career. 'I got very close to the family and used to go rugby touring with the husband,' he says. Another two hectares are in Mâcon, where he has planted mostly Chardonnay, some Gamay, and a third of a hectare of Shiraz: 'I want to see what we can do with Shiraz in a northern climate.' The fact that he was even offered the land is testament to his talent. In typically humble fashion, Mark takes nothing for granted. 'I've got the most remarkable opportunity for an outsider here in Burgundy, to make wines at this level; to farm pieces of land which I only dreamed of when I was in Yarra Yering,' he says.

Unlike many Burgundian wines, which need to be laid down for years to reach their full glory, Mark's gentler hand (meaning maximum expression of the fruit and terroir) is perfect for the impatient wine lover. Certainly, his wines will age elegantly but what Mark produces is approachable, fun and a pure joy to drink while still young, with all the best features of a modern Burgundy Pinot Noir – not just for the elite with a cellar full of dusty, decades-old Burgundy. 'I'm looking for some of that delicious Pinot fruit and freshness and vibrancy. I'm not very extractive in the vinification,' he says. 'Winemakers are the ultimate fiddlers and tinkerers. We're always trying to fix something. I'm pretty hands-off at times. Knowing when not to work the fruit is the biggest lesson I teach my *stagiaires* [interns].'

Mark describes himself as 'a feel it, taste it, smell it, touch it, kind of winemaker' and much of what he does is based on intuition and experience. Instead of sending samples off to labs to figure out when to pick he uses 'the most fundamental analytic tool we have: the palate. I make a decision about picking times simply on taste.' He's also a fan of chaptalization – adding sugar during fermentation to boost the wine's final alcohol content – where necessary. 'It's one of our greatest tools. [By chaptalizing] I'm able to continue my fermentation for another couple of days. Those little yeasty babies are the essence of my winemaking. If we can continue that fermentation we get a huge opportunity to build complexity into the wine.'

Mark has a side project making wine in the Northern Rhône in the Cornas appellation and he also works with Dagon Clan, a venture based in Dealu Mare, Romania.

WORD FROM THE WINEMAKER

A restaurant that represents your region?

Premnord in Premeaux-Prissey. Céline Dedinger is the chef and she cooks the most amazing stuff: fresh, vibrant and unfiddled with. They've got all kinds of things on the wine list, mine included.

Go-to restaurants for a meal with friends?

Bissoh is a super Japanese place in Beaune. La Table du Square in Beaune is classic and fun.

Where would you go for a late-night drink?

I think one of the greatest wine bars in the world is Bruno's in Dijon. Bruno has one of the best lists. There's hardly any space because of the boxes of wine, but it's brilliant. And the boulangerie/bar in Morey-Saint-Denis (Les Gourmandises de Morey) is one of the most honest places to have a drink in Burgundy. It's all locals.

Is there a local sports team to look out for?

I support the local rugby teams in Gevrey-Chambertin and Nuits-Saint-Georges. There's a great ambiance and camaraderie at the matches.

Quote a phrase that often gets used in Burgundy winemaking.

'*C'est compliqué*'. Used when one is not wanting to talk about a subject, or commit. Very often used when buyers are looking for a bigger allocation.

SOUTHERN RHÔNE

The Rhône Valley wine region extends 200km (125 miles) from Vienne to Avignon: in the northern stretch, steep slopes along the river produce perfumed red wines from the Syrah grape and equally fragrant whites from Viognier; the best reds are ageworthy and expensive. The southern Rhône is known for its opulent red wines made predominantly from (blends of) Grenache, Syrah and Mourvèdre. Anyone vaguely interested in French wine will have heard of Châteauneuf-du-Pape, the southern Rhône's best-known Appellation d'Origine Contrôlée (AOC) and the cream of the crop; on the other hand there's the vast Côtes du Rhône AOC, which ranges from juicy, spicy, food-friendly wines to the frankly dire.

The region makes a diverse range of wines – red, white, pink – from a variety of grapes and soil types, at all sorts of price points. There's a lot to choose from in the southern Rhône: as well as Châteauneuf-du-Pape, there are great wines from Gigondas and Vacqueyras.

Producers to look out for include Beaucastel, La Biscarelle, Clos des Papes, Gramenon, Rayas, Roucas Toumba, Vieux Télégraphe.

We're focusing on the exciting Ventoux appellation in the foothills of Mont Ventoux in the south-east of the region, roughly 90 minutes' drive north from Marseille. Ventoux is better known as one of the most gruelling climbs in the Tour de France bicycle race and remains a relatively obscure appellation. Even if the name doesn't ring a bell, you might have already tried the Ventoux gateway drug from your local off-licence – the chicken on the front of a bottle of La Vieille Ferme is instantly recognizable.

Although Ventoux is just 30km (18 miles) to the east of Châteauneuf-du-Pape, its climate and terroir are quite different. The soil is limestone-dominated and it can get incredibly windy in the vineyards. Ventoux's white wines have a wonderfully floral nose and long mouthfeel, while the pinks speak of fresh, vibrant fruit on the palate. The reds are identifiably Rhône in style with a lovely, lifted freshness.

Historically, Ventoux's cooler climate meant red grape ripening was less reliable and its reputation within France wasn't great. The untapped potential and relatively cheap land prices have attracted a diverse troupe of wine-growers from all over the world: winemaker Even Bakke swapped California for Clos de Trias; the ex-German Riesling extraordinaire Corinna Faravel crafts elegant reds at Martinelle; while Scottish couple James and Joanna King have spent the past two decades restoring and replanting the Château Unang estate.

Alex and Fred Chaudière
Château Pesquié

Trundling up the driveway to Château Pesquié, flanked on either side by 300-year-old plane trees, feels like the ultimate French fantasy: the honeyed facade of a beautiful bastide with white-shuttered windows and more than a dozen spring-fed gurgling fountains in the manicured grounds, while Mont Ventoux's wind-whipped, white limestone peak provides the backdrop. Only over the past couple of decades has Ventoux's wine-growing potential really been recognized, but there is evidence of Roman viticulture here stretching right back to the first century BC.

Affable brothers Frédéric and Alexandre Chaudière are the third generation of their family to make Ventoux wine, cementing the name Pesquié (Provençal dialect for pond, probably down to all the springs on site) as one of the region's star producers. Their maternal grandparents Odette and René moved to Mont Ventoux just before it became an AOC in 1973, renovating the château and growing grapes to sell to the local cooperative. By the mid-1980s, their daughter Edith and her husband Paul Chaudière had quit their careers (in physiotherapy and speech therapy respectively) and taken over the running of the estate. They ditched the co-op to set up their own cellar and bottled their first wines in 1990 under the Château Pesquié label, at a point when there were around ten other independent wineries in Ventoux. Today there are 150.

Fred and Alex couldn't be more different but they complement one another like Syrah and Grenache in a classic Ventoux blend, both essential parts which make the other better. Since boyhood, Alex has been helping his father and driving tractors around the vineyard. 'I was always sure I'd be working in wine,' he says, and took a classic route of studying oenology followed by nearly seven years of hands-on experience all over Europe and Australia. Alex's younger brother, Fred, left home at 16 to pursue the academic avenues of literature, philosophy and history before returning to Ventoux aged 23 for what he thought would be a temporary spell. It wasn't, and we don't blame him. 'A brief stay turned into the

birth of a sincere passion. I studied at The Paris Institute of
Political Studies, which would have prepared me for a brilliant
political future that hopefully I will never embrace,' Fred says.
Together the pair have converted the vineyard to organic and
biodynamic agriculture, officially taking the reins from papa
Paul in 2006. 'We've changed many things within the vinification
process and ageing,' says Alex. For instance, the use of concrete
eggs and larger neutral barrels as well as gentler extractions and
more whole-cluster fermentations.

The mountain creates a kind of natural amphitheatre and, while
the temperature can hit 30°C during summer days, at night the
hot air rises towards its summit and cooler air falls to the foothills.
This contrast gives the wines freshness and acidity, thanks to a
longer and slower ripening of fruit, which is especially important
for their two most-planted varieties, Syrah and Grenache.
'Our cooler climate is really what makes us different from our
immediate neighbours. It's been helping us to make better wines,'
says Fred.

The Chaudière estate now totals 100 hectares (247 acres). Just
like the rest of Ventoux, the wines they produce are accessible and
diverse. Pesquié's top wines can be found on the best restaurant
lists in 40 countries. Quintessence is one of the finest wines in the
appellation: a concentrated blend of 80 per cent Syrah and 20 per
cent Grenache from 50-year-old vines grown on clay-limestone
soils. The wine is barrel-aged for 12 to 15 months. The nose grabs
you and pulls you in with ripe raspberries and black truffles. The
juicy tannins pair perfectly with local meat, such as Sisteron lamb.

Later-ripening Cinsault, Mourvèdre and Carignan are used for
the estate's red and rosé blends. White production is based
on Grenache Blanc, Roussanne and Clairette plus plantings of
Marsanne, Vermentino and Viognier. You can't go wrong with
their entry-level wines produced under their Le Paradou label.
The Viognier, for instance, is easy drinking with a fleshy texture
that is the essence of the Rhône, with a white floral nose like
freshly washed sheets. You'll often find Le Paradou at brilliant
restaurants and Bert regularly puts them on his wine lists simply
because you get so much for your money.

So far, climate change has smiled upon the region's producers, with hotter and drier growing seasons meaning winemakers here can achieve the ripeness they struggled to get 30 years ago. 'We are thinking of planting some new areas higher up. It's not that easy as there is less water reserve, but there is some really interesting terroir in the north-east part of the Ventoux,' says Alex. 'We are afraid of the frost, but it's going to happen one way or another,' adds Fred. 'In terms of planting Sicilian or Portuguese grapes [as they are doing in Bordeaux in reaction to warming temperatures], I think we should really understand how far we can go with the ones that have been here for so long. There will be less Syrah and Grenache in our wines in the future. No doubt. But if we start making Verdejo–Assyrtiko blends, who will we be anyway? It would be so far from what we have always done, it doesn't make any sense.'

Trust us – drinking a glass of pink Ventoux on a summer evening in the gardens of Château Pesquié is the place to be.

WORD FROM THE WINEMAKER

Your go-to restaurants for a meal with friends?

There are many around us. Hard to decide between La Table du Ventoux, La Colombe in Bédoin on the way up to the Ventoux, [headed up by] a young French chef trained in Aspen, California, La Calade in Blauvac, Vin Ensen in Caromb and Chez Serge in Carpentras. In terms of an all-time favourite dish, perhaps the pigeon from Chef Christophe Schuffenecker at La Colombe.

Any recommendations for lunch in Ventoux?

A local favourite is the truffle 'brouillade' from Serge Ghoukassian (of restaurant Chez Serge in Carpentras, a town which has the oldest black truffle market in France). Truffle is one of the signature products in the Ventoux, and Serge is one of its greatest ambassadors.

Where would you go for a late-night drink?

Vin Ensen in Caromb offers an incredible range of great wines. Vin Ensen means 'wine together' in Provençal dialect. It was created by two young sommeliers, Philippe Sébire and Hugo Boulay.

Where's the best market for fresh produce?

The most iconic market is the one in L'Isle-sur-la-Sorgue, held on Thursdays and Sundays.

Your favourite producers for cheese and meat?

For cheeses, Fromagerie Mercy in Carpentras. They are all taken care of with incredible passion and professionalism. For meat and charcuterie, Brunet in Carpentras or La Boucherie des Halles in Pernes-les-Fontaines.

Which local delicacy should you not miss?

Nougat, made with the local almonds and lavender honey. Check out the ones from Silvain in Saint-Didier, a 'paysan-nougatier'. And a local cheese called Banon, wrapped in chestnut leaves.

A local dish to look out for?

L'agneau de sept heures [leg of lamb cooked at a l ow heat for seven hours], as we have amazing lamb in the area (particularly the lamb from Sisteron, north-east of the Ventoux mountain), paired with a ratatouille made with vegetables from the Comtat Venaissin plain nearby.

Any insider tips for Ventoux?

The most famous [and toughest] cycling route goes from the village of Bédoin to the summit of the Ventoux. If you are a little less trained, you might want to tackle it from Sault (and in June and July you'll see the incredible colours of the lavender fields). The third route to the summit goes up from Malaucène. If you are not in shape to cycle the Ventoux mountain, you must still walk on its summit: on a clear day there are outstanding views of the Alps to the north and the Mediterranean to the south; standing on the bare limestone rocks feels like being on the Moon.

GEORGIA

For many wine lovers, a visit to this mountainous country between Europe and Asia is more of a pilgrimage. You can thank Georgia for the current craze for orange wine: skin-contact amber wine fermented in *qvevri* – big-bellied terracotta pots buried to their necks underground – is a source of national pride. The Georgians have been making wine this way for centuries and the country owes much of its cult following to this ancient way of natural winemaking, despite the fact that less than five per cent of its wines are produced this way today.

Bordering the south-eastern shores of the Black Sea, the country is one of Europe's most diverse: you'll find the rare temperate Colchic rainforest in the country's west; the Chalaadi glacier in western Svaneti near the Russian border; and Kakheti's Gareja desert in the south. Part of the Soviet Union between 1922 and 1991, Georgia counts Turkey, Armenia, Azerbaijan and Russia as its neighbours, a situation which its president Salome Zourabichvili describes as both blessing and curse: 'Blessed because the country is a lush intersection on the Silk Roads between Europe and Asia; cursed because it is hemmed in by mighty empires with a penchant for invading: Persians, Turks and Arabs from the south, Mongols and Russians from the north. Moscow ruled Georgia for most of the nineteenth and twentieth centuries, and invaded briefly in 2008.' Indeed, in 2008 Russia seized control of two breakaway borderland enclaves within Georgia, Abkhazia and South Ossetia, both of which are still occupied by Russian troops.

Winemaking in Georgia stretches back at least 8,000 years and its history is interwoven with the vines. Its language may have given us the word for wine (from the Georgian *gvino*) and there's even a legend that says the cursive script used to write the Georgian language is derived from the tendrils of grapevines. What we can say with more certainty is that Georgia can lay claim to being the ancestral home of viticulture. Archaeologists discovered ceramic fragments which were parts of *qvevri* used to ferment and store wine in 6000 BC in a Neolithic settlement about 32km (20 miles) south of Tbilisi, the cosmopolitan capital. It's the world's oldest evidence of winemaking, and you can see the reconstructed *qvevri* on display in the Georgian National Museum, adorned with its rudimentary bunches of grapes.

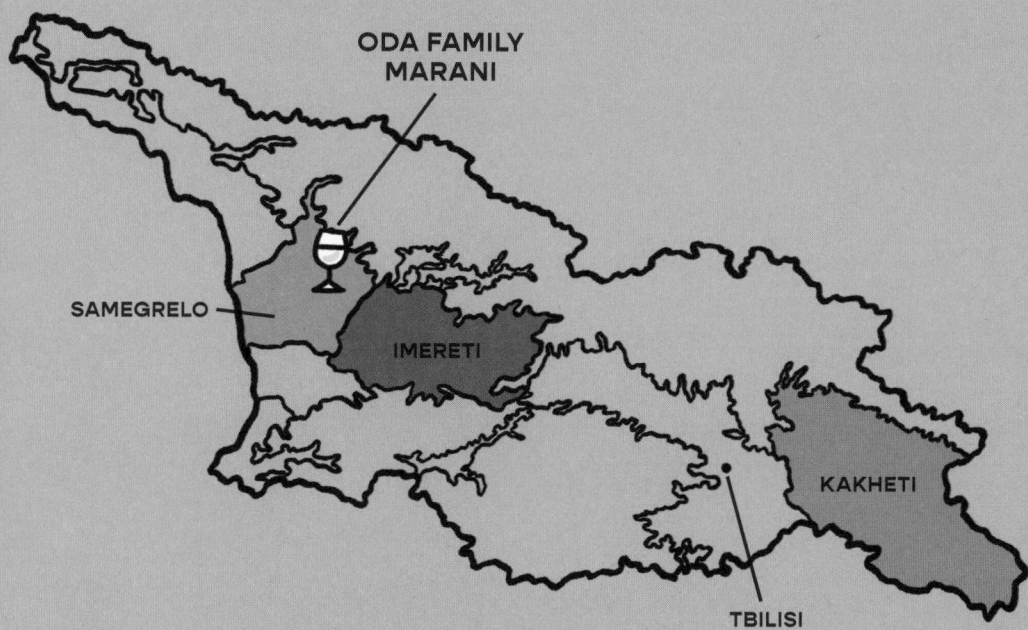

ODA FAMILY
MARANI

SAMEGRELO

IMERETI

KAKHETI

TBILISI

What's most refreshing is that the country is so completely itself – there's not been much influence from mass plantings of international varieties, and many winemakers are focusing on nurturing their own Georgian-ness. But Georgia also demonstrates the devastation of the wine industry by the Russians. Under Communism, the small country of just 3.7 million people became a powerhouse of production, supplying almost the entire USSR with lakes of low-quality wine and eroding centuries of traditional winemaking culture and knowledge in the process. Georgia has at least 525 indigenous grape varieties – more than anywhere else in the world and about a sixth of the global total – but thanks to the USSR's exclusive focus on a few high-yielding varieties, many have been lost and forgotten. Slowly, though, they are being rediscovered. Here are two you'll encounter most often:

Rkatsiteli (რქაწითელი) – A versatile white grape grown throughout Georgia. Its naturally high acidity makes refreshing, balanced wines (sparkling, still and sweet) with notes of lime zest, Cox's apples, honeydew melon and fresh walnuts.

Saperavi (საფერავი) – Georgia's favourite red grape has a name meaning 'dye' due to its deep colour. It makes high-quality wine with a fleshy, dense, juicy core, good natural acidity and grippy, grainy tannins. Best enjoyed alongside grilled meats or charcuterie.

If you're just staying in the capital, go ahead and roam freely to your heart's content, but to explore the wine-growing regions we'd suggest travelling with a wine guide. The roads can be a bit hairy and English isn't always spoken – we can recommend Maka Tarashvili or Mari Tinashvili.

Georgian hospitality is legendary, and you'll go to bed every night with both belly and heart full – there's a saying that guests are a gift from God, and your hosts will proceed to bring out plates of food until you beg them to stop (they won't). Pack trousers with elastic waistbands and thank us later.

KAKHETI

Read any wine list featuring a Georgian section, or attend a tasting of the country's wines, and you're almost certain to encounter Kakheti's offerings, often characterized by their strong tannins and heavy body. Kakheti is the largest of Georgia's ten wine regions, and produces about three-quarters of the country's wines. There are hundreds of wineries here, from tiny family *maranis* (cellars) to wine-producing monasteries (including the cave monastery of David Gareja near the Azerbaijani border) and established commercial estates.

Chock-a-block with monasteries, fortresses and waterfalls, Kakheti's diverse climate encompasses both subtropical and steppe within its vast plains, from semi-arid desert to alpine lakes. In the key wine-growing pockets, an almost Martian, rust-coloured landscape features iron-rich cinnamonic soil which translates – especially in the Saperavi wines – to a rustic, earthy character which balances out the pretty fruit notes.

We stopped by Sighnaghi, a terracotta-roofed hilltop town on the ancient Silk Road with countless traditional turquoise-painted wooden balconies overlooking the Alazani Valley. Here, we tasted wines at the cellar door of one of the biggest names in Georgian wine: Pheasant's Tears. The name is a nod to a Georgian legend that says only the very best wines are good enough to make a pheasant cry. It's an enterprise co-run by the American John Wurdeman, a restaurateur and painter turned winemaker who first fell in love with Georgia when he heard the country's polyphonic folk music on a CD as a 16-year-old skateboarder in 1991. John was one of the first to introduce the world to the wonders of Georgian wine. His on-site restaurant gets popular, so make a reservation to try the wines alongside dishes constructed from the daily bounties of Sighnaghi farmers' market.

Other names to know include Giorgi (Gogi) Dakishvili, a much-respected third-generation winemaker who runs Orgo in Shalauri, a village near the region's capital, Telavi, and also consults for the large Schuchmann estate. Gogi's *qvevri* Saperavi made from 80-year-old vines was the best red we tasted on our trip, with rich notes of blackcurrant, cherry and leather. His son Temuri also has a separate project called Vita Vinea. History geeks should drop by the Ikalto Monastery, a sixth-century complex near Telavi with a *qvevri* graveyard and eighth-century stone wine press; and there's a super-kooky display of wine-

related artefacts at the family-run hotel and museum at Dimitri Wine House in Telavi. Then there's Winery Rtoni (Georgian for branches) run by ex-lawyer and gaming enthusiast Giorgi Skhirtladze, whose wines are stocked at the brilliant 8000 Vintages wine bar in Tbilisi.

The Shumi winery is one of Kakheti's biggest estates, based in the Alazani Valley. We stopped by for plates of Kakhetian *mtsvadi* (pork skewers cooked over flame) and *khinkali* (broth-filled dumplings reminiscent of Chinese *xiaolongbao*) – Georgia's incredible cuisine is a mash-up of thousands of years of trading and invasion. The manicured grounds include a living museum of more than 400 grape varieties. These are blended together into a somewhat lethal fortified wine called Zigu, which we toasted with the Georgian version of cheers, *gaumarjos*, which translates as 'to our victory'.

IMERETI

Kutaisi, the capital of the Imereti region, is one of the oldest cities in Europe and a great jumping-off point for loads of natural wonders and historical sites. It's a quirky spot on the banks of the Rioni River, full of faded metalwork, hipsterish cafés and a vegetable-heavy cuisine rich in wild greens, herbs and salads doused with crushed walnut dressings (we ate at Lilestan, Sisters and Tina's Ethno Winehouse). The city has its own airport (worth checking out as lots of budget airlines fly in here) and on its outskirts the UNESCO World Heritage-listed Gelati Monastery is a medieval beauty adorned with elaborate frescoes. A little further out, you'll find massive cave complexes and the semi-abandoned Soviet-era sanatoriums at Tskaltubo, built around the radon-carbonated spring waters that Joseph Stalin used to

frequent. Many are surprised that the ruthless revolutionary was a Georgian, born Ioseb Besarionis dze Jughashvili into a poor family in Gori, about an 80-minute drive from Tbilisi.

The Imeretian countryside is a patchwork of vines, mulberry bushes and swaying cornfields (Mchadi cornbread is a local staple) to a soundtrack of clanging bells and hooves as processions of cows hold up cars on the rural roads. There are fruit trees laden with peaches, persimmons and pomegranates, and to the west, around Khoni, tea plantations produce a delicate black tea which goes nicely after a meal with some slices of *churchkhela* – chewy sweet treats in the shape of a sausage made from dried grape must and filled with walnuts.

Imereti's key indigenous white grape varieties include Tsolikauri, which has a full-bodied, oily character similar to Vermentino; Tsitska, with high acidity and a herbal, aromatic nose a bit like a good Pinot Gris; and the late-blooming Krakhuna (meaning 'crisp'), which develops rich and complex aromas in the right vintage. These wines typically have a fresh, cool-climate character that's more of an entry-point to a western European palate than Kakheti's richer, tannin-heavy amber wines. Here in Imereti, wines benefit from the warm ripening season and develop mandarin and tropical fruit flavours; the amber wines especially have lots of structure and body.

A name to look out for is Gaioz Sopromadze, a family-run winery in Baghdati. Fourth-generation Lasha Sopromadze makes wonderful low-intervention *qvevri* wines from local varietals grown on sandy, iron- and flint-rich soils.

SAMEGRELO

The Black Sea influences the maritime and subtropical climate of Samegrelo, one of Georgia's prettiest provinces, in the far west of the country. It's also one of the country's oldest wine-growing regions. The best grapes are grown in the foothills of the Caucasus Mountains, where cooling breezes lessen the effects of high humidity, which makes vines susceptible to rot and disease. To combat humidity, the *maghlari* method of grape cultivation – where vines are trained to grow up tree trunks as nature intended – was widespread here until the twentieth century.

The lush region is known as 'the land of the Mingrelians', after an ethnic subgroup of Georgian people with their own language, Mingrelian or Megrelian. Legend lies heavily here. Samegrelo was once part of the Kingdom of Colchis, an ancient land rich in gold, which in Greek mythology was the destination of Jason and the Argonauts, who sailed here in search of the Golden Fleece.

Exotic fruits such as mandarins, kiwis and chillies grow successfully, but Samegrelo is best known for its hazelnuts – Georgia is one of the top global exporters of the nut. The valuable crop has helped to turn around the cash-poor region's fortunes but an invasive Asian pest called the brown marmorated stink bug, first spotted in Georgia in 2015, has wreaked havoc on harvests.

Some of Samegrelo's dishes can have a kick. Look out for Megrelian adjika: a chilli paste seasoned with garlic, fenugreek and coriander that accompanies all sorts of foods.

Keto Ninidze
Oda Family Marani

One of the winemakers who left the biggest impression on us during our travels was Keto. A passionate proponent of women's rights, the self-taught winemaker uses her labels as vehicles for political and social commentary.

The wine that put Keto on the map is her Samegrelo-grown salmon-pink rosé wine, Naked Ojaleshi. The variety's Mingrelian name means 'grows on trees' – referring to the way that the vines were once grown – and the wine is 'naked' because the dark-skinned grapes are fermented and aged in *qvevri* without their skins. 'Terroir vs. Terror' is written on the label with artworks of two nude women: one beautiful and proud, standing surrounded by vines, and the other crammed into a glass, like a cage. Keto tells us this label is a nod to the high levels of gender-based violence in Georgia and also the way women are trapped in kitchens because of *supra* – extravagant multi-course feasts to mark special occasions. A Georgian *supra* always has a toastmaster, a *tamada*, who leads the party and introduces each toast. '*Supra* culture is a lot of work,' Keto explains. 'Today, a *supra* with a toastmaster has become quite a touristic thing.'

Meanwhile, '20 per cent of Georgia is occupied by Russia' is printed across the front of her dry white Tsolikouri *qvevri* wine (made from grapes grown in Orbeli, in Samegrelo's neighbouring Lechkhumi region) along with an illustration of Georgia's outline filled with grapes; the sections of dead fruit represent the Russian-occupied territories of South Ossetia and Abkhazia. Her Dzelshavi is made from 60-year-old vines in the Racha region; the ancient thin-skinned red grape can be compared to Pinot Noir or Beaujolais. The label shows a pregnant woman with her arms around her *qvevri*-shaped belly: 'I see the *qvevri* as a symbol of fertility,' Keto says. 'In the same way a woman gives birth to a child, *qvevris* give birth to wine.'

Tbilisi-born Keto is an eloquent writer. She worked for ten years as a researcher for the Institute of Georgian Literature and began writing about wine in 2015, while studying for her doctoral thesis on the sociology of literature at the capital's Ilia State University. She is married to Zaza Gagua, a geographer by profession, and one of the co-founders of Marani Martvili, a small winery making low-intervention wines since 2012 using traditional Georgian methods in his family's village, Targameuli in Samegrelo. Keto's own sidestep into winemaking came about in late 2015, after hearing how another farmer in Targameuli was struggling to sell 500kg (80st) of top-quality Ojaleshi grapes. She bought them and began her first experiments.

Fortuitously, in 2016 Zaza was offered a top administrative job at Martvili Canyon national park – an otherworldly river gorge with waterfalls and turquoise waters that feels like something out of a Studio Ghibli movie. We paddled through it on an inflatable boat, and suggest you should too.

For the nature-loving couple and their two daughters, relocating to rural Samegrelo was a no-brainer. 'We always wanted to live here, in Zaza's ancestral home,' Keto says. They settled in an *oda* built by Zaza's great-grandfather in 1935; it's a wooden house with an elaborate balcony raised on stilts, traditionally found in western Georgia, where the climate is humid and warm. Keto's business, Oda Family Marani, is named in its honour, and she runs her cellar entirely independently of Zaza. 'Though my husband's winemaking experience and my own are two different stories, Oda is generally perceived as his project. Family and wine rest on patriarchal values [in Georgia],' Keto writes in her 2019 book, *A Gently Fermenting Revolution: women in the Georgian wine business.*

When the couple cut down a hazelnut plantation to make way for their vineyard in 2016, their neighbours looked on with incredulity. They planted old Megrelian and Abkhazian grape varieties: Chvitiluri, Koloshi, Dudghushi, Lakvazhi and Ashugazhi. Many of these were lost and forgotten during Soviet rule.

We try Keto's wines at her on-site Oda Family Restaurant
alongside a bounty of Megrelian delicacies brought out by local
women, made from produce grown in their permaculture vegetable
garden or from nearby farmers. It's some of the best food either
of us have ever tasted at a winery and their Megrelian *khachapuri*
(with grated cheese on top as well as inside the bread) is worth
the trip alone. Be sure to call and book ahead. 'The women in the
kitchen also help with the winery. It's a completely female-run
operation,' she says.

Keto follows an organic, low-intervention philosophy without
being dogmatic – if a wine needs sulphur dioxide before bottling,
she'll add a bit, and if the grapes are struggling with disease
in humid conditions, she'll intervene with some (organically
approved) copper. 'We don't filter. We don't use caps on the corks;
it's pointless plastic. For me the most important thing is to express
the character of the terroir with minimal intervention,' she says.
As of 2024, Keto's annual production hovers around the 7,000 bottle
mark and much of this is exported, including to Sager + Wilde in
east London.

WORD FROM THE WINEMAKER

Your local restaurant recommendations?

We eat Megrelian food at Sanapiro in Martvili and Diaroni in Zugdidi. Papavero in Kutaisi also has tasty food.

Dining favourites in Tbilisi?

I always prefer a casual, light meal with friends. My favourite places in Tbilisi are Craft Wine Restaurant and Ninia's Garden.

What are the best food pairings with your wines?

Western Georgia's acidic, fresh and crisp wines are very food-friendly and go well with dairy, which is dominant in Megrelian cuisine.

Your favourite family dish?

In Samegrelo, where hunger was often a problem, the most important dish was *ghomi*. *Ghomi* is rather like polenta: before Columbus, it was made from a variety of millet and then it was replaced with corn. Megrelians are very conservative about cooking this sacred meal. It has to be shiny white, properly cleaned and with a certain consistency. I love to serve *ghomi* with melted Sulguni (qvervi-aged Megrelian cheese) inside, and also with Gebzhalia cheese (Sulguni-style cheese seasoned with fresh mint), which also has to be bright white. 'Bzha' (in Ge-bzha-lia) in Megrelian language means both 'sun' and 'milk' – and Gebzhalia is usually made in the shape of a spiral (eternal sunshine). I also love to cook *ghomi* with wine, like Italians do with risotto. I use Tsolikouri wine, cream, grated smoked Sulguni cheese, fresh herbs and green apples from my garden.

Any insider tips for Samegrelo?

The most beautiful places in Martvili are the Oniore waterfall (but it's a pretty long hike), Balda Canyon and Martvili Canyon. There are lots of beautiful swimming places on the Abasha River near Martvili Canyon. Half an hour's drive from us, over the border in Imereti, are the Okatse Canyon and Okatse waterfall – both places are very special and a must to experience while visiting our area.

What do you do on a rare day off?

My number one passion is writing. I also love singing.

Can you tell us a bit more about Georgian music?

What I love about Georgian songs is their diversity: Tushetian songs have nothing in common with Gurian ones; Kakhetian folk songs are very different from Megrelian songs. Most of all I love Gurian songs with their musical thinking articulated in polyphony. My grandmother's sister was a wonderful performer of Gurian Krimanchuli – which is something like yodelling.

GERMANY

Most of Germany's 13 wine regions are clustered in the south-west of the country, the spiritual home of our beloved Riesling grape, which was first recorded in the Rheingau region in 1435, and is Germany's most planted grape – a fragrant, fresh and elegant variety which develops in complexity as it ripens late in these cool climes. Two-thirds of German wine production is white and apart from Riesling you'll encounter Gewürztraminer, Müller-Thurgau, Pinot Blanc (Weissburgunder), Pinot Gris (Grauburgunder), Scheurebe and Silvaner. Dornfelder and Pinot Noir (Spätburgunder) are two reds you'll see frequently. The fact that the Germans are the world's third largest producers of Pinot Noir still seems to fly under the radar (is it the idiosyncratic labelling?), a shame given they make some superb quality examples.

Victoria fell in love with Germany's stonking Rieslings while working front of house at Som Saa, the Thai restaurant in east London. The food-friendly wine list – at the time put together by a badass Berliner sommelier called Christina Schneider – still lives rent-free in her mind. These are relatively full-bodied wines with an acidity that makes them much more refreshing than most Chardonnays and thus pairing perfection for bold, spicy and/or aromatic dishes. And don't be afraid of a touch of residual sugar (sugar that has not been converted into alcohol during the fermentation process) because the fresh acidity in these wines balances out the sweetness. Keller's trocken (dry) Riesling from Rheinhessen is so zesty it tastes almost like biting into a lime.

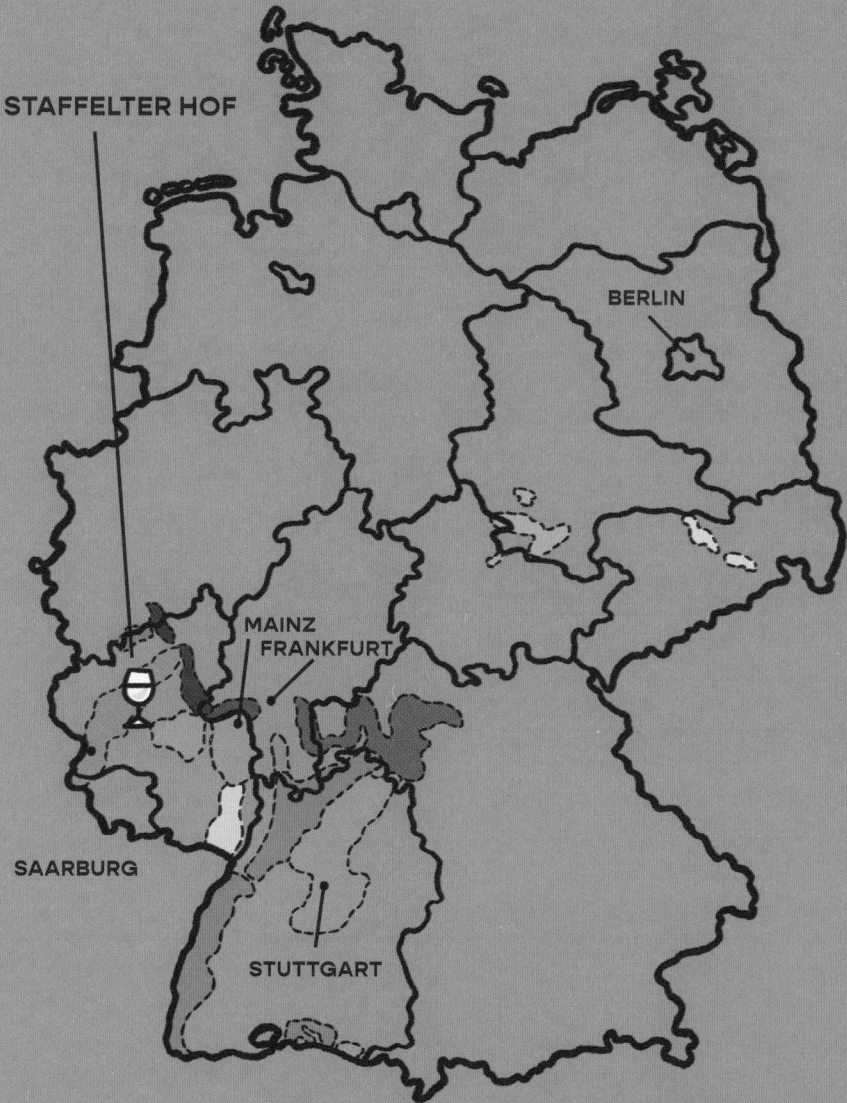

STAFFELTER HOF

BERLIN

MAINZ
FRANKFURT

SAARBURG

STUTTGART

GERMAN CLASSIFICATIONS

Germany's wine classification systems are probably the most complicated in the world. The lowest-quality categories are **Landwein** and **Deutscher Wein**. However, as in other parts of Europe, some modern winemakers use these terms for excellent wines as they choose to work outside the many constraints of the higher-quality levels.

Qualitätswein – the grapes for these wines must come entirely from one of Germany's 13 wine regions. Sugar may be added during fermentation to boost the alcohol if the grapes are not ripe and sweet enough. Levels of sweetness may be indicated on the label: Trocken (or Selection) is the driest, containing less than 9 grams of residual sugar per litre. Halbtrocken, Feinherb or Classic describe off-dry styles.

Prädikatswein is the main category for high-quality wines. Traditionally, as a cool-climate country, Germany's grapes often struggled to achieve ripeness, so this became the determining factor of wine quality. The grapes are picked when fully ripe; no sugar may be added to these wines. In ascending order of ripeness these are:

Kabinett – dry or off-dry, usually light-bodied; a great aperitif, thirst-quenching and super drinkable.

Spätlese (*'late harvest'*) – the grapes are left on the vine after they've ripened; the wines are usually off-dry, but are sometimes 'trocken' (dry); richer and fuller-bodied than Kabinett, we love pairing these wines with pork.

Auslese (*'selection'*) – the very ripest, late-harvested grapes are used. Nearly always sweet, these wines pair well with fresh fruits or savoury, spicy dishes.

Beerenauslese (BA), or 'berry selection' is made from shrivelled grapes, which develop lush tropical fruit and honeysuckle notes. These sweet wines can be enjoyed alongside desserts or salty or funky cheeses.

Trockenbeerenauslese (TA) – three words glued together as 'dry berry selection': the raisined grapes are very high in sugar, and noble rot concentrates the sweetness even further, resulting in intensely sweet, decadent wine to sip on its own and which also works in synchronicity with cheesecake.

Eiswein ('ice wine') – the grapes are frozen on the vines and picked when the temperature dips to -7°C or -8°C. The berries must be pressed immediately, resulting in a super-concentrated nectar to make a rare, expensive treat.

VDP (Verband Deutscher Prädikatsweingüter), the Association of German Prädikat Wine Estates, is a group of more than 200 German wineries. Members must follow strict rules; the system was inspired by France's fine wine classifications where the site or vineyard is of importance. Bottles or their capsules will show the VDP logo of a stylized eagle with a cluster of grapes, linked with one of the following terms:

Gutswein – estate-grown wines, labelled with the region and grape variety.

Ortswein – grapes come from a particular village and the wines express plenty of regional character. It's the equivalent of village wine in Burgundy.

Erste Lage ('first site') – the equivalent of a Premier Cru in France; wines are labelled with the name of the village and vineyard. Abbreviated on labels to 1G.

Grosse Lage ('great site') – the very finest vineyards, equivalent to the French Grand Cru: dry, ageworthy wines from these sites can, if they meet the VDP criteria, be labelled Grosses Gewächs ('great growth'), abbreviated to GG.

MOSEL

The deeply meandering Mosel River has flowed through France and Luxembourg before it reaches Germany, where it eventually joins the River Rhine at Koblenz. The banks that rise from the river are home to some of the most dizzyingly steep and labour-intensive vineyards in the world, some so treacherous that no machine can work here. The southerly-facing slopes, with heat-retaining soils made up of blue and red slate, produce wines that are up there with the very best.

The Mosel is an ancient winemaking region; the Romans cultivated vines here in the first century BC and modern-day Trier, Germany's oldest city, sits at the head of the Mosel Valley. Founded around 15 BC as Augusta Treverorum, it later became one of the Roman Empire's flourishing capitals, and you can still see the evidence, from an amphitheatre that entertained a 22,000-strong crowd with gladiator fights and executions, to Porta Nigra, one of the best-preserved Roman city gates in the world.

We dropped by the Peter Lauer estate in the Mosel's Saar region on our travels, but Bert had visited the family-run winery founded in 1830 a few years prior for a tasting with Florian Lauer, the head winemaker. It was an eventful trip in which Bert perfected his sabrage – the technique for opening sparkling wine with a sabre – even managing to sabrage a bottle of Sekt with a bin lid. On Bert's birthday, as a surprise, Florian disgorged a bottle of 1988 birth year sekt for him to try (no bin lid involved). The '88 vintage hits the kind of highs that most Champagnes can only dream about – the finest bubbles, with hints of

THE '88 Vintage Sekt HITS Highs Champagnes Can ONLY Dream About

smokey bacon and yellow apple purée on the nose. And the palate? Sensory overload with aged Parmesan flavours and golden pears.

Another visit was made to quintessential Mosel producer Weingut Joh. Jos. Prüm – hosted by the lawyer-turned-winemaker Dr Katharina Prüm, whose family has been growing grapes here for hundreds of years. We clambered up the slate terraces to see the sundial in the vineyard of Wehlen ('Wehlener Sonnenuhr') which appears on every J J Prüm label. Lunch started with a glass of Kabinett Riesling and white asparagus. A main course of sausages and pork terrine was paired with Spätlese and for dessert, piles of the most spectacular in-season strawberries alongside an incredibly fresh and vibrant off-dry Auslese from 2007.

Jan Matthias Klein
Staffelter Hof

Little Bastard. Party Panda. It's Müller Time. These are not the names of wines you expect to come out of one of the world's oldest wineries, let alone one of the most traditional winemaking regions in Europe. But Jan Klein, seventh-generation winemaker at Staffelter Hof, is not your everyday producer.

Records for the Staffelter Hof estate go back to 862 CE, when it was owned by the Belgian Benedictine Abbey of Stavelot. Secularized in the early nineteenth century, the historic winery – with its Play Doh yellow riverside manor tucked into a sweeping bend of the Mosel River – has been Klein family property ever since. 'Mostly, this area is known for old people and oompah music,' says Jan. 'Things are slowly changing.' And he's been instrumental in the Mosel's reinvention. Staffelter Hof is in Kröv, a village roughly halfway between the cities of Trier and Koblenz, in the Mittelmosel (middle Mosel), where many of the biggest and best German producers are located. Think Dr Loosen, Joh. Jos. Prum, and Willi Schaefer.

A nine-year-old Jan's earliest wine memory was a dulcet sip of a 1983 Auslese Riesling made by his father. 'I can't say I was hooked but I was definitely interested,' he says. His childhood spent helping out his perfectionist father Gerd at the family winery was almost enough to put Jan off the industry altogether, but not quite. 'When I finished high school I thought, my parents have a cool place here and they put their heart and soul in it. I should at least try.' So he worked a harvest at Weingut Sander, in Rheinhessen, one of the first organic wineries in Germany, helped by his mentor, the late Daniel Vollenweider at Weingut Vollenweider – a pioneering producer from Switzerland who came to the region with nothing and ended up as a benchmark of great Mosel Riesling.

Jan polished his craft at Winburndale Vineyard in Australia and Domaine des Planes in Provence, and aged 28 took over at Staffelter Hof in 2005. He ceased herbicide application

immediately and embarked on an arduous path to organic
conversion (eventually gaining certification in 2014). You could
compare it to a giant game of Tetris: a six-year process of buying,
swapping and selling pieces of land next to existing parcels (now
14 hectares, or 35 acres in total). If you have loads of small plots
scattered across the dramatic slopes (as is the norm in Mosel)
and your neighbours on both sides are applying conventional
treatments via pesticide-spraying helicopter, a mere gust of wind
can take the preparations in the wrong direction. So you need
enough land together that going organic makes sense.

His next mission was to go back to basics with winemaking. 'In
the 1990s it was all the rage to use all selected yeasts, enzymes
and fining agents,' he says. In a radical departure from the Mosel
mainstream, Jan created his first unsulphured and unfiltered
Naturwein in 2014 (released in 2016): Madcap Magnus, a hand-
bottled bone-dry Riesling, spontaneously fermented (i.e. made
without added yeasts) until all the sugar was converted to alcohol.
Magnus the wolf appears on Staffelter Hof's coat of arms – legend
has it that a donkey once worked the perilous slopes of Kröv until
a wolf killed it. Magnus was captured by the monks, who put him
to work on the vineyards as penance.

By 2015, Jan's entire production was made in a low-intervention
way. The sole differences between the Jan Matthias Klein (low
intervention) wines and the Staffelter Hof classics? The latter get
sulphured and filtered. That's all.

His early industry fans include Nic Rizzi (music mogul turned
Modal Wines founder) and the orange wine expert Simon Wolf.
Bolstered by a bumper harvest in 2018, the low-intervention side
of the winery has proliferated – today outselling the traditional
wines. Jan insists that both lines get just as much love, even
though they seem so different.

The dynamic international team includes viticulturist Kosie
Van Der Merwe, from South Africa's only Demeter-certified
winery, Nomad Wines, based in Elgin. Yamile Abad was Jan's
cellarmaster between 2018 and 2021, a Peruvian woman crazy
about fermentation.

Music is a big deal here: Jan loves rock, metal and punk, while his brother Ernst is in a band and writes music and lyrics. 'Together we started a cultural association at the winery,' Jan says – check the website for events; you can also stay on-site in apartments.

You'll notice the tongue-in-cheek *Naturweine* labels designed by local artist (and upcycling enthusiast) Aaron Scheuer are odes to music, politics and alt-culture. There's Rizzy Starmust, an ancestral method pét-nat Riesling inspired by Ziggy Stardust (David Bowie), fermented in oak, then transferred with residual sugar for a bottle fermentation of between 18 and 24 months to make the natural bubbles. It has brilliant texture and looks and smells wild, but has pure flavours on the palate of honeysuckle, pear and stem ginger.

Kiss Kiss Maddies Lips, a dark rosé fizz which takes its name from the Nirvana song *Molly's lips*, is a blend of Pinot Noir and Pinot Madeleine bursting with cranberry and cherry flavours which makes for a fun, crushable summer wine to share with friends.

Sandersstruck is an aromatic Müller-Thurgau skin-contact wine with lots of weight and richness on the palate, and a wonderful mineral core which brings it all together. 'I got a bit too excited about making that label,' Jan laughs. 'The original name of the wine was 'It's Müller Time'. The label was a drawing of Robert Müller, the guy investigating Donald Trump for meddling with Russia to win the 2016 election. The wine was banned in North Carolina. For the next vintage I changed the name to Sandersstruck as a tribute to Bernie Sanders.'

Staffelter Hof is part of the international Slow Food association and the winegrowers' association *Der klitzekleine Ring* (a group dedicated to the recovery and preservation of the Mosel's steepest hillside vineyards – many have been abandoned, wiping away centuries of knowledge). Jan also provides a platform for up-and-coming organic winemakers to experiment (via his Pandamonium sideline). Sustainability and future-proofing is at the forefront: from planting herbs, shrubs and trees among the vineyards as part of an agroforestry project, to engaging flocks of sheep to help with trimming of the weeds and the application of natural fertilizer, as well as experimenting with three hectares (seven acres) of hybrid grapes and, in 2015, plantings of Portuguese varieties. 'It's a small project with a [winemaker] friend, Pedro Marques from the Lisbon area (see pages 228–30), to see if climate change has made it possible to grow them here. The Fernão Pires is usually straightforward but the Arinto is very late ripening – Riesling comparable. The wine control came here this spring and said, "Oh, but you cannot write Portugieser [a type of red grape grown in Germany] on the label when it has Portuguese grapes in there." I said, "I'm not writing Portugieser, I'm writing it this way – PortuGeezer." And she looked at it and said, you and your funny labels.'

WORD FROM THE WINEMAKER

What are your favourite spots to eat in the Mosel?

Die Mosel in Traben-Trarbach is an amazing place, very creative Iza-Tapa cuisine, with small dishes to share and a great selection of wines.

My favourite place in Kröv is Nikos restaurant in the Panorama Hotel. They do Mediterranean food (mainly Greek-influenced). I adore their fried aubergine with Mizithra cheese, walnuts and Romesco sauce.

The best typical Mosel dishes to look out for?

I love filled potatoes (with minced meat), *Deppekoche* (made from potato, leek, eggs and sausages), and wild boar prepared in all sorts of ways.

Where do you recommend for local specialities?

The butcher Kutscheid in Ürzig for wild boar sausages. My friend Thorsten Melsheimer is an affineur for a great local cheesemaker, he rubs the cheeses with his wines or with our marc.

Do you have any insider tips?

The walk from Kröv to Traben through the vineyards and forest has stunning views of the Mosel River bend. A good place for breakfast in Kröv is called Dooscht. Marcello's ice cream place is a favourite as well.

Are there any local architectural gems?

Impressive Art Deco architecture in Traben-Trarbach: the Hotel Bellevue, Villa Huesgen and Villa Breucker to name a few. These are from the glory days when Traben-Trarbach was one of the biggest wine-trading cities in the world.

GREECE

The most obvious choice for a chapter on Greek wine regions would be Santorini, the glitzy Cycladic island famous for its cliff-clinging white-washed towns and inky volcanic soils. Santorini's wines (and its flagship grape variety, Assyrtiko) have captured the hearts of sommeliers across the globe (shoutouts to Estate Argyros, Hatzidakis Winery and Artemis Karamolegos). We love this grape: in Santorini it produces a white wine that's wonderfully seaweed-saline and mineral. Some of the world's top winemakers adore Assyrtiko too: Alois Lageder in Italy's Alto Adige, Eben Sadie in South Africa, and Jim Barry in Australia's Clare Valley are all growing the grape on their home turf.

Mark Andrew MW, co-founder of Noble Rot (the brilliant restaurant group and wine magazine) and one half of the duo behind the importers Keeling Andrew & Co, is a longtime cheerleader for Greece's new-gen winemakers. Like many, he first fell in love with the world-class wines made from Assyrtiko on Santorini. 'Haridimos Hatzidakis was the master, but since his death in 2017 a number of exciting new wineries have launched on the island, including Akra Chryssos, with some superb biodynamic wines, and Oeno P, an amphora-only project from the great Paris Sigalas,' says Mark.

'Over the past few years it has been fantastic to witness the development of other Greek regions. On Crete, the genius Gianni Economou is finally getting the credit he deserves for his idiosyncratic but brilliant wines. Newcomer Iliana Malihin (see pages 146–48) is doing amazing work helping local growers convert to organic farming, and using their fruit to make wines that rewire expectations of what the Vidiano grape is capable of. In Naoussa, Xinomavro wines have undergone a revolution in quality: the rustic tannin bombs of yesteryear have given way to the silky, elegant wines of Thymiopoulos and Domaine Dalamara, two of the most underrated red-wine-producing estates in Europe.

'Even more exciting are those regions and grapes on the cusp of wider recognition. The white wines made from Robola on Kefalonia are a minerality-lover's dream, especially those from Sclavos, Sarris and Petrakopoulos. Likewise, Christos Zafeirakis in Thessaly is making a case for Limniona being Greece's top red variety, crafting sumptuous wines of harmony and finesse just down the road from Mount Olympus.'

THESSALONIKI

ATHENS

PATRAS

HERAKLION

ILIANA MALIHIN
WINERY

CRETE

On a visit to Greece in spring 2023 we heard through the grapevine that Cretan wines are where it's at. A sommelier at The Zillers Roof Garden (the Michelin-starred restaurant atop a boutique hotel in Athens), some pals at a bar called Galaxy (a 1970s timewarp near Syntagma Square in Athens) and the owner of Loggia (an unpretentious bar perched on a clifftop on the island of Sifnos, with tunes as good as the wine list) all agreed.

Crete is by far the largest of Greece's 227(ish) inhabited islands. Its position at the crossroads of Europe, Africa and Asia means it has been a hotspot of invasion and occupation over the centuries. It was the birthplace of Europe's first advanced civilization,

the Minoan, and a hub for viticulture throughout its history. A 3,500-year-old wine press – Europe's oldest – was discovered at Vathypetro, not far from the archaeological marvel that is the Minoan Palace of Knossos, just south of Heraklion.

The present-day wine industry in Crete has only been finding its feet over the past two decades. Various factors have delayed its ascent, including forest fires and the destructive arrival of phylloxera in the late 1970s (well over a century after the rest of Europe). Today, several enterprising vintners are at the forefront of Crete's renaissance. Look out for the wines of Lyrarakis, cult winemaker Gianni Economou, and Iliana Malihin (see pages 146–48).

CRETAN GRAPES

Greece produces more white wine than red, from more than 300 indigenous varieties, many of them confined to their native region. Some of our favourite Cretan mainstays to get on your radar include:

Dafni (white)
Mainly grown in the mountainous areas near Heraklion, Dafni is named after the Greek for laurel or bay tree, thanks to comparable herbaceous aromas and flavours. We paired it with *revithia*, a chickpea stew seasoned with caramelized onions and woody herbs such as rosemary, thyme and oregano. It's a very old grape: in Chania's Archaeological Museum you can admire a Bronze Age copper vessel with the inscription 'Dafnitos Oinos', meaning wine made of Dafni grapes.

Liatiko (red)
An ancient Cretan variety and the island's most widely planted red grape. Crete's cooler spots (close to the coast or at altitude) result in elegant wines. Liatiko makes an earthy, pink wine with bite, or a lovely light red a bit like Pinot Noir, perfect alongside simply grilled meats. Whack a bottle in the fridge for 30 minutes before serving to get it to what's called cellar temperature: around 12–16°C.

Thrapsathiri (white)
The grape makes well-balanced wines with heaps of natural acidity, a full body and overtones of lemon zest. Its fresh citrus notes cut through oily fish such as sardines or mackerel.

Vidiano (white)
Slowly making a comeback from near extinction, Vidiano is often referred to as Greece's answer to Viognier. Its floral nose, stone fruit flavours (in particular apricots) and a big, silky-textured finish make it super-versatile when it comes to food pairings. Douloufakis Winery makes a good, affordable example.

Iliana Malihin
Iliana Malihin Winery

You can't talk about Crete's wine scene without mentioning Iliana.
She's a true force in the revival of winemaking in south-central
Crete, and her exceptional wines made from old, sometimes
forgotten, vineyards are among the very best we tasted.

Sipping Iliana's old-vine Vidiano alongside slices of *spanakopita*
(feta and spinach pie), the wine had so much Cretan character
that opened up in the glass. The smells and tastes transport you
straight to the island: olive brine notes, flavours of stone fruit
skins and the heady perfume of sun-baked herbs.

Iliana creates all-Greek, low-intervention wines from her HQ in
Melampes, a village between Mount Kedros and Mount Vouvala
(with the Libyan Sea about 20 minutes' drive away) in the south of
Rethymno, a region between the Chania and Heraklion prefectures.
'I came across Melampes by accident. The terroir was so special,'
Iliana recalls, noting its unusually complex soils (a rocky
combination of schist layered with sand and clay), quite unlike the
island's typical limestone. 'It was the first time I saw something
like this in Crete.'

Aged 26, the Athens-born winemaker set up her winery in 2019. 'I
always wanted to live in Crete,' confesses Iliana. 'I had some of the
best moments of my life here with my grandparents in summer.
That's why I studied agriculture at university.' Her grandfather
Emmanuel had always produced his own wine from a plot of vines
in Lampini, a village in Crete's central mountain range, and the
whole family would muck in during harvest. Around the dinner
table Iliana observed everyone tasting and comparing past vintages,
and became curious about how wine worked.

For her postgraduate degree in oenology, Iliana hit headlines with
a thesis on the yeast strains native to the Vidiano vineyards in
Fourfouras on the slopes of Mount Ida, Crete's highest mountain.
She created one of her first wines while working on Santorini in

collaboration with winemaker Spyros Chryssos – a limited edition, experimental blend of Assyrtiko from the ancient Louros vineyard on Santorini and a Cretan old-vine Vidiano from Fourfouras. Part of her 2021 harvest was spent at the brilliant Burgundian winemaker Sylvain Pataille, who is leading a resurgence of the underrated white grape, Aligoté.

Iliana began her enterprise working with five growers. Today, her expanded network of 40 is clustered around the high-altitude villages of Melampes, Fourfouras and Meronas. 'We have a very hot climate, so acidity is not an easy thing to achieve. I blend a range of wines grown on different expositions of the south and north side to give a good acidity,' Iliana says. 'I'm not part of Wines of Crete [an association for the island's winemakers] because I don't think our philosophy is similar, but I have a great connection with some other natural winemakers in Greece: Sclavos in Kefalonia and Tetramythos in the Peloponnese.'

She keeps things low intervention at the winery, bar the addition of minimal sulphur dioxide at bottling to 'keep the wine alive'. She vinifies the wine from each grower separately, working with indigenous yeasts and stainless steel tanks for cool fermentations – techniques which mean that her unfined, unfiltered blends capture the essence of the sunny terraces they come from.

Each winegrower works to her strict stipulations of organic agriculture, many tending to ungrafted pre-phylloxera vineyards older than a century, although some of the plantings are much younger. 'Now, the most important thing they need to cultivate is respect for nature,' she says. Forty years ago, Rethymno was home to more than 283 hectares (700 acres) of old vines, but the vast majority have been razed by forest fires over the past 20 years, and Iliana is on a constant quest to find and protect what's left.

This is no mean feat. In July 2022 she was dealt a massive blow. Almost 90 per cent of the historic vineyards in Melampes were devastated by three days of wildfires. These old vines have roots that run deep but even if the ancient plants do survive, it may take at least three years for them to fruit again. The state has been slow to offer support so Iliana has taken matters into her own hands, pouring her efforts into consultations with experts, publicizing the issue and even catching the attention of NASA. She is determined this tragedy will not repeat itself, and is raising funds for a specialized fire protection and prevention programme for the vines.

After only a handful of vintages Iliana's wines can already be found in some of the best restaurants around the world. In the UK, try them at Noble Rot, the wine-lover's go-to, Brat, Chez Bruce and 1905 London, the city's first Cretan restaurant and at Angela's in Margate. In New York, they're on the list at Daniel (the eponymous restaurant from chef Daniel Boulud) and all over the place in Athens, including Annie Fine Cooking and Jerár. Her artist-cousin, Vassiliki Metheniti, created the wine labels, while Iliana designed her chic, concrete winery together with her mother. It's strongly recommended to phone or email before visiting, but here you can taste the wines alongside homemade bread, village cheese, and olive oil from Lampini, as well as Iliana's *tsikoudia* (a local grape-based spirit) called Omadi, the Greek word for together.

WORD FROM THE WINEMAKER

Any insider tips for the Rethymno region?

Nero in Spili is the best delicatessen. To the south-west of Spili is the Kourtaliotiko Gorge, with a hidden waterfall and river pools. I recommend the beaches of south Rethymno such as Agios Pavlos, Triopetra and Ammoudaki.

Somewhere you'd recommend for lunch in Melampes?

Nostos is a good taverna.

Which restaurant represents Rethymno?

Hasika in Rethymno Old Town.

Any more Rethymno restaurant recommendations?

Ali Vafi's Garden; Avli; H17 (bar and grill); Lemonokipos; Prima Plora (organic produce and chichi vibes, to the west of the town); Veneto (excellent food in a hotel in a fifteenth-century Venetian mansion).

Any tips for eating in Heraklion?

7 Thalasses (meaning 'seven seas' and serving top seafood); Apiri (contemporary Greek); Ladókolla (seafood-heavy menu); Il Pazzo (divine Neapolitan bites); Peskesi (Cretan cuisine served in a historic mansion); Thigaterra (carefully sourced Greek food).

ITALY

Where do we even begin with Italian wine? You can go very deep as, when it comes to drinking and dining, each of Italy's 20 regions is ferocious in its individuality. We're keeping things simple by focusing on what we believe to be the greatest terroirs in the country, and quite possibly the world: Piedmont, Tuscany, Veneto and Sicily. A few of the many reasons why we love Italian wines is their food-friendliness, great value (very often, but not always) and dazzling diversity of native grapes. About 500 varieties of grapes are grown from Italy's cooler mountainous north through to the toe of that southerly sun-baked boot.

This variety of Italian wines can be complicated to get to grips with, especially given that the country was only unified in 1871, so it's almost easier to consider it as a collection of discrete zones. There is much to be discovered beyond Italy's best-known regions and grapes. We love Alto Adige, a region of subalpine splendour bordering Switzerland and Austria, in particular the ALMA XX produced by Alois Lageder. The grape is Manzoni Bianco, a super–fresh crossing of Riesling and Pinot Bianco created in the 1920s, which is set to be your new favourite variety. In north-west Sardinia, Alessandro Dettori's one-of-a-kind wines are unlike anything else. A generous and punchy red, his Tuderi is made from 100 per cent Cannonau and aged in concrete vats. Depending on the vintage, it can reach 15–16 per cent ABV and yet retains a seriously refreshing edge and heady, herbal aromas.

If you love high-quality Nebbiolo, check out a DOCG called Valtellina, in Lombardy (the region with Milan as its glossy capital). Our favourite producers here are Ar.Pe.Pe, Sandro Fay and Dirupi. Le Marche is a hugely underrated region that runs alongside the Adriatic Sea in central Italy. You can find good-quality, generous Sangiovese and Montepulciano here, but it's the whites that are really worth the trip. Aurora, Accadia, Ca'Liptra, Malacari and Bucci are producers that excel at making wines from the Verdicchio grape, a dream pairing with rich, fishy dishes. The masters of skin contact are Radikon and Gravner from Friuli-Venezia Giulia, in Italy's northernmost corner. We also love the wines of Skerk, Miani and Le Pianure made here.

Italy's wine classification system is a pretty straightforward pyramid but a higher category does not automatically mean you're getting a superior wine.

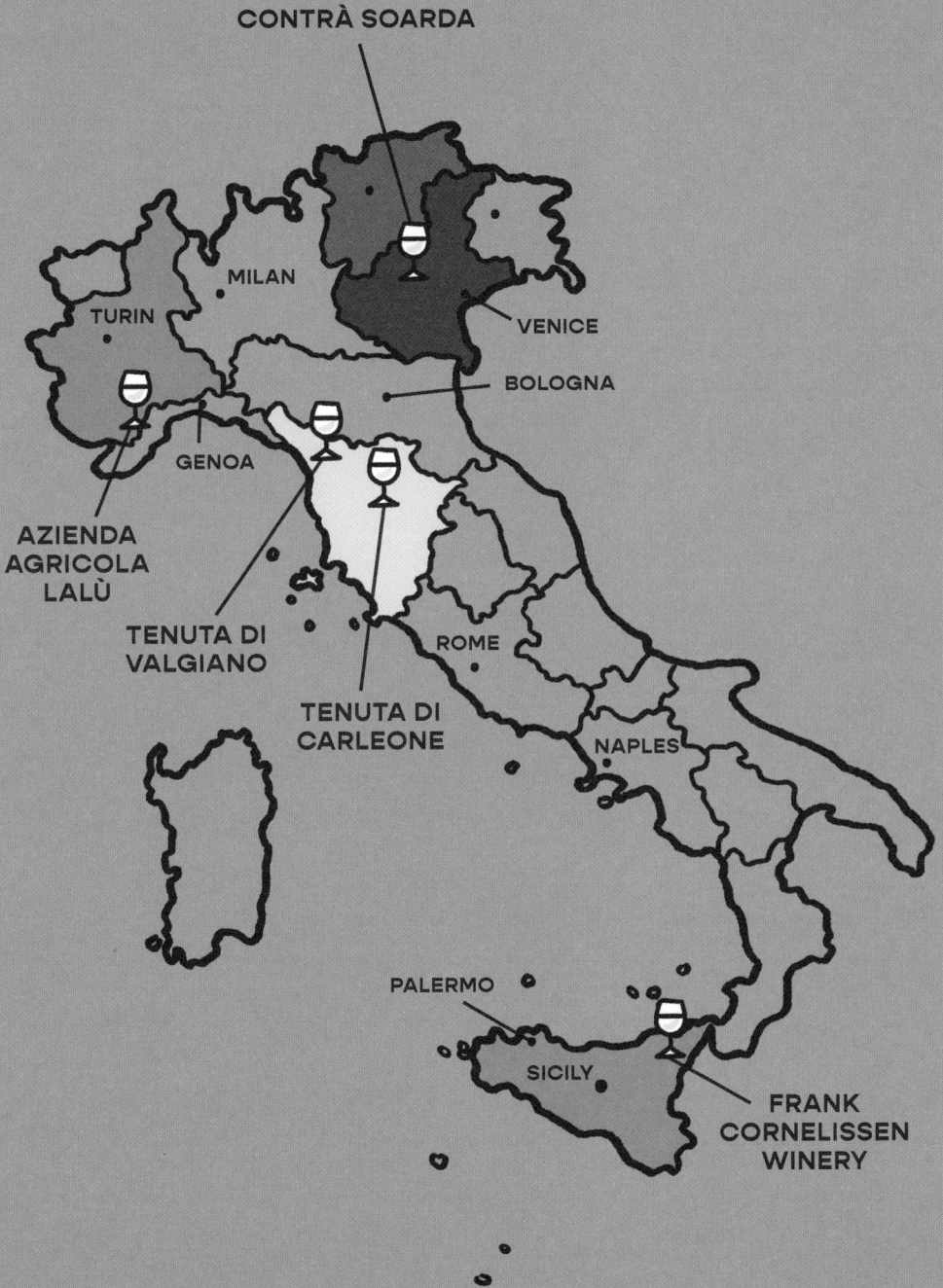

CONTRÀ SOARDA

MILAN

TURIN

VENICE

BOLOGNA

GENOA

AZIENDA
AGRICOLA
LALÙ

TENUTA DI
VALGIANO

TENUTA DI
CARLEONE

ROME

NAPLES

PALERMO

SICILY

FRANK
CORNELISSEN
WINERY

VdT/Vino da tavola (table wine)
At the base of the pyramid sits Vino da tavola (VdT), which is usually an affordable wine made to be enjoyed while young. A VdT doesn't meet the specific requirements of a geographic or classification designation like a DOC or DOCG. It's the kind of unfussy wine you'd drink from a plastic beaker with a quick plate of pasta on holiday. A brilliant, super-gluggable example is Fiasco! Vino Rosso from Monte Bernardi, a quirky blend of organic fruit from all over Italy – Tuscany, Le Marche and Sicily. About 20 quid for a litre.

IGT/Indicazione geografica tipica (indication of geographical typicality)
These wines are labelled with the place they were made. A wide range of quality and prices is represented under this umbrella: not all IGTs are created equal.

DOC/Denominazione di origine controllata (designation of origin)
There are 329 different DOC wines, encompassing some famous names like Soave, Valpolicella and Montepulciano d'Abruzzo. Again, there are world-class DOCs, but some terrible examples too. Seeking out the smaller, lesser-known DOCs can be more rewarding, such as Boca or Gattinara in Alto Piemonte.

DOCG/Denominazione di origine controllata e garantita (controlled and guaranteed designation of origin)
The DOCG classification is reserved for Italy's best wines from the most respected vineyards. We're talking Barolo, Barbaresco, Chianti and Brunello. Being part of the DOCG club means you can charge primo prices and command maximum respect. The high standards are often accompanied by restrictive rules, such as being forced to age in oak for a specified amount of time. If the winemaker doesn't jump through hoops to meet the judges' criteria and they don't approve of the wine, its certification is declined and then the winemaker is forced to declassify their wine. Anyone brave enough to leave the DOCG to forge their own path is taking a huge risk with their livelihood. You essentially have to create your own style of wine that's different from convention while also being respectful. This is why a lot of so-called natural winemakers are hated, because others toeing the line will say 'No, it's supposed to be like this'. In 2005, a bureaucratic mix-up meant A&G Fantino, a top Piedmontese producer, didn't pass the DOCG test with one of their top Barolos made from 60-year-old vines. The Fantino brothers (Alessandro and Gian Natale) looked on with a sense of humour. Instead, they released this declassified Barolo Riserva as a humble *Vino Rosso* called *Laboro Disubbidiente*. An anagram of Barolo, *laboro* means 'labour' in Italian while *disubbidiente* means 'disobedient'. Complete with an illustration of a snooty DOCG judge on the label, these bottles continue to sell out and this fantastic cuvée has since become a tradition.

PIEDMONT

Bordering France and Switzerland, this north-west corner of Italy is a picturesque patchwork of misty woodlands and rolling vineyards interspersed with the occasional hazelnut grove (this is Ferrero Rocher country, after all). The region is cosseted by mountains on three sides: the snow-tipped Alps to the north and west and the Apennine range in the south. For the full *Piemonte* experience visit in autumn – white truffle season – when vines will be ablaze with myriad shades of pink, auburn and gold. (Victoria uncovered a truffle the size of a fist on a hunt with Cascina Burroni on her visit in autumn 2024.)

Bert's most recent tour of Piedmont started as each one should – thrashing around the narrow, windy roads in a convertible Fiat 500, stopping off for winery visits and double-taking at the bill in every restaurant after each spectacular meal, thinking he'd been undercharged. He was crashing at Dave Fletcher (the Aussie winemaker)'s place and partying every night with David Lobe, a Canadian wine importer living in the middle of Rognas vineyards, just outside Barbaresco, who loves mature wines. David and the crew would be up until the early hours tasting his collection of bottles from the 1960s, 1970s and 1980s. Road biking comes a close second to the Fiat 500 – expect brutal climbs, but it's probably the best way to figure out the lie of the land and take in those enviable views.

Piedmont has a backstory of contrasting wealth and poverty. For centuries it was ruled by the monied House of Savoy, but throughout much of its past the

Piedmontese were dirt poor. These days it's a land of gastronomic luxury. The restaurants possess a heavy smattering of Michelin stars and the wines are the most revered in Italy – its most hallowed, Barolo, is routinely described as 'the wine of kings, the king of wines'.

Winemaking is centred to the south-east of the region's capital, Turin, encompassing the long, narrow strip called the Langhe Hills (from the Latin for 'tongue'), which is home to the Barolo and Barbaresco DOCG. This is the epicentre of the region's top wine production, which is often compared with Burgundy. Both Barolo and Barbaresco are made from 100 per cent Nebbiolo, a fickle, late-ripening red grape. Generally speaking, Barbaresco vineyards lie at a lower altitude than those in Barolo, which means it's warmer, so harvest tends to start earlier. The tannins tend to be a touch softer and juicier in Barbaresco.

Long ageing requirements for both Barolo (38 months, of which 18 must be in wood) and Barbaresco (24 months; at least 9 in wood) brings up a dilemma. Are the wines so consistently great because of these tight regulations? Or would they be even better if winemakers had more creative freedom? It's hard to say, but it certainly makes it much more difficult for new wineries to start up without piles of cash. Oh, and it takes

seven years for newly planted vines to be eligible for DOCG status.

Speak to any sommelier and they're likely obsessed with Nebbiolo (Bert certainly is). It's a very special grape. Crunchy, grainy tannins seem to turn into silk on the palate. Tart, damson skin flavours giving way to red cherries and roses. These wines get better and better with age, developing an earthiness that's almost like sun-baked clay and mushrooms. It sounds like it shouldn't work, but it really does. Nebbiolo is sometimes compared to Pinot Noir – both show pure and elegant fruit with a rose petal nose. It's the tannin structure that sets them apart, with Neb having a bigger profile that needs time and patience.

Besides our favourites below, some crème de la crème producers of Barolo include Giuseppe Mascarello e Figlio, G.B. Burlotto, Giuseppe Rinaldi, Poderi Aldo Conterno and Gaja. And for Barbaresco, Sottimano, Roagna, Roberto Voerzio, Cigliuti and Produttori del Barbaresco.

In the 1980s, modernist and traditionalist winemakers butted heads in a figurative battle dubbed The Barolo Wars. In one camp, a group of forward-leaning producers including Elio Altare and Domenico Clerico took their cue from the popularity of Burgundian wines and began making wines aged for less time in new French barriques (gasp!) that were more polished and less austere. By using shorter periods for maceration and fermentation (days as opposed to weeks), their wines were fruitier and ready to drink at an earlier stage. In the opposing camp, the arch old-schoolers led by Giuseppe Rinaldi and Bartolo Mascarello regarded these attempts to make their precious Nebbiolo more accessible to modern palates as an affront, sticking to long-ageing in old Slavonian oak casks, creating intense flavours and rich tannins. These days the sides have met somewhere in the middle; the wines have never been better.

The best examples can set you back hundreds of euros, but look out for Langhe Nebbiolo, Nebbiolo d'Alba on the bottle for a way more affordable alternative. Alternative local grapes such as Dolcetto or Barbera are great options too. Dolcetto translates as 'little sweet one', which it isn't – it has a black cherry character and soft tannins. Barbera is Piedmont's most-planted grape, an easy-drinking red that doesn't need much ageing – at homestyle trattorias you'll get a glass of lively, local Barbera for a few euros. You can pick up Rinaldi's Dolcetto for around £40 a bottle and drink it straight away, whereas a Barolo from the top crus can set you back £250–£300, plus you'll have to age it for 10 years until it's ready to drink. A lot of the big Barolo and Barbaresco houses are snapping up land in the Barbera del Monferrato Superiore DOCG as we see climate change take effect.

Beyond the two big Bs, another winemaking DOC is Monferrato. It's less touristy and also responsible for the deliciously crisp and oily grape Cortese – famous for its use in Gavi or Cortese di Gavi, a DOCG, arguably Piedmont's best white wine. The best Gavi producers are La Raia, Ernesto Picollo and Giordano Lombardo. The Asti DOC is best known for its slightly sweet sparkling wines made from Moscato Bianco.

The wine-growing areas on Piedmont's northern fringes, Alto Piemonte, lie about 145km (90 miles) north-west of Alba. This high-altitude zone sits in the foothills of the Italian Alps and was once Piedmont's biggest producer of wine. Post phylloxera and the Second World War, it struggled to recover, but it's now on the rise once more. Sub regions of the Alto Piedmont such as Gattinara, Bramaterra, Lessona and Boca are brilliant value for money here; expect fresh, interesting wines often blending indigenous red varieties with Nebbiolo. Favourite producers include Le Piane, Proprietà Sperino and Travaglini.

Lara Rocchetti and Luisa Sala
Azienda Agricola Lalù

A few years ago, Bert had dinner with Silvia Altare, the daughter of the Barolo pioneer Elio Altare, widely regarded as one of the best winemakers in Italy (and one of the original Barolo Boys). Silvia had recently taken over her father's estate and was saying how lucky she was to own some of the most desirable vineyards in the world. 'But it wasn't always like this,' she explained. When Silvia was growing up in the 1980s, the wines of the Langhe weren't all that desirable. Young people scarpered to Turin for urban life, many to work in factories like Fiat as there weren't many opportunities for them locally. College pals Lara Rocchetti and Luisa Sala made this move in reverse.

By chance, the Turin city girls sat next to each other on their first day of university in 2010 and hit it off immediately. Neither had a family background in agriculture – let alone wine – but were studying at the University of Gastronomic Sciences in Pollenzo. The university had close links to the Slow Food movement, the (now international) non-profit organisation founded in Piedmont to prevent the disappearance of local food cultures and traditions.

Though not solely studying wine, the duo ended up submitting a joint thesis on building a carbon-neutral cantina. After graduation, they split up to experience harvest in the vast wineries of South Africa and Argentina. On their return to Italy, they dished out 200 CVs with zero success. 'No one believed we could work out on the fields in the snow. We were desperate,' says Lara. 'We begged Nicola Oberti from Trediberri to hire us. He said yes. And after that, people started to know that we were good, hard-working employees,' says Luisa.

After a year tending to Trediberri's 5 hectares (12 acres), the duo was fully enamoured by the Langhe. Nicola Oberti's father offered the pair a 0.5-hectare (1-acre) plot in Roncaglie, one of the best crus in the whole of Barbaresco, which they promptly bought aged just 24 with their combined inheritance. It's notoriously difficult to buy land in Piedmont and so Trediberri's offer to sell to them is a real validation of their dedication and talent. Owning such a killer plot was a huge moment for the pair; they had their foot in the door to make them a legit Barbaresco producer.

After planting vines on their new plot in 2014, the following four formative years were spent working in Langhe and across Europe, including two Burgundy winemakers with a cult following in the trade: with Cécile Tremblay and with Dominique Lafon at Domaine des Comtes Lafon. 'A lot of our inspiration comes from the harvests we did in Burgundy. The way they respect the fruit and terroir is unique,' says Lara.

With Piedmont's astronomical land prices (second only to Burgundy and Bordeaux), getting a foothold in this part of Italy is as difficult as it gets, but despite this Lara and Luisa were able to set up Azienda Agricola Lalù in 2018. 'Lalù started as a dream of two girls who wanted to produce wine,' Luisa says. 'We didn't meet when we were two fully formed winemakers, we grew together with wine. Without La or Lu, Lalù doesn't exist,' says Lara. Initially, rural life was tough and each credits the support of the other for their success. 'Every Friday when we finished work, we were running back to our life in Turin, going back and forth in the car. We were living the city-girl life at the weekend, we wanted to see people and party,' says Lara.

'Relationships are at the heart of our story,' Luisa explains. 'Firstly, our friendship with each other, and the relationships we cultivated around us.' The pair admit the Piedmontese were 'quite hard' at the beginning. 'It was very difficult to make new friends here, but once you demonstrate to them that you're capable and determined, and you work with passion, they open up a lot,' says Lara. They appreciate the wisdom of their newly made friends, many of whom are in their 60s and 70s, who saw Piedmont's rise from poverty to wine superstardom firsthand.

Lara and Luisa's estate now totals 3.5 hectares (7.5 acres). Remaining super-aligned, they share every responsibility, from cellar duties to technical winemaking and agriculture. They have been organic in the vineyard from the very beginning, but now the focus is on mitigating monoculture and improving biodiversity by employing techniques like drone spraying to avoid compacting the soil and to foster a rich microbiome. They bought a new property in 2022 and are practising living off the land with their summer and winter vegetable gardens. 'Buying this land and property was a really big deal for us. We have always supported each other.'

The ageing criteria for Barolo before release are strict – at least 38 months, with 18 of those months in wood. There are grumblings among several producers that they'd like to reduce this. It makes it harder for start-ups to get going, oak is expensive and leaving wine to rest for three years is bad for cash flow. 'For our personal winemaking style, we would choose less oak, but it's important for us to stay in the community to represent our interpretation of the Barolo,' Lara says.

Anyone who can't afford a Barolo should try their Langhe Nebbiolo; it's bright and soft with an immediacy that is rarely found in Piedmont. We were lucky enough to glimpse their eagerly awaited 2019 Barolo Le Coste Di Monforte. The wines are everything you'd want from the great wines of the world. You can feel the application of their techniques and ideas learned during their time in Burgundy. Beguiling, inviting aromas of dried flowers, pomegranate and strawberry. Super integrated tannins. And the grapes have captured such a pure identity and superb sense of place. And they're just getting started. Future superstars, for sure.

WORD FROM THE WINEMAKER

Which restaurant would you visit if you were celebrating?

La Terrazza da Renza in Castiglione Falletto. We don't need fancy places to celebrate, instead we search for good vibes, great people, tasty food and an astonishing view. Da Renza specialises in antipasti, and our favourite is the *insalata langarola*, a classic Langhe salad made from celery, cheese and nuts. There is a really strong community between producers, restaurants and bars here. It's really alive.

Any must-try restaurants in La Morra?

You can always count on More e Macine; the selection of wine is incredible and the *vitello tonnato* (sliced veal covered in a creamy tuna sauce) is one of the best. [This is a local winemaker's favourite, so be sure to make a reservation.] In Vineria Sociale, we go for the focaccia. Stefano is a master! And for the selection of new wines from around the world. [It's a wine bar-shop-restaurant with outdoor seating.] La Fontanazza is an incredible restaurant that changes their menu every week following what's seasonal, good and ethical. The wine list is personal and unique. [The restaurant also operates a B&B.]

Which restaurant makes the best agnolotti, Piedmont's signature tiny stuffed pasta?

A hundred people will give you a hundred different answers, but some great *agnolotti* are the ones at restaurant Guido Ristorante in Fontanafredda, Serralunga d'Alba.

Do you have a winery mascot?

Our chocolate labradors, Moka and Orsa, are an important part of Lalù. They share life with us, in the vineyards, during the tastings and harvest.

Any insider tips for Piedmont?

We go to Chiesa della Madonna di Loreto in La Morra for short walks with our dogs. Sunsets there are amazing.

What's your all-time favourite bottle of Barolo?

Barolo Brunate 2016 Rinaldi. In 2016, we had just started understanding viticulture, climate and vintages. Marta and Carlotta Rinaldi's wines are often (always, really!) on another level, but the 2016 has a special meaning to us.

What's a local saying that you identify with?

Sagrinte nen ('Don't worry'). When we were buying our house and our land, the process was complicated and lasted over a year. We had doubts and we were scared too. In the beginning we weren't sure that we would succeed. One day, we noticed in front of the main door of that house, there was a small sign saying '*Sagrinte nen*'... It was a sign!

TUSCANY

Oh, *Toscana* – a land of gently undulating hills and sweeping vineyards, where many of Italy's most heavy-hitting wines are produced. With a coastline lapped by the Tyrrhenian Sea, Tuscany is the country's oldest wine region thanks to the Etruscans, the ancient civilization that cultivated vines on the land from the eighth century BC and went on to establish a flourishing wine trade.

The undisputed top dog of Tuscan wine is Sangiovese. With a name that comes from the Latin *sanguis Jovis*, meaning 'blood of Jupiter', the Sangiovese grape makes up two of Tuscany's most revered fine wine DOCGs: Chianti Classico and Brunello di Montalcino. These are widely considered to be the region's best appellations, but a DOCG is not the be all and end all.

One of Bert's all-time favourite Tuscan wines is bottled as Rosso di Toscana. It's an IGT – so only one up from table wine on the classification system – by a producer in Radda called Montevertine. In the late 1970s, Montevertine's Sergio Manetti turned his back on the constrictions of Chianti Classico. At the time, the appellation forced producers to add white Trebbiano grapes to the blend. Sergio said no thanks, preferring to demonstrate what 100 per cent Sangiovese could do. It's up there with the best Chianti ever produced. His move inspired many others to follow suit, when the appellation's tight rules didn't work for them. Gianfranco Soldera did the same in Brunello in 2006, bottling as an IGT. Again, these wines are some of the most sought-after in Italy (with prices to match).

Sangiovese is a bit of a chameleon; it makes a super-distinctive wine with unmistakable notes of tart sour cherries and balsamic vinegar on the nose, with a finish ranging anywhere from medium to full-bodied. The Biondi-Santi estate makes a benchmark Brunello di Montalcino: bold and rich with lots of oak influence and tannins – the kind of classic Sangiovese that needs to be aged. Just a ten-minute drive down the road, Stella di Campalto is a much smaller producer employing more of a DIY approach. Her vineyards are at a higher altitude, surrounded by forest, and face a different orientation, meaning they are less exposed to the hot Tuscan sunshine. In the glass, Stella's interpretation of Brunello looks so light, almost like you're about to drink a Beaujolais, but it still has that trademark Sangiovese power, elegance and purity. In the best possible way, Sangiovese will always have a slight rustic edge. Although much like Nebbiolo, the grape making up fine Barolo and Barbaresco, Sangiovese contradicts itself as the best examples will often smell simultaneously like dirt or tar and also roses.

The Tuscan kitchen is often simple, centred around tomato-heavy peasant dishes or meaty plates of wild boar, sausages and, for the perfect pairing with Sangiovese, that famous Bistecca alla Fiorentina (Florentine-style steak made from local Chianina cattle). The grape's rustic, grainy tannins love fat and protein, while the tart, chewy red fruits graciously complement rich food. In one of the quintessential dishes of Tuscan farmers, day-old bread is combined with onions and tomatoes, which is then transformed by olive oil and vinegar into *panzanella*, designed to

be scooped into the mouth and gobbled like gelato.

Tuscany's wines are so much more than just its two most famous appellations. Head east to the province of Arezzo and the Pratomagno massif, peaking at almost 1,600m (5,250 feet) above sea level, where those milk-white Chianina cows graze on the plateau. A producer to look for is Ornina, who make experimental, low-intervention wines at altitude and even a cool Tuscan fizz. In the north, there's Lucca (see pages 164–66); here we sampled the ultimate piece of toasted bread slathered with rosemary-cured *lardo* (pig fat) in a random deli with four seats. Laura di Collobiano of Valgiano is making some phenomenal reds in Lucca. Meanwhile, the Tuscan archipelago is home to its own clutch of native varieties and a long history of wine production. The largest and best-known is Isola d'Elba, the island where Napoleon was exiled (and where many mainlanders now spend their summer holidays). Another is Isola del Giglio, which lies a one-hour ferry ride from Porto Santo Stefano. Check out the wines of Altura, made from vines on Giglio, scattered across the scant soils atop granite bedrock by Francesco Carfagna, a former mathematics professor. Made from Ansonaco, a nearly extinct native grape, the wine is deep and golden, which Francesco compares to an iced tea. We think it's a bit like drinking the sun.

You also have to try Vin Santo, the local, late-harvest sweet wine. Dip a *biscotto* in the cheap stuff so the biscuit soaks up the dulcet liquid. However, with a top-notch version like Isole Olenas, try pairing a glass with a slice of *castagnaccio*, the typical Tuscan cake made with chestnut flour.

Laura di Collobiano
Tenuta di Valgiano

We can confirm that the Lucca Hills, in the coastal north-west of Tuscany, is a destination that merits multiple visits. The first time Bert came here, to a tiny hamlet called Valgiano, he watched the sun set over the city of Lucca before heading to a Slow Food party with Laura di Collobiano, where wine flowed and artisan producers exchanged their bottles to the soundtrack of *Bam Bam* by Sister Nancy.

Lucca is Tuscan through and through, but the walled city dances to the beat of its own drum. Many years of separation from the rest of the region, both physical and political, have left it with a distinct personality. Its fortunes were founded on silk and banking; you can taste Lucca's monied past in its complex, rich dishes, none more so than its speciality of *tordelli lucchese*, a vivid egg-yellow pasta topped with a meaty ragù, and generously stuffed with yet more meat.

The Lucca Hills (*Colline Lucchesi denominazione di origine controllata*) is the wine-producing region surrounding the city. Sandwiched between the foothills of the Apennines – the backbone of Italy – and the Tyrrhenian Sea, this varied, verdant and wild place is a stark foil to the expanses of monoculture and manicured estates of Montalcino to the south of Tuscany.

A native of Turin, the capital city of Piedmont, Laura moved to Tuscany at the end of the 1980s to work at a shipyard in the seaside city of Viareggio. Hankering for a slice of rural life, she moved inland in 1991 and two years later bought a dilapidated sixteenth-century palazzo surrounded by some much-exploited vines with her husband, Moreno Petrini, the owner of a tempered glass factory who had grown up close to Valgiano. The couple's initial aim was simply to produce a red and white wine to contribute to the upkeep of their newly purchased estate, but 30 years later things are quite different. You can now find their bottles on the best wine lists around the world.

Refined and silky, they aren't what you'd expect from a classic Tuscan red and never fail to surprise.

The evolution of Valgiano's wines has been just as glorious as the palazzo, which Laura periodically rents out to glitzy guests (sometimes Hollywood A-listers). Today, Villa di Valgiano is filled with beautiful antiques and Murano chandeliers. Candy-coloured Neoclassical murals and trompe d'œil frescos adorn the walls, many dating from the early nineteenth century, when Lucca was a principality led by its Princess, Elisa Bonaparte, Napoleon's younger sister. The settlement of French dignitaries and troops in the region during the 1800s would also influence its wine, bringing with them grape varieties such as Merlot, Syrah and Sauvignon.

Tenuta di Valgiano produces four wines from grapes picked and vinified together. Their flagship Tenuta di Valgiano Rosso and Palistorti di Valgiano Rosso are both made predominantly from Sangiovese with Merlot, Syrah, Ciliegiolo and Canaiolo, the former produced from older vines. A small run of Palistorti di Valgiano Bianco is made from a blend of Trebbiano, Vermentino and Malvasia, which goes nicely with anchovies, bread and butter.

Of the estate's 55 hectares (136 acres), only 16 are under vine. Ripening is slow thanks to a combination of sea breezes and cooling mountain air. Laura and Moreno initially enlisted the help of Saverio Petrilli (the oenologist at Tenuta di Valgiano for 28 years) to begin its transformation, with a new aim to create 'a liquid expression of this beautiful landscape'. Along the way, they learned a lot from the Australian winemaker Michael Dhillon, who, like the couple, started out in a completely different field and had to learn his craft from scratch.

Obtaining certification in 2000, Laura started with their organic conversion back in 1997 when she began following the methods of the Aussie biodynamic guru Alex Podolinsky. 'I try to be a creator of health and not a fighter of disease,' Laura says. During 'the Dark Ages', their first few years of conventional agriculture, Laura explains 'we would fight parasites, masked and gloved, with the application of expensive products with unpronounceable names'.

The choice to eschew noxious chemical preparations is not stated on the bottle, instead Laura sees it simply as 'an instrument to enhance the fertility of the soil and reproduce the humus, which retains water and rehabilitates the soil'. The majority of winemakers within the appellation have followed suit and no longer farm conventionally. 'It's probably the most efficient way to do so.'

Perhaps it's the elevation of the Lucca Hills, 250m (820 feet) above sea level, or maybe it's Laura's Piedmont heritage that is evident in the wines, but there's an elegance here that complements the more typically rustic Tuscan charm. This has a lot to do with the winemaking – everything is done with care and a great deal of patience – but the terroir plays its part too. 'A fine wine cannot be made anywhere,' Laura says. The two main soil types are an alkaline calcareous marl and an acidic alluvial sandstone covering, which are common as muck in Tuscany. What is incredibly unusual, however, is to find them one on top of the other in what geologists call a 'reverse duplex'. The sandstone, the older pre-glacial soil, was exposed when the African tectonic plate started to bump into the European one. This contrast brings complexity to the wines. Another example of this reverse duplex sitch can be found in Vosne-Romanée in Burgundy's Côte de Nuits subregion, whose top vineyards produce some of the world's priciest Pinot Noir-based wines.

The rest of the estate comprises forests, wheat fields, pastureland and olive groves (yielding a fine olive oil from the ripe, dark purple fruits of the 3,000 trees). There are also 90 beehives producing spectacular honeys from chestnut, alfalfa and acacia blossoms. 'We started making honey because a swarm landed on one of our olive trees 15 years ago, so we took care of it. Three days later, a second swarm landed on another. Man is a kleptoparasite of these fantastic little animals. We feel less guilty because they came to us,' explains Laura. On a different visit, Laura brought out a flight of Zalto glasses with a smidge of each honey inside, to properly smell the expressions from each of these locations. The favourite was a spicy honey gathered from a plant called *Helichrysum italicum* (curry plant) with notes of liquorice and hazelnut. Laura agrees. 'It's a very sexy honey,' she says.

WORD FROM THE WINEMAKER

A restaurant you'd visit if you were celebrating?	Il Giglio in Lucca.
The must-eat dishes at your favourite restaurants?	*La trippa* (tripe) and *baccalà con bietole* (salt cod with chard) at Osteria di Lammari. In May, they make the best *garmugia* (Tuscan spring soup). For *tordelli lucchesi*, go to Trattoria Bimbotto in Vorno.
Any insider tips?	Tereglio, a tiny village in the Mediavalle (mid-valley) area, a 40-minute drive away, spread on the tip of a hill. It's a magical place where I love spending a day doing nothing in the local locanda called La Fagiana.
Let us in on a bit of Tuscan slang.	When you have a problem in your garden – such as the lemon tree looks a bit miserable – you go to the local agraria shop and ask '*Che ni dai?*'. That's slang for 'What can I add?' to solve the problem. Often you hear people saying 'he uses the *che ni dai* way to solve his problems'.
Name a book that has inspired you.	*Silent Spring* by Rachel Carson and *Eating to Extinction* by Dan Saladino.

Sean O'Callaghan
Tenuta di Carleone

One of our favourite people in the industry, John Baum, was
first to put Sean O'Callaghan's wines in front of Bert. John is the
owner of Winemakers Club, a wine bar and importer hidden below
the Victorian archways of Holborn Viaduct in London. John has
seriously great taste. Sean's Sangiovese challenged everything Bert
knew and expected from Chianti and now, without fail, he buys a
case every year.

Born blind in his right eye, Sean goes by the affectionate nickname
of *Il Guercio* ('the one-eyed bandit') among friends in Italy. He has
been making wine in Tuscany for more than three decades, but a
hint of a West Country accent belies his Somerset roots. In fact,
his early years were spent in Sri Lanka; his father, mother and her
brother were managing tea plantations in what was then Ceylon
until they went back to south-west England in the 1970s. Sean
credits his uncle, 'a real horticulturist', as his OG winemaking
inspiration. 'He started Castle Cary vineyard after we all returned
to England. I was in boarding school in Worthing and my uncle
said, why don't you take a year off, go to Germany and work on a
vineyard before you go study something stupid?'

That one year turned into eight. Sean flung a rucksack on his back
and, through a connection, ended up doing an apprenticeship for
Schlossgut Diel in Dorsheim's Nahe region and got an initiation
into all things Riesling. Next, he hitchhiked across to the other side
of the Rhine for a degree at Geisenheim University. 'My thesis was
on English vineyards. There were only about five of them at the
time, so it was quite easy,' he quips.

Sean's path to Italy was fortuitous. He drove down to Tuscany
in an old, beaten-up VW Golf for a holiday, while also keeping a
lookout for a new gig. He was seeking 'something small, artisanal',
unlike many of his fellow graduates who'd ended up at big wineries
or co-ops. 'I tried to go to Montalcino, but nobody understood
English and I didn't speak any Italian in those days,' he recalls.

'The only guy I could talk to was John Dunkley, who started Riecine. We drank a bottle of red wine under a pergola and then he offered me a job.'

John Dunkley's much-respected enterprise, Riecine, was comparatively minute back in 1991 – just 2 hectares (5 acres) on stony, alluvial soils in the forest-shrouded upper levels of Gaiole in Chianti. The landscape is even more breathtaking than the typical Tuscan patchwork of rolling arable land and cypress trees. 'Up here in the hills, there's woodland interspersed with little bits of vineyard and some olive trees. In a way it's similar to the tea hills of Sri Lanka,' Sean says.

At Riecine, the pair's focus was on 100 per cent Sangiovese, rather than the blending of Merlot and Cabernet Sauvignon (which is allowed under Chianti DOCG rules), going against the fashion during the 1990s and early 2000s to make big, dark wines for an American palate. Sean was initially working solo. 'I had to do everything myself, which is an amazing way to learn and make mistakes,' he says.

Sean spent 25 years as Riecine's head winemaker, until ownership passed into Russian hands in 2012, to Putin's former transport secretary. 'We didn't get on,' Sean says. 'I left Riecine in 2016. I'd been experimenting with this high vineyard [about 430–600m/1,400–1,900 feet above sea level], long-maceration wine in cement and I managed to persuade the Russian guy to sell me 1,700 litres of it. And that was the first Guercio, bottled under my name.' Instead of labels he simply drew his logo on the bottle – a winking, one-eyed face, of course. Within seconds of posting this first batch on Instagram, it sold out.

Meanwhile, an Austrian businessman called Karl Egger and his family had fallen in love with a crumbling old estate near the medieval town of Radda in the heart of Chianti. The Egger's 100-acre grounds include vineyards, woodlands and olive groves, plus a (now-restored) old farmhouse, Villa Pian Vecchio. 'We were introduced by an architect, who had built the cellar at Riecine and was helping them with their estate. We got on like a house on fire,' Sean says. The Eggers set up Tenuta di Carleone in 2012 (producing not just wine but also grappa and olive oil). Sean came on board as head winemaker in 2016. 'I have total freehand to do what I like. I'm trying to make the wines exactly how I want Sangiovese to taste,' he says.

When you stop by Radda, have lunch or dinner at Bar Dante for local dishes served casually alongside a wine list that is unbelievably good value for money. Top tip? Go a couple of times, drink well and make friends... and then ask if there's anything not on the wine list. They may just offer you something from their special stash.

Sean's winemaking approach? *Fingerspitzengefühl.* There's no direct translation from the German, but in essence this 'fingertips feeling' alludes to a blend of intuition, instinct and flair; as well as a certain amount of sensitivity and patience that comes with experience. 'Making wine is similar to cooking. If you've got the right recipe and grapes that are beautiful, it's much easier,' he says. Tenuta di Carleone's vineyards now total 32 hectares (79 acres), all organically farmed ('with some biodynamic stuff'). You can describe Sean's wines as natural: no yeasts or fining agents are used; just small amounts of sulphites are added pre-bottling. 'I'd like to say my wine's a wine, not fermented grape juice,' Sean says.

'I was told: your wine tastes like Pinot Noir and Nebbiolo had a baby.'

At his last visit to Frenchie's restaurant in London's Covent Garden, Tenuta di Carleone's Il Guercio was being poured by the glass. 'I walked in and felt like Mick Jagger,' Sean says. 'Julie Barbero – who was the sommelier there – told me, your wine tastes like Pinot Noir and Nebbiolo had a baby. I'm going to have that tattooed. That's exactly what I'm trying to do – prove to everybody that Sangiovese shouldn't be made in a Bordeaux style. It should be made in a Burgundian style – fresh and elegant. We're doing minimal extraction but over a long period, which means you get much more integration of the tannins and a light, fresh fruit flavour.'

Each vintage is always special, incredibly well-priced and has its own distinct character. Sean appreciates tradition but loves to tinker. With the top wine, Uno, he's aiming to make it like

Le Pergole from Morevertine was in 1990s. Sean also produces
a super-drinkable red pét-nat (aka 'pétillant naturel', is a
naturally sparkling wine made using the ancestral method, where
fermentation finishes in the bottle without added yeast or sugar)
made from the Alicante Bouschet grape, inspired by another fizzy
red called Vinho Verdo Tinto from northern Portugal, which they
serve in ceramic cups and is a bit like a Lambrusco. 'I'm very good
friends with Dirk Niepoort from Portugal,' Sean says. 'I almost
moved out there after the Riecine thing didn't work out. I've got
an amazing picture of Dirk when I let him taste the first one,
with a huge smile on his face, he says, "you're a complete bastard.
You managed to do it first time around."'

If you haven't tried any of Sean's wines, the Chianti Classico is a
must – 100 per cent Sangiovese fermented for 60 days in stainless
steel and then aged in cement and old oak, tasting so vibrant with
wonderful Campari-like tart flavours. It might be our favourite
Chianti of all time.

WORD FROM THE WINEMAKER

A local restaurant you'd visit if you were celebrating?

Trattoria del Pesce, Bargino.

Do you have a hobby or something you enjoy doing on a rare day off work?

Cooking, biking.

Any insider tips for the local area?

I would suggest a walk around Siena.

What are your favourite nearby restaurants?

Le Panzanelle, Lucarelli – get the spaghetti alla pesticida – and Barlesh, Montevarchi, where any dish is amazing.

Best local bar for well-priced bottles?

Enoteca Baldi in Panzano, also serves great food.

What is your favourite piece of local slang?

Boh, which means 'I have no idea'.

Name a book that has inspired you.

Sten Nadolny, *The Discovery of Slowness*. Read in German: *Die Entdeckung der Langsamkeit*.

VENETO

There's a lot to say about Veneto, a super-diverse region in the north-east of Italy. Its capital, Venice, built on 118 islands in the middle of the Venetian Lagoon, was once the world's richest city and an axis of global trade. Winemaking in the city stretches back 2,500 years and until 1100 CE there was even a vineyard in Venice's famous square, Piazza San Marco. The climate is a medley of alpine and Mediterranean, governed by the Dolomites to the north, Lake Garda to the west and the Adriatic Sea in the east. Today Veneto is a powerhouse of wine production, churning out a quarter of the total wine produced in Italy in 2021.

Veneto's most famous vinous export is Prosecco. This easy-going fizz is made from the Glera grape throughout a vast swathe of northern Italy, but originally it hails from a small heartland called Conegliano Valdobbiadene. For a fuller-flavoured, more interesting sparkler look out for the Col Fondo style, which translates as 'with the bottom', because the sediment (or lees) is left in on purpose. Fermented in the bottle, it is a textural and classy delight that works as the ultimate *apero* wine or harmoniously with Venetian favourites such as wet, mash-like polenta alongside hard cheese. Check out producers such Riccardo Zanotto, Malibran, Adami and Mongarda for guaranteed bangers.

Verona, the romantic city home to the star-crossed lovers Romeo and Juliet, is surrounded by hilly vineyards, with Valpolicella on one side and the castle-topped town of Soave on the other. Soave is also the name of the dry white wine made predominantly from

HEADY NOTES OF

ALMOND

& GREEN

FRUIT

Garganega, an aromatic grape called Grecanico in Sicily, grown on a complex mix of limestone and volcanic soils. In the wrong hands, it results in insipid, bottom-shelf supermarket plonk. Soave proper (which will probably have Classico or Superiore written on the label) can result in a lively, straw-coloured wine with heady notes of almond and green fruit. Dodge the dull stuff to seek out star producers such as Filippi, Pieropan, Gini and Monte Tondo. Some of the top wines from these estates age well too. For another great example of white wine, try the Turbiana grape from the Lugana DOC, which straddles both Veneto and Lombardy along the southern banks of Lake Garda. A favourite winemaker here is Ca' Lojera, for old-vine Turbiana with rich stone fruits and a beautiful balanced, salty finish.

Corvina is the grape of choice in Valpolicella blends. A great starting point is Valpolicella Classico, a light and crunchy red that makes the perfect picnic wine. The more intense variation is Valpolicella Rispasso, where the juice is passed through the dried-out grape skins left over from Amarone production for a second maceration. Amarone della Valpolicella is a complex, bitter and unctuous wine which can near 17 per cent ABV. It needs a hearty pairing – think roast duck or slow-cooked beef – or enjoy it after a meal. Brilliant Valpolicella producers to note are Meroni, Antolini, Monte dall'Ora and the legendary Giuseppe Quintarelli.

Marcello and Eleonora Gottardi, *Contrà Soarda*

We're heading to the volcanic hills of Breganze DOC in Vicenza, a lesser-known part of Veneto, for one of our all-time favourite whites: Vespaiolo. A beguiling wine with plenty of mouth-watering juiciness and salinity, it references a well-made dry Riesling and Soave, but it's completely its own thing. Its name comes from the Italian word for 'wasp' as the grapes have to be harvested as soon as they're ripe, otherwise these *vespe* will devour them. Few producers make dry examples of Vespaiolo; its better-known incarnation is as a sweet wine called Breganze Torcolato. However, the versions made here at Contrà Soarda by the Gottardis are knock-out, whether you go for their young, zippy Breganze or the longer-aged Vignasilan.

The family has been Veneto restaurateurs since 1904. 'In the old times, they ran a typical trattoria, producing most of the food they were serving,' says Eleonora, a fifth generation Gottardi who runs the estate with her elder brother Marcello and their mother and father. 'They had horse meat on the menu and grew vegetables such as white asparagus, a traditional local speciality from our hometown Bassano del Grappa, and a few rows of vines for the production of house wine.' In 1986, their parents Mirco and Gloria took over restaurant Da Pulierin ('little horse' in Venetian dialect) and made it a household name in Bassano. However, the high-school sweethearts had always dreamt of a life in the vineyards, so in 1999 they began transforming a precipitous abandoned wilderness nearby with 60,000 vines and 1,000 olive trees. It didn't take them long to achieve critical acclaim.

The Gottardis christened their new winery Contrà Soarda, which means 'on the slope'. In 2003, they constructed their spectacular cellars cut into the hillside, literally moving mountains to do so. The slick building takes inspiration from the double-curved vaulted systems of Antonì Gaudì and Eladio Dieste, architectural icons of Modernism, and blends seamlessly into the landscape, making use of gravity rather than pumps and geothermal temperature control. Their first vintage was 2005.

Some 40 miles from Venice, the family now farms 19 hectares (47 acres) of organically certified vines planted on these mineral-rich Lapillus volcanic soils, with a climate tempered by the cooling breezes from the Valsugana Valley. They produce a splendidly diversified and high-quality range of wines, championing native grape varieties including the white Vespaiolo and Garganega and the red Marzemino Nero, grown in the area since the seventeenth century, as well as Pinot Noir, Merlot and late-ripening Carménère.

Serafino, Poméa, Burrito, Vitae and Roccia are the family's five donkeys, which help out with mowing between the vines during the spring months. 'We treat our donkeys as pets, but donkey salami is quite popular in Veneto. There's also a place nearby that has a whole tasting menu made exclusively of donkey meat, Osteria alla Chiesa,' says Eleonora. These winery mascots are the inspiration for Musso (Venetian dialect for 'donkey'), limited-edition wines made from a blend of Carménère, Groppello and Marzemino grapes.

In 2010, Pulierin Enotavola was reopened as an on-site, farm-to-table restaurant with gorgeous views over the surrounding hills. 'We serve our own interpretation of *pasta alla carbonara*. Fresh *tagliolini*, made by our chef Erica, dressed with a goose egg sauce and crunchy *fiocco di torello*, a home-cured bull's meat made from a local breed of Rendena cattle from our farm,' says Marcello. 'Maybe it's my father's mid-life crisis, but also we brought back the old-times concept and started growing vegetables again,' adds Eleonora.

According to the siblings, Venetians are typically 'tough, open-minded and hardworking, but always big dreamers'. It's clear they've inherited this work ethic and vision. Marcello left home for wine school aged 15 to become an oenologist and is now Contrà Soarda's head winemaker. 'I grew up with the cellar,' he says. 'It was always work, study, work, study. I'm lucky that I gained experience all over the world, from Argentina to California to Armenia.' Meanwhile, Eleonora travelled the globe as a wine exporter, but she has since settled back home in Italy. Together, they work with as much determination as their parents and are continuing to experiment year on year, for instance producing a range of BC (Before Christ) wines made using neither electricity nor added sulphites, as well as partnering with the environmental start-up Carbon Jacked to create Terra, a Veneto Rosso IGT blend of Marzemino Nero and Merlot: Europe's first carbon-negative wine.

WORD FROM THE WINEMAKER

Any insider tips for the local area?

Eremo Di San Bovo: it's a short 20-minute trail that brings you to a little old church on the hills of Bassano. The trail starts from the road and in a few minutes it takes you into the woods down a small slope where at the end you can find the Eremo, a little construction from where you can get a lovely panorama over the Altopiano of Sette Comuni. Curiosity: San Bovo is the guardian saint of domestic animals.

Cascate Del Silan (either 15 or 60 minutes): this trail starts in San Michele di Bassano (just a couple of kilometers away from our vineyards) and takes you to the Silan waterfalls. It's a very short walk until you reach the beautiful waterfalls surrounded by the woods, but you can also consider continuing the trail that takes you all the way up to Valrovina through a very old path to the Silan spring. Curiosity: 'Silan' derives from the word *Sil*, which means watercourse. During the World War this spring was added to the aqueduct system that supplied the front.

Do you have a go-to traditional dish from the local area?

Pastasciutta [pasta, cooked in boiling salted water, drained then seasoned]. Maybe more traditional Italian comfort food rather than typical from the area. But as an Italian, pasta is what comes to my mind every time I'm hungry. It's extremely versatile, so pastasciutta is always fantastic with any type of sauce, at any time of the day!

Do you have a winery mascot?	Four dogs: Uva, Barrique, Vigna and Buccia; and five donkeys: Serafino, Poméa, Burrito, Vitae, Roccia.
What do you enjoy doing on a rare day off work?	Diving. This is something I do together with my wife Greta. When we travel for holidays we always look for a destination where we can practise our mutual passion!
Any insider tips for eating in Venice?	Highly recommend Vini da Gigio; L'osteria di Santa Marina; Antiche Carampane.
What's your favourite Venetian phrase?	'Sbasa a testa e urta come un mus' ('Head down and work hard like a donkey!').

SICILY

There's something undeniably alluring about Sicily, a jewelbox island ruled by its ill-tempered, active volcano, Mount Etna. Everyone wants a piece. Its strategic position at the crossroads of Europe saw the capital, Palermo, become the most conquered city in the world. Phoenicians, Greeks, Arabs, Vandals, Normans and Spaniards have each left their successive thumbprints on Sicily, resulting in a distinct culture and character that's quite unlike the rest of Italy.

The Med's largest isle has got it all: 965km (600 miles) of extraordinarily beautiful coastline, film-set-ready cities and an idyllic countryside encompassing wildly varying climes, altitudes and soils. For an idea of range, the late Nicolas Belfrage (a titan of Italian wine) said Sicily has the potential to be 'California, Australia, Chile, southern France, Jerez and middle Italy all rolled into one'.

Back in the 1980s and 1990s, a lot of Sicilian wine was rough – simple stuff shipped off to the mainland to bulk out blends. Today it's a completely different story. The past couple of decades have seen a wave of quality-minded makers homing in on the reasons why wine has been made here for thousands of years. What's great about Sicilian wine is that it's so real – good-value bottles sing of island sunshine and sea breezes – and seriously varied – harvest can begin in the searing heat of August in the west and end as late as November on Etna's highest elevations.

The island's ubiquitous red is Nero d'Avola, a dark grape with lots of range.

Frappato has long played second fiddle to Sicily's premier red and is considered more of a simple trattoria wine. Yet the Frappatos (or Frappati?!) made by producers like COS (started by Giusto Occhipinti with two classmates in the early 1980s) and Arianna Occhipinti on the chestnut-coloured sands of Vittoria, in the island's south-east, have revolutionized its rep. Meanwhile, the wind-whipped west is best-known for its fortified Marsala wine – Marco De Bartoli is the name to know here. There are also some interesting whites – look out for Alessandro Viola's examples of Grillo, made near Trapani, for smashable, saline wines with lovely notes of pear skin.

Perhaps it's the simmering threat of eruption, but the wines produced up on the slopes of the Etna DOC get our pulses racing. Here, you'll frequently find two indigenous varieties, Nerello Mascalese and Nerello Cappuccio. Both result in aromatic wines with lifted, ripe raspberry notes, dried herbs with slightly smoked, earthy vibes.

Carricante, a zesty and herbal white, is almost exclusively grown on Etna.

If a coastline besieged by sunseeking tourists is not your jam, there's much off the beaten track to be discovered, especially in Sicily's rural core. On a trip in 2022, Victoria discovered her all-time ultimate *cannoli* stuffed with just-made sheep's ricotta at Caseificio Pasini, near Sambuca di Sicilia, about an hour's drive south of Palermo. If you squint, the views from this hilltop dairy and cheese shop stretch out over Lago Arancio, across the sea and as far as Pantelleria, a tiny volcanic island 60km (37 miles) from the Tunisian coast. Here, an unbelievably delicious UNESCO-listed sweet wine, Passito di Pantelleria, is made from dried Zibibbo, a grape that is called Muscat of Alexandria elsewhere. Our absolute favourite version is called Ben Ryé and is made by Donnafugata, one of the larger Sicilian producers, which makes wines all over the island. Victoria came home with several bottles stuffed in her suitcase.

Frank Cornelissen
Frank Cornelissen Winery

Action Bronson was the first person to get Victoria on to Frank
Cornelissen's wines. The New York rapper (slash ex-chef slash
bon vivant) behind the Viceland series *F*ck, That's Delicious*
launched in 2016, repeatedly professes his adoration of Frank's
Susucaru Rossato, a low-intervention rosé akin to a light red
from Jura. Susucaru is named after a Sicilian expression meaning
'they stole it'. Made from a skin-macerated blend of native island
grapes (Malvasia, Moscadella, Insolia and Nerello Mascalese), the
wine is fermented in epoxy tanks. It's no exaggeration to call it
the ultimate cult wine among a certain tranche of natural wine-
drinkers, with its notes of red cherry, paprika and iron-rich smoke
from the volcanic soil.

Frank has been living in the northern valley of Mount Etna
since 2000, but he is not Sicilian, originally hailing from Hasselt
in Flemish-speaking Belgium. A polyglot prone to extremes
– whether climbing alpine mountains in the depths of winter
or following the strictest macrobiotic diet – Frank's fervent
individualism is the reason for his runaway success. The adjective
often used to describe the winemaker is unyielding. 'My life has
got these high-frequency ups and downs,' Frank admits. 'I'm called
a bit of a *spigoloso* (sharp-edged person).'

Growing up, food and wine were always intermingled for Frank.
'My mother was the director of a hotel school in my hometown
and my father was a fighter pilot,' he says. 'My father passed on his
love of wine to me. I started tasting consciously, seriously, with
him in a pragmatic way from the age of 12 in an era where you
could still buy top Bordeaux and Burgundy. He allowed me to use
my savings to buy a case of 1972 Domaine de la Romanée Conti
and a few bottles of 1961 Château Canon, my birth year.'

And so Frank got hooked on fine wine and began working as a specialist importer, handling some of the greatest bottles in the world, including those made by Gianfranco Soldera in Montalcino, Tuscany (see page 161). Frank credits this somewhat controversial figure as the one winemaker who left the greatest mark on him. 'He was provocative, extremely intelligent and analytical – and usually always right.'

All the while, Frank was 'searching for a place to make a really great wine, potentially without adding anything'. The hunt began, like all good wine pilgrimages should, around the Black Sea: the birthplace of winemaking. 'I had to see what and how. A gymnast from Georgia picked us up in Tbilisi and drove us around on the craziest trip in Kakheti. We slept in the midst of lentils that were drying in a house. We were embraced by people in the most unbelievably gentle way,' Frank says. In particular, one of the qvevri wines he tasted was a revelation. 'It had character, personality; a serious wine made with zero technology.'

Fresh from his escapades in Georgia, Frank was catching up with a friend over lunch in Modica, south-east Sicily. The sommelier brought out a wine from Etna which was so special that Frank got in the car first thing the next morning to hunt out the vineyard it came from. It was May 2000 and the volcano was still covered with snow. After many local tip-offs and wrong turns, Frank found the remote spot between Randazzo and Linguaglossa, an area ravaged by harsh winters and untouched by commercial winemaking infrastructure. Stone walls, old, ungrafted vines, half-abandoned buildings... 'Boom. That's the place. It was perfect. And it looked like Kahketi, in some ways,' he says, wistfully. Frank bought this vineyard, Barbabecchi, a small site sitting a little over 900m (3,000 feet) above sea level. It now produces the grapes for his most celebrated wine: Magma.

'A serious wine made with zero technology'

From his first 2001 vintage, Frank set out to extract an expression of 'liquid rock'. He avoided spraying copper or sulphur on the vines, with no additions of any kind during the winemaking. The wine was aged either in fibreglass or epoxy tanks, or in epoxy-coated terracotta amphoras buried up to their necks in the cellar's volcanic soil.

In the early days, the results from his almost-zero-intervention experiments were unpredictable, but often magnificent. However, it was a struggle: Frank almost bankrupted himself several times. 'You start with something as a passion, it gets out of hand and turns into an operation that you have to manage. The winemaking was the least of our worries; it was the regulations in terms of labels and vinification. In 23 years, I've gone from 500 to 150,000 bottles. We still are a seriously artisanal winery. The evolution has been very gradual and, actually, we make better wines today,' he says. 'My wines are essential. I don't use wood. I want the purest fruit from that specific vineyard transferred into a bottle which is recognizable as a wine from that specific site.'

The wiry, white-haired winemaker compares this sloping terrain to the top areas for *contrada* (single-vineyard) red wines, such as the Côtes-de-Nuits in Burgundy or Piedmont's Barolo region. 'What's so special is the complexity of the geology, the subsoils. The different lava streams have literally spat out different compounds and minerals.'

Frank's 'wolf pack' now totals 30 employees, as well as his Japanese wife, Akiko Nakadai, who hand paints the crimson calligraphy-like logo on each individual bottle of Magma. The estate has expanded to 24 hectares (60 acres), chiefly of Nerello Mascalese, but Frank does not produce under the Etna DOC, rather the Terre Siciliane IGT designation. Around 13 hectares (32 acres) are old vines grown in the traditional, free-standing Alberello system (as a low-level bush), a further 9 (22 acres) are old vines trained up into modern, Guyot-style rows, plus 2 hectares (5 acres) of olive groves. The remainder are orchards, vegetable plots and wilderness.

Usually, there is little need for anti-fungal treatments in these climes: it rains, but there's plenty of wind, meaning vines dry quickly. Frank does, in tough years, spray copper sulphate on the vines, for example during the 2023 outbreak of powdery mildew, a fungal disease which ravaged many of Mount Etna's vines. 'Lowest crop ever,' he recalls. 'Nature gives and takes.'

His ruthless dedication is palpable, but Frank is mellow and contemplative throughout our chat. 'People must think I'm

arrogant in some ways, but I'm not. I'm downright simple,'
he insists. Perhaps, but the conversation soon veers towards the
philosophical, emphasizing the importance of the vine within
Western and Orthodox cultures. 'The vine shuts down with the sap
stream, like humans [start to] shut down at 38 degrees. Basically,
the vine is the vegetable counterpart of the human body, which
is something very special. Like kids, you have to raise them. You
have to experience difficulty. There's a bond with the vines. It's
not a crop, like cereals or potatoes. It's about nursing, caring
and nurturing a vegetal being.' His distinctive bottles feature an
elegant brushstroke outline of Mount Etna as the logo. 'My labels
are basically who I am,' says Frank. 'I don't have an oenologist.
It's just me. I have a lot of great people around me, but in the
end, I decide. It's my wine.'

These days you're more likely to see Frank cycling between his
vines on his e-bike or waiting for snow. 'For me, winter is a period
when I regenerate. I love Telemark skiing. I need physical activity
otherwise I will go crazy.' And macrobiotics? 'It is by far the most
efficient diet for high-performance sports, like putting serious
fuel in a race car, but it has social pitfalls. Life is not just being on
your own.'

He adds: 'When people discuss *terroir* they talk about the climate,
varietals, geology and surroundings. Usually, they forget the most
important part of *terroir*, which is man. The person who interprets
all of those elements. You have to belong there, in a place that
you love. That's something fundamental. And I have found a place
where I'd love to die.'

WORD FROM THE WINEMAKER

What's your favourite Sicilian dish/snack/comfort food?

I have no particular favourite dish, really. Sicily is not simply an island, rather it's a continent in terms of diversity... If I had to choose, I would go for *macco di fave* (soup made from broad beans) with a fantastic olive oil.

Where would you go for a casual lunch?

As the best man at my wedding has a restaurant with a huge wine list, Pizzeria-Osteria Cave Ox, I usually go there. His wife Lucia is a great cook and she always pulls off wonderfully simple dishes – for example, bruschetta with burrata and anchovies. I order her *paccheri con baccalà e capperi* (pasta with cod and capers), but also the lamb with juniper berries.

Could you recommend some local places for dinner?

Sicily has a lot of special places. For an entry-level restaurant, I recommend Ristorante da Antonio. The owners are fantastic, and their antipasti are absolutely top. For a mid-level restaurant, head to Ristorante Al Fogher. Angelo is a gifted person with a sensitive palate and a respect for history. He searches for local produce with a sense of place: his best dishes are the vegetarian ones where the natural tastes really shine. Shalai is an elegant restaurant with a Michelin star and good Etna wine list.

Where would you go for a late-night glass?

Enoteca Il Buongustaio is a wine shop where you pick your bottle, the owner opens it and pours the glasses. They also serve small plates of ham and cheese. Great people with a monstrously wide selection of wines. It's a dangerous place!

JAPAN

Yes, we do mean wine, not sake! But before we dive in, let us say that no trip to Japan is complete without sampling the country's signature rice wine. Some unmissable sake producers include Heiwa Shuzo – their plum and yuzu sakes, made just outside Kainan City in Wakayama, are next level – and Senkin, based about two hours' drive north of Tokyo in Sakura City, Tochigi Prefecture, which makes terrific Junmai ('pure rice') sake. The Junmai Daiginjo Urara is so juicy, fine and complex – the kind of sake that can carry you through a whole meal and even pair with beefsteak. Exotic fruits and warming spice balanced with razor-sharp freshness.

Japanese drinkers have long been enthusiastic importers of wine, in particular top-quality Burgundy and fizz (both prestige house Champagnes and cool-grower Champagne), but the country was also an early adopter of low-intervention styles, and among the first to snub conventional and commercially made wines in favour of artisanal bottles that sing of the terroir and place they come from. Small-scale, off-piste producers are popular – for instance Servaas Blockeel (our super-low-intervention Belgian winemaker, see pages 48–51) only makes a few hundred bottles in each carefully crafted vintage, and a significant chunk is sold to Japan.

Grape growing is by no means new to Japan. Koshu, a grape with somewhat mysterious origins, has been grown here for more than a thousand years. Classified as *Vitis vinifera*, the distinctive varietal is related to stock which made its way here from the Caucasus, via the Silk Road, interbreeding with other wild Asian grapes en route. Koshu's thick skin and rot resistance makes it well suited to Japan's often humid climate. The chubby, dusky-pink-skinned fruit results in a crisp, delicate wine that is quintessentially Japanese: a fragrant citrus nose (a bit like yuzu zest) with lots of jasmine on the palate, and a flinty finish. Often served young and fresh, it goes splendidly with fish and lighter Asian fare.

Beyond Koshu, Japan has embraced a host of hybrids and international varieties. A particularly popular red grape is Muscat Bailey A, an unusual crossing of American and European grapes, bred in the 1920s for disease resistance and to counter humidity. A great example we tried comes from Kurambon in the Yamanashi Prefecture, which was founded in 1913 and follows the Masanobu

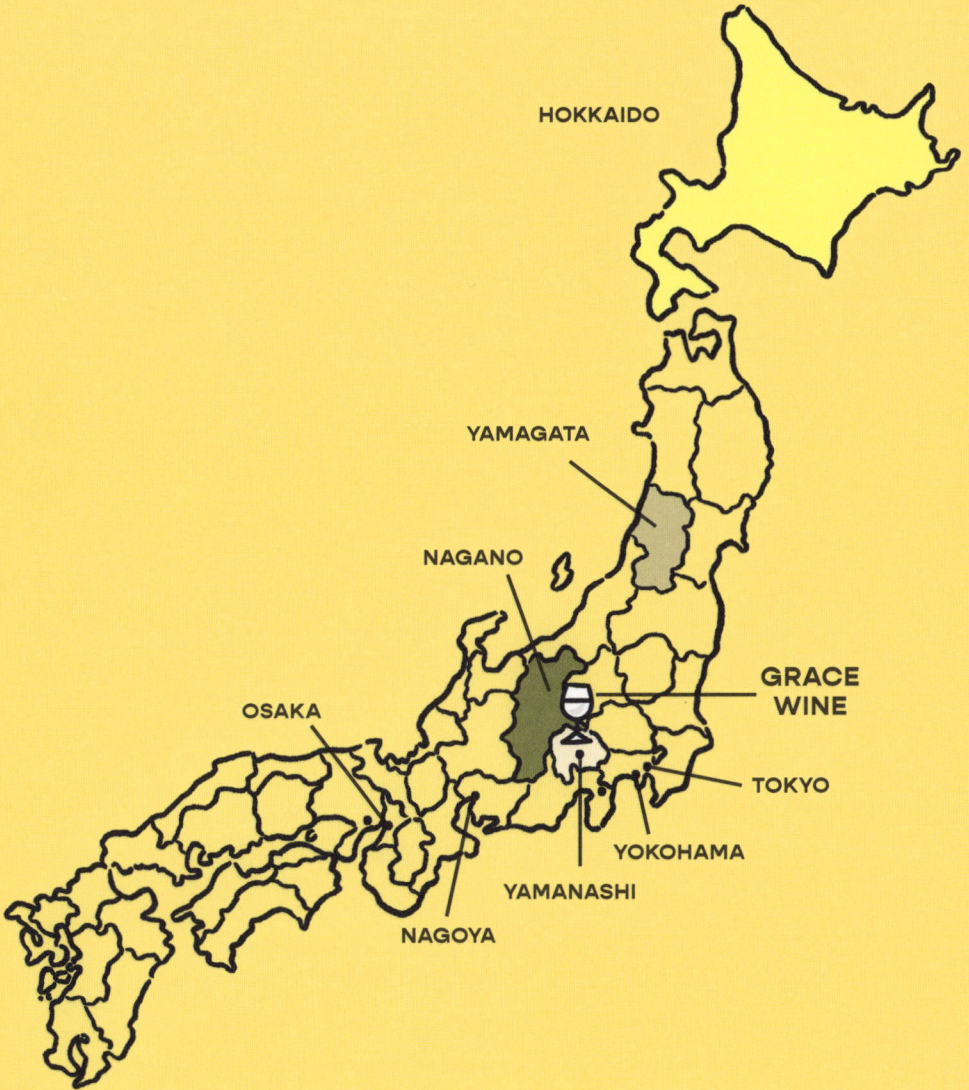

HOKKAIDO

YAMAGATA

NAGANO

OSAKA

GRACE
WINE

TOKYO

YOKOHAMA

YAMANASHI

NAGOYA

Fukuoka method – he was a farmer and philosopher who advocated no ploughing, spraying or weeding.

The Yamanashi Valley, on Japan's largest island, Honshu, lies about an hour or so to the west of Tokyo. This inland valley is the heartland of the country's commercial wine industry, encouraged by the Yamanashi Prefectural government in the Meiji Period (1868–1912). It is famous for its fruit (grapes, of course, but also peaches, apples and kiwis, among others) and was the first Japanese region to be awarded a GI (Geographical Indication) in 2013. Yamanashi's biggest city is Kofu, with a population of 188,000, and wineries tend to be clustered around a handful of villages.

Some 80 per cent of Yamanashi is forest or mountain. Picture a bucolic fantasy, drier and more open than much of Japan. Lush slopes, petite parcels of vines interspersed with orchards and hot springs, all flanked by the three highest peaks in the country: snow-tipped Mount Fuji, Kitadake and Ainodake, which offer a dose of protection from typhoons. Yamanashi has all the hallmarks of a great wine region; incredibly complex soils thanks to a setting where four tectonic plates meet, lots of sun and big shifts in temperature from day to night. Wineries will often protect each precious bunch of grapes from the summer monsoons with a little waxed-paper hat. Yamanashi's Lumière Winery, one of the region's oldest, was founded in 1885 and says it can take as long as a month to cover all the fruit this way. Lumière's great orange wine captures all flavours of Koshu skin, and the sparkling Koshu is particularly smart, bottle-fermented using the Champagne method. It reminds us of Crémant d'Alsace with an aromatic, multi–layered nose.

Exciting things are happening throughout this country that puts precision at the heart of much of what it does.

In central Honshu, **Nagano** is made up of a series of wine valleys: Chikumagawa, Tenruugawa, Kikyogahara and Nihon Alps. Like Yamanashi, it sits in a rain shadow surrounded by mountain ranges. Most agricultural land lies higher than 500m (1,640 feet) above sea level. Many winemakers here favour international varieties and take influence from France (Merlot is one of the most commonly planted grapes); other up-and-coming producers are trialling hybrids with dynamic results.

The northern island of **Hokkaidō** is a hub of whisky production, with its crystal-clear waters and harsh winters drawing parallels with the Scottish Highlands. One of our favourite expressions is Nikka from the barrel, a great gateway to Japanese whisky with a rich body and slight citrus sweetness. Hokkaidō is also home to a growing clutch of creative winemakers producing distinct, cool-climate wines (in particular Pinot Noir, Chardonnay and Zweigelt). Check out Domaine Takahiko: Takahiko Soga is one of the top-billing producers here, who has been on a quest to bring umami to Pinot Noir. His was the first Japanese vineyard to make the wine list of Noma, the cult Copenhagen restaurant.

In the far northeast of Honshu, the cooler climes of **Yamagata** suit hybrid varieties like Niagara, Delaware and Muscat Bailey A. Here, smaller growers like Kunoh, Sakai Winery and Yellow Magic Winery are experimenting with low-intervention techniques to make fun low-intervention and skin-contact wines.

Ayana Misawa
Grace Wine

The most impressive Japanese wines that we tasted on our travels come from Grace ('Chuo Budoshu' in Japanese), made by fifth-generation winemaker Ayana Misawa. She has been helping out in her family's Yamanashi vineyards and ivy-clad winery since childhood, and always wanted to follow the path laid out by her father and grandfather before her. 'I have a younger brother, and honestly, it was not expected for me to be a winemaker because I am a female. Normally, in Japan, leaders are passed down through the paternal line,' Ayana explains. 'If I were a man, I probably would have had more responsibility and would have had to come back [to Japan] earlier. I wouldn't have the opportunity to explore my winemaking.'

This lack of expectation has turned out to be a blessing. Ayana studied oenology and viticulture at both Bordeaux and Stellenbosch universities, also slotting in six southern-hemisphere vintages across Chile, Argentina, Australia, New Zealand and South Africa, including Duncan Savage, who makes our all-time favourite South African Savignon Blanc from his urban winery in Cape Town. Duncan comes across as a super-chilled out guy, 'but his winemaking is very precise,' says Ayana.

The Misawa family have been making wine here for more than a hundred years and Ayana has been head winemaker since 2007. 'My ancestors' first vintage in 1923 was Koshu,' she says. 'We are relatively old compared to other producers in Japan, but I think it's very important to bring innovation and also to respect the variety and region. I don't want to simply stick to tradition. For example, I changed the training system of Koshu to get more concentration from the fruit. Traditionally, Koshu was trained in the *tanashiki* pergola system with overhead wires [a technique to counteract intense humidity], resulting in much higher yields, but I changed to a Vertical Shoot Positioning (VSP) system to get more concentration from the fruit.'

Ayana follows a low-intervention, organic philosophy and makes wines from about 20 hectares (49 acres) of grapes grown in two pockets of Yamanashi: the more mountainous Akeno and Katsunuma, where most of the prefecture's wineries are centred. Grace's Katsunuma vineyards are around 500m (1,640 feet) above sea level on clay-granite soils, resulting in crunchy and complex terroir wines.

The focus is on minimal meddling but a meticulous approach here. Ayana also eschews other more conventional techniques like chaptalization (the addition of sugar) and acid adjustment. She certainly knows what she's doing – Grace's Koshu is served as part of a wine pairing to the fish course in Heston Blumenthal's triple-Michelin-starred restaurant in Bray in England, The Fat Duck. Ayana's greater challenges seem to be around being sufficiently bossy in what many see as a man's job. 'A winemaker needs to be resolute and clear in the direction [of staff],' she says diplomatically.

At a London tasting in 2024, Ayana's wines stood head and shoulders above others made in the Yamanashi Prefecture. 'I want to bring some of the beauty of Japan into the wine glass,' she says. 'Some people say climatically, we have a disadvantage because of the humidity and rainfall. I don't agree. I did vintages in Australia's Hunter Valley, which had a similar situation.'

We are particularly smitten with Grace's 2021 Koshu Misawa, a spectacular, sunny vineyard 700m (2,297 feet) above sea level surrounded by mountains – Mount Kayagatake to the east, Mount Yatsugatake to the north and Mount Fuji to the south. The combination of volcanic soils, its position in a rain shadow and the most sunshine in Japan results in something very special. Everything is hand picked and whole bunch pressed; fermentation is done with indigenous yeasts followed by maturation in neutral French oak barrels. The delicate nose is awash with jasmine. On the palate it has lots of texture and peach skin – a precise and beautifully balanced delight. There's a real sense of purity here, a nod to Ayana's considerate craft.

Koshu (and white wine more generally) is the star, but Grace
also produces sparkling wine, red and rosé. Ayana grows a
selection of hybrid grapes and international varieties such as
Muscat Bailey A, Chardonnay, Merlot, Cabernet Sauvignon,
Cabernet Franc and Petit Verdot. A country girl through
and through, she is a champion not just of Koshu but her
province more widely. 'If you want to escape from the city,
I highly recommend that you come to Yamanashi for fresh air,
nature, food and wine. There are some great restaurants with
local food and diverse ingredients like mountain vegetables,
especially early in spring. The cuisine is very varied – it's not
all sushi, tempura and kaiseki. We have a lot of meat and
game too.'

WORD FROM THE WINEMAKER

Which wineries and locations have you previously made wine at?

As an intern student, Alsace and Macon (Saint Veran). As a vintage cellar hand, Mountford (Waipara, NZ) in 2008. I also made wine at Brokenwood (Hunter Valley) and Woodlands Wines (Margaret River) in 2009; Vina Errazuriz (Chile) in 2010; Catena Zapata (Argentina) in 2011; Cape Point Vineyards (South Africa) in 2012; and Bay of Fires, House of Arras (Tasmania) in 2013.

A local restaurant that represents your region?

If I were to pick the most authentic restaurant in my region, I would choose Esaki. Chef Esaki gave up his three Michelin stars in Tokyo and opened his dream restaurant by himself at the foot of Mount Yatsugatake in Yamanashi. Whenever I go to Esaki, I always feel a lot of energy from the local nature and mountains.

Which local produce do you enjoy pairing with your wine?

Mountain vegetables with Koshu.

Do you have any insider tips for Yamanashi?

Given that 80 per cent of the land in Yamanashi is covered by mountains, there are beautiful places to enjoy hiking and walking here. There are also nice onsen (hot springs). Yamanashi's unique geology results in nine types of spring quality, which is very rare in Japan.

A favourite walk?	Nishizawa Gorge.

Which foods remind you of home and why?

Houtou is the locals' favourite: thick, ribbon-like noodles [a variant of udon] simmered with pumpkins, *negi* [Japanese onions], shiitake mushrooms and potatoes in a miso-based soup. This noodle dish has several origin stories, including one about the local Samurai Shingen Takeda, who is thought to have invented it in the sixteenth century when rice was scarce during the Age of Provincial Wars.

My mother's dried persimmon (a local tradition, Yamanashi is famous not only for its grapes but also its orchards). Just after the harvest, persimmons are hung up to dry in the mountain winds for about two months.

Your favourite family dish?

Wine *shabu shabu*, a Japanese hotpot dish of thinly sliced meat and vegetables boiled in water and served alongside dipping sauces. At home, we use white wine and dashi soup stock instead of water.

What are your favourite local restaurants?

Goshiki, a lovely Izakaya restaurant in Kofu city. Cueillette, a family-owned authentic French restaurant, in Nirasaki city. Bistro Mille Printemps (focusing on local wines) in Katsunuma Village. Unagi Yokouchi, Kofu city (their speciality is eel). Tempura Tenmatsu (a family-owned tempura restaurant with counter seats) and Sushi Tatsumi (a family-owned sushi restaurant with counter seats), both also in Kofu city.

Your favourite restaurants in Tokyo?	Kaiseki Komuro (Kagurazaka); Kojyu (Ginza); Kuroiwa (Ebisu); L'Osier (Ginza); Igarashi (Ebisu); Kazu (Akebonobashi); and Kintsugi (Yotsuya).
What's your best wine memory in Yamanashi?	I once had a bottle of Koshu at the top of Mount Fuji.
What is the best thing about making wine in Yamanashi?	Koshu, family, comrades and my homeland.

LUXEMBOURG

Tiny, landlocked Luxembourg is arguably more famous for its lax tax laws and impressive GDP than its wine. The Grand Duchy of Luxembourg, to give the country its full name, nestles between Belgium, France and Germany.

Much of its winemaking is concentrated in the picture-book south-east of the country, where the Moselle river (known as Musel in Luxembourgish and Mosel in German) forms the border with Germany. The Romans appreciated the terroir of this slender 42-km (26-mile) strip, one of the northernmost latitudes for winegrowing in the world. The serene region stretches from Wasserbillig (a town built on the Roman settlement of Biliacum) in the north to Schengen in the south.

Despite a history of winemaking going back 2,000 years, the country's wines are still finding their footing in the global sphere: we think they are supremely underappreciated. Much of Central Europe unfairly knows the country for bulk winemaking or knock-off Champagne. But the quality of wines from growers who bottle their own wines has increased dramatically in recent decades.

Before the First World War, the majority of its vineyards were planted with the high-yielding Elbling variety, sold to German wineries for bulk blending into sparkling wine. Post-war, Luxembourg focused on quality and the first classification system was introduced in 1935. Today, 34 varieties are permitted under the Moselle Luxembourgeoise AOP; around 90 per cent of the grapes are white wine varieties, many with German ancestry. The most-planted grape is Rivaner (also known as Müller-Thurgau) which, in the hands of the right winemaker, exhibits complex aromas of peach skin and rose petals and a great mineral edge. Other popular varieties include Auxerrois, Riesling, Pinot Gris, Pinot Blanc and Gewürztraminer.

If there's one wine Luxembourg is particularly renowned for it is crémant, a sparkling wine made in the same way as Champagne (secondary fermentation in the bottle); the Grand Duchy is the only country besides France where crémant is produced. Its history here dates back to 1885, when the French company Champagne Mercier cannily began to make Champagne in Luxembourg to save on taxes. These days, a Crémant de Luxembourg must follow a number of strict

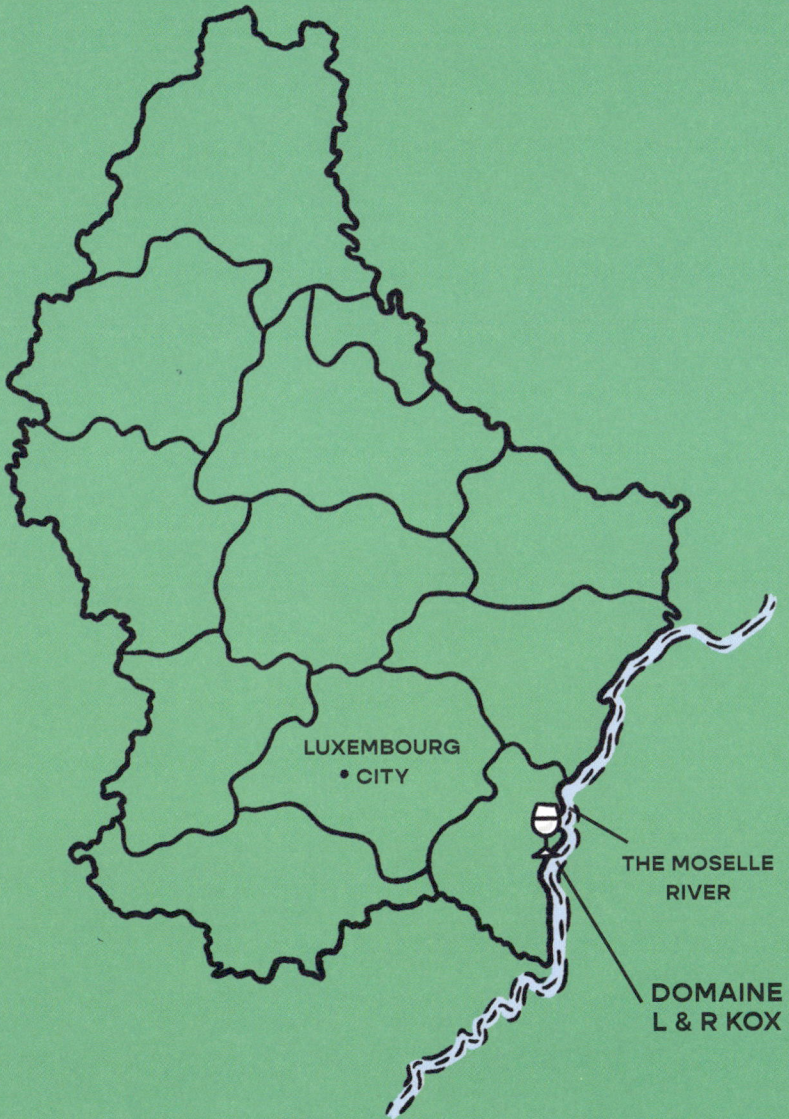

LUXEMBOURG
• CITY

THE MOSELLE
RIVER

DOMAINE
L & R KOX

guidelines, with at least nine months ageing on the lees. We love it because it offers incredible value for money, and a different expression to Champagne: think heady aromas packed with jasmine and peach skin on the palate plus an excellent structure and backbone thanks to Riesling-dominant blends.

Crémant de Luxembourg deserves a proper pairing. It's perfect with *friture de la Moselle* – the ultimate Luxembourgish finger food – battered and deep-fried small freshwater fish, to be devoured whole (bones included) and served alongside lemon wedges.

Corinne Kox:
Domaine L & R Kox

A doctor of microbiology and the eldest daughter in a family with a history of winemaking stretching back to the seventeenth century, Corinne grew up convinced that the last thing she'd ever be doing is working in wine. 'I did not plan to come back,' Corinne admits. 'I always criticized viticulture as a monoculture. Biodiversity was actually my motivation to take over the winery.'

Scientific study and employment abroad kept her away from the Grand Duchy for more than a decade, but Corinne eventually moved back to Luxembourg for love. She started helping out at the estate in 2012 alongside her day job in the Ministry of Higher Education and Research and by 2019 she had taken over as head winemaker from her father, Laurent. The 12-hectare (30-acre) estate, set up by Corinne's parents in 1977, is divided into 50 parcels dotted across Remich, a picturesque town a 30-minute drive from the capital, Luxembourg City. If you're not driving, you can hop on the 411 bus from the Gare Routière all the way to Remich – public transport across Luxembourg has been free since 2020.

Corinne is experimenting with the power of polyculture: planting fig and peach trees, historic varieties of tulips and aromatic herbs among the vines of a glorious south-facing terraced site overlooking the Moselle. A north-facing parcel abuts a nature conservation area: verdant, buzzing with bees and planted with berry bushes. 'The scenery here is less dramatic and more romantic than the German side of the Mosel,' she says.

Biodiversity results in better soils, which improve the quality and complexity of Domaine Kox's wines. Incorporating trees in the vineyard – vitiforestry – means deep roots that prevent erosion, while leafy canopies provide shade, reducing the impact of heatwaves and retaining moisture in the soil, in turn encouraging birds and rare species of bats. Corinne harvests wild plants such as comfrey and nettle to make fertilizer; instead of plastic ties she uses whips of willow to secure vines to their line, just as her grandfather once did. Embracing these old-school approaches is not just an environmentally friendly decision, but an economical one. Corinne's newer vines are grown more slowly so that they can compete with other plants during their first years of life. They might look stunted now compared with the identikit rows belonging to her conventionally farmed neighbours, seemingly flourishing with help from man-made fertilizers and herbicides, but Corinne hopes hers will be stronger and more resilient in the long term.

'Slowly but surely we're going to switch to more resistant varieties, such as Sauvignac [a crossing of Sauvignon Blanc and Riesling]', says Corinne, quick to stress that as an independent operation, she has the luxury of larger margins (and hence more experimentation) than a winemaker simply growing grapes to supply a cooperative: 'I don't want to judge.'

In the late nineteenth century the vine pest phylloxera appeared in Luxembourg, wiping out long-established vineyards and decimating red varieties. Their replanting was outlawed and red wine vines pulled out, but now the tide is slowly turning. At Domaine Kox, for instance, St Laurent was previously grown on certain sites, so the domaine was permitted to replant this variety in the Moselle in 2004.

Innovation is in Corinne's DNA: Laurent was the first independent winemaker to make crémant in the Grand Duchy and now his daughter is carving out a path with more risk, more work, but ultimately more freedom. She plucks inspiration from the ancient and modern: her travels across Georgia led her to install a pair of qvevris (clay vessels used for the fermentation and ageing of wine) in her back garden, yet Corinne has also pioneered the use of drones in Europe to apply treatments on steeply sloping sites and to track disease and drought. She tells us that she's also got a ground-spraying robot in the works. In the winery, however, she takes a hands-off approach, investing in top-tier equipment so she can focus all her energies outdoors: 'We automate everything we can in the cellar, so that we can use our brains in the vineyard'.

Bold and curious, Corinne's personality shines through in her wines. We love her Kvevri Riesling [her spelling of *qvevri*], hand-harvested from vines planted in 1985 then fermented on skins in *qvevri* for five months, where it gains its beautiful copper colour, intense beeswax aroma and a long, generous mouthfeel with super-integrated tannins.

Corinne also manages to translate the fruit precisely in her crémants, which make up about 40 per cent of the production at Domaine Kox. Her non-vintage Cuvée Sans Sulfites Ajoutés (without added sulphites) spends 48 months ageing on the lees and is packed full of character, a far more complex and rewarding fizz than many Champagnes.

WORD FROM THE WINEMAKER

Name some local restaurants you'd visit if you were celebrating.

Brasserie B13 in Bertrange for modern bistro-style cuisine with a twist; Guillou Campagne, a family-run restaurant with a welcoming atmosphere, garden terrace and classic cuisine (with a Michelin star) in Schouweiler Dippach.

Where are the best places to eat in Luxembourg City?

Restaurants that serve a nice selection of Luxembourg wines include Le Bouquet Garni, a gastronomic restaurant in an old building in a historic neighbourhood, and Public House at Casino, a beautiful restaurant in the old casino building, now a contemporary art museum.

Which local restaurants represent Moselle?

Restaurant de l'Ecluse in Stadtbredimus, for generous portions of traditional fare – get the *friture de la Moselle*! – in a sleek setting, surrounded by vineyards, or Koeppchen in Wormeldange, open since 1907, with panoramic views of the Moselle, serving hearty Luxembourgish classics.

Name your favourite bar for a late-night glass of Luxembourgish wine.

Bonne Nouvelle in Luxembourg City.

What's your ultimate comfort food?

Bouneschlupp, the national dish: a traditional Luxembourgish green bean soup with potatoes, bacon and onions.

Who are your go-to local food producers?

Meyrishaff, in the countryside near Bastendorf, for products from eggs to chicken (fresh, or fresh from the rotisserie) to fruit and veg.

Bio-Haff Baltes for goats' cheeses (from their own herd of goats on this organic farm near the village of Stegen).

Haff Muller-Lemmer (in Contern) for fruit, vegetables and eaux de vie; Les Paniers de Sandrine for fruit, vegetables and other products; check lespaniersdesandrine.lu for opening times of the farm shop in Münsbach.

Michel Collette at Beiemich, 11 rue de Michelbouch, Merzig, for honey.

Any insider tips for Luxembourg?

I love the north of the country, the Luxembourgish 'Ardennes', with many hiking and biking tours. Beautiful landscapes and castles to visit!

What are your favourite Luxembourgish phrases?

Wann ech gelift is the Luxembourgish way to say 'please': it literally means 'if it pleases you'. Another word that Luxembourgish people use very often is 'tiptop', meaning 'great' or 'excellent'. Some of my favourite expressions include 'Du gees mir op d'Strëmp' – 'you're getting on my socks', which means 'you're getting on my nerves'. And one which sounds like we are talking about wine, but we are not: 'Ech hu kee Rouden a kee Wäisse méi' – 'I have no more red and no more white' means 'I don't have any money left': red and white refer to red and white coins (copper and silver).

POLAND

Europe has long been divvied up into three assumed factions: vodka, beer or wine. Geographically speaking, vodka rules the northern countries while wine dominates the south, and a 'beer wedge' (including the UK, Germany and Belgium) slots in between these two bands.

Poland stands firmly in the vodka camp, and given Victoria's Polish family background, it seemed inexcusable not to explore her homeland's wines for this book. They did not disappoint, and the winemakers we spoke to are doing everything they can to shake off this cliché.

While living in Warsaw between 2015 and 2016, Victoria found much more beyond shot bars and cheap *pierogi* joints. The Polish capital has a contemporary art and design scene to rival any modern metropolis, cracking cuisine and all sorts of surprises like a botanical garden on top of the postmodern pink-and-green BUW (University of Warsaw) library and freely roaming red squirrels and peacocks in Łazienki Park. Back then it wasn't as easy to find homegrown wine on a restaurant list in the city, but things have changed.

Stereotypes run deep and our initial discourse around Polish winemaking raised a lot of quizzical brows (among Poles included). Many see the country as a land of potato and grain; shot glasses filled with Wyborowa and Żubrówka; tinnies of Tyskie and Zywiec.

It is not common knowledge that viticulture is old hat in Poland: archaeological digs uncovered ninth-century vineyards at the foot of Wawel Hill, in Kraków, but the country's most fruitful winemaking era was about 500 years later, when wineries could be found across the entire country. A dip in global temperatures (aka The Little Ice Age, somewhere around the sixteenth century) combined with an inordinate number of economic upheavals, political crises and wars have suppressed Poland's winemaking potential for centuries.

In the 1920s and 1930s, Grempler & Co in Zielona Góra ('Green Mountain') in western Poland's Lubuskie region churned out hundreds of thousands of bottles of Sekt. At the time it competed with Champagne and was adored by the European bourgeoisie. This city, formerly part of Prussia, was known as

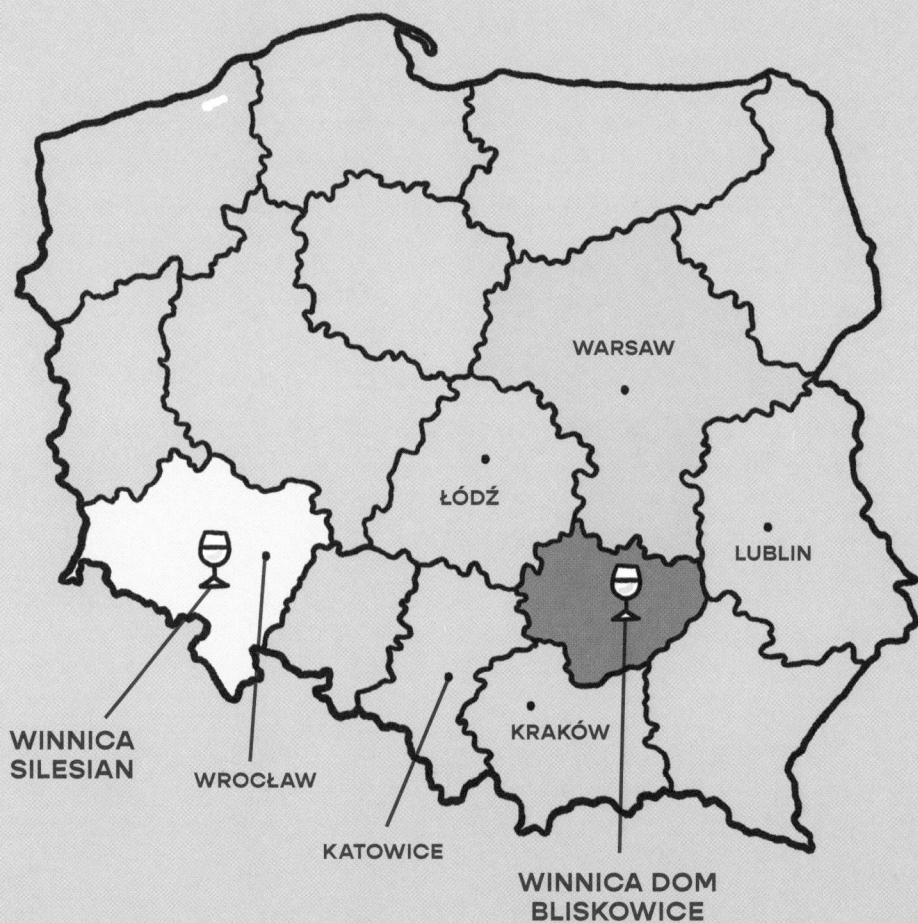

209

WARSAW

ŁÓDŹ

LUBLIN

KRAKÓW

WINNICA
SILESIAN

WROCŁAW

KATOWICE

WINNICA DOM
BLISKOWICE

Grünberg for 200 years until it was handed back to the Poles at the end of the Second World War in 1945. Under collectivization, nationalized wineries changed tack to make generic juices, vinegar or fruit wine; chichi fizz didn't exactly fit with communist ideology.

The country's contemporary winemaking revival began again in earnest during the late twentieth century. Its evolution has been swift. Wineries can now be found in each of its 16 administrative regions (*voivode*) and in June 2023, the National Support Centre for Agriculture reported more than 500 registered vineyards in Poland. In 2025, the number is closer to 600. White wines (and hybrid varieties) dominate the output (as they do in other northerly countries sharing similar climes) but Poland's scale, complexity of terroirs and vast range of varietals mean seriously exciting times ahead.

LOWER SILESIA

Wine is woven into the history of Lower Silesia – Dolny Śląsk – a *voivode* sharing a border with Germany and the Czech Republic in the country's far southwest, where you can pretty much find a fortress, palace or castle (ruined or otherwise) in every other village. The fairytale thirteenth-century Książ Castle in Wałbrzych, perched on a rocky promontory in the Sudeten Mountains, is its most famous, lying about 80 minutes' drive from Lower Silesia's capital, Wrocław. This moochable city, packed with pastel-hued buildings, is sometimes nicknamed the Polish Venice thanks to its setting along the banks of the River Oder and on 12 islands. Hungry in Wrocław? Head to Pod Trumienką Bakery for dreamy Advocat-filled doughnuts or Restaurant IDA is a smart spot tucked away in a tenement house where the famous Rura jazz club used to be.

A cluster of winemakers such as Winnica L'Opera and Winnica Moderna have set up shop in the mild climate and undulating landscape of the Trzebnica Hills, about 40-minutes' drive to the north of Wrocław (or somewhat longer if you fancy cycling via a rented bike to properly admire their beauty).

When European borders were redrawn post 1945, Poland shifted westwards. A hunk of what was West Germany became Polish and a portion of eastern Poland became Ukraine. Many Lower Silesians come from places like Lviv in present-day Ukraine (aka Polish prewar Lwów; the same story within Victoria's family) and this is why you'll spot

Ukrainian-style dishes on many restaurant menus in Wrocław (known as Breslau during its German era), harking back to those *babcie* (grandmas) used to cook.

Cistercian and Benedictine monks managed vineyards in the region from the twelfth century onwards – Lubiąż is a glorious example of Baroque architecture and the largest (former) Cistercian monastery in the world – and many places founded during that period have names that nod to Lower Silesia's grape-growing legacy, for instance Winna Góra (Wine Hill) and Winne Wzgórze (Wine Hillock). Planted in 2001, the 23-hectare Winnica Jaworek is the biggest winery in this region; Jaworek's Feniks (phoenix) 2008 was the very first wine registered with Agencji Rynku Rolnego (ARR, Poland's Agency for Agricultural Market) to go officially on sale in the whole of the country in June 2009.

Esben Madsen
Winnica Silesian

There aren't many Danes making wine right now full stop, fewer still in the foothills of the Sudeten Mountain range in Poland. Esben, an oceanography scientist originally from Copenhagen, describes his recent foray into winemaking as 'pretty intense'. We'd probably opt for something more strongly worded.

He and his now wife Sonia were living in a shoebox in Dalston, east London, disillusioned with their day jobs (Esben at a climate change NGO, Sonia in the media industry) and fantasizing about an escape from the rat race. 'The initial plan was a lavender farm,' Sonia explains, but that soon went out the window when her floppy-haired father, Jarek Mazurek, floated the idea of planting vines at the family farm in Bagieniec, a teeny village 48km (30 miles) southwest of Wrocław, in early 2016. 'He's a dreamer, and a doer,' she says, and indeed by the end of that year Winnica Silesian had been born: Jarek had planted the vineyard and the couple had packed in their east London life and returned to Sonia's birthplace.

Jarek tends to the vines, but Esben was thrown in at the deep end as head winemaker. 'My father-in-law has green fingers and makes sure we have really good fruit. He trusted us to learn and do. I started working in 2017 and my first winemaking vintage was 2018,' he says. Aside from some help in that first year from two young winemakers, Michał Pajdosz from Winnica Jakubow, and Matthias Schuh from Dresden, he and Sonia were on their own.

Fast-forward to today, and it's obvious Esben is in his happy place tinkering with his shiny equipment in the winery, a former stable building with beautiful brick arches. As we visited he was in the middle of deep-cleaning a filter, patting it affectionately while admitting: 'I've cried because of this filter. I'm not ashamed to say that it brought me to tears.'

The winery is named after the Silesian horse, an enormous and elegant local breed known for its athleticism, while the labels tell the horse-breeding history of Sonia's family in black and white photographs. Sonia's great-grandfather (on Jarek's side) came from Ternopil in what is now western Ukraine; for generations they bred horses for tsars and the Emperor of Austria-Hungary. When the Second World War ended, they had to leave everything behind and start from scratch in southwest Poland. 'They re-established their horse-breeding enterprise here by buying five Silesian mares,' Esben says. Those equine links were still apparent as we pulled up in our rented Skoda; Sonia's cousin is trotting a chestnut mare around the dressage arena beside the winery.

The Mazureks' farm, formerly a communist collective, was 'a bit of ruin' when Sonia's parents took over. Historically, it was part of the castle of Bagieniec, a moated chateau. We sip their wines in a just-constructed tasting-room-cum-wine-bar (whipped up in a mere two weeks by the always-tinkering Jarek) while a stork pads slowly through a nearby field. Some winemakers take generations to achieve what Winnica Silesian has managed to do in their first five years. 'It's been stressful, but amazing,' Esben says. At 2022's *Decanter* awards, Winnica Silesian's Rotor Riesling 2019 scooped 92 points and a silver medal: quite the feat, but they don't take themselves too seriously. On the label, the wine is labelled 'young, dumb and full of sun', with recommended pairings including *gołąbki* (stuffed cabbage leaves in tomato sauce) as well as smoked fish and cheeses. Ever the scientist, Esben explains that this blushing wine is made from an obscure pink-skinned mutation of Riesling grown solely in a few tiny pockets of Germany and Austria, where it is used almost exclusively for the production of white wine. Esben says: 'The only real difference [between Rotor Riesling and regular Riesling] is the skin pigmentation. We had this idea to make a skin-contact wine with it. You get all kinds of exotic notes: pomelo peel, strawberry and rose on the nose – it's opened our eyes to playing around.'

When we visited, Winnica Silesian's 4 hectares (10.5 acres) of vines were in the process of a three-year-old journey towards organic certification. Grown on rolling granite hills (a similar situation to Beaujolais) beside a mountain range running for more than 305km (190 miles) along the Czech–Polish border. These granite soils are made up of three main minerals. 'Feldspar and mica weather quickly to make a clay, while the quartz stays as little granules, so soil that is derived from granite is well-draining but because of the mica and feldspar, you also have good water retention,' Esben says.

Their sideline of low-intervention wines is emblazoned with a dinky castle and named Szato Bagno: *szato* is the Polish phonetic spelling for chateau; *bagno* means swamp, because there's a lot of standing water in the area. 'It's kind of tongue in cheek,' Esben grins. 'Wine is such a mysterious product. I apply science to my winemaking; I read all the textbooks, but it's so complex. You can't say for sure that because you did one thing one way that the wine is a certain way. There's a lot of art in it – you do your best, but ultimately, what comes out is a bit of a mystery.'

Taking in the views over the vineyards from a platform mounted on top of a ramshackle VW campervan, we spot Sonia's cousin cantering on a horse in the distance. Everything the couple does has a playful undercurrent with an almost Wes Anderson aesthetic. The winery also puts on parties and picnics in collaboration with chefs from Poland and beyond. We'll be back for sure.

WORD FROM THE WINEMAKER

Name a local restaurant you'd visit if you were celebrating.

Tremonti in Świdnica. I adore Italian food (who doesn't?) and this place does it best in our area. The pasta is made in-house, the ingredients are fresh, the menu is seasonal and the restaurant is beautiful.

Which authentic restaurant represents your region?

I am neither a Pole nor a Silesian, so I have to be careful about making pronouncements of authenticity. For me, Boreczna, situated in the Owl Mountains not far from here, authentically represents Lower Silesia, because the chefs are innovative, modern and world-class. Lower Silesia has a fluid, multicultural history extending into the present, which is reflected in Boreczna's kitchen and menu.

Your favourite local bar?

Ambasada San EscoBAR in Świdnica. They serve great local beer, and the place is named after a non-existent country made up on the fly by a former Polish Minister of Foreign Affairs during a press conference. The internet went wild (at least in Poland) spawning memes and jokes – and a bar! Inside features a detailed map of the mighty island-nation of San Escobar.

Which dishes do you love cooking to pair with your wines?

I love Chinese food, especially the mouth-numbingly spicy dishes of Hunan and Sichuan. So I enjoy cooking Kung Pao chicken from time to time, using Fuchsia Dunlop's recipe, of course. This dish goes perfectly with dry and off-dry Rieslings from Lower Silesia.

Any insider tips?

A quirky feature of Wrocław are the hundreds of dwarf statues found all over the city. They commemorate an anti-communist movement started in the 1980s, whose symbol was an orange dwarf. Political protests were arranged for the rights and freedoms of the statues. The authorities didn't know how to react, due to the absurdity of the demands, knowing that they'd be a laughing stock had it initiated a crackdown. Brilliant.

Best spots for local delicacies?

Delikatesy Kamienica in Świdnica is a one-stop-shop for many local products like honey, cheese, cured meats and wines from our region. I also recommend visiting Kozłonoga, which is a goat dairy and farm shop – Joanna's cheeses are to die for! Last but not least, near our winery is a family-run riding school, Biały Las, which also has a great Polish restaurant. We like to walk there through our local woods, and it's only about 10 minutes on foot.

What is your favourite filling for pierogi?

I love them all equally, but I'm craving the ones filled with sauerkraut and forest mushrooms. Each bite is bursting with umami and earthy fermented flavours.

Your ultimate Polish comfort food dish?

Gołąbki, rolled cabbage leaves stuffed with minced pork or beef and rice or buckwheat, and served with a light tomato sauce and sour cream. The first time I tried them I was completely underwhelmed, but they've really grown on me and now I find their mild flavour delicious, and absolutely comforting. My grandmothers-in-law both make excellent versions, and usually in large enough amounts that we get to take some home.

What's your favourite Polish phrase?

Szlachcic na zagrodzie równy wojewodzie – a nobleman on his homestead is equal to the *voivode* (local governor). To me this proverb means 'I am independent, I make the decisions here' and 'you can't tell me what to do'; it beautifully reflects a centuries-old Polish cultural sentiment of free thought and liberty to make your own living and live your best life – something that shouldn't be forgotten in today's political climate! For me it also speaks to Polish winemaking, which is unconstrained by appellations and rules, and therefore full of creative, fun wines.

SANDOMIERZ AND MPW

(MAŁOPOLSKI PRZEŁOM WISŁY, VISTULA RIVER GORGE OF LESSER POLAND)

These twin microregions lie roughly halfway between Warsaw and Krakow, running alongside the light and bright environs on either side of the Wisła river. Both have established a dynamic wine scene, with various official wine trails and associations and an annual festival dedicated to the wines of MPW held in Janowiec Castle since 2010. Aside from our pick, there are tons more brilliant vintners to look out for here, including the wine wunderkind Kamil Barczentewicz who works a 12-hectare (30-acre) site atop a south-facing limestone hill in Dobre, MPW, not far from the historical town of Kazimierz Dolny, where he ferments his organic fruit in concrete eggs, oak vats and barrels. It's a gorgeous setting; his wife, Anna, has an on-site ceramics studio, and the pair host tastings of their terroir-driven Pinot Noirs and Chardonnays alongside local cheeses from Mleczna Droga or Sebastian Podleśny at Żeby Kózka.

Maciej Sondij
Winnica Dom Bliskowice

'Being a wine producer is like being a rock star, battling your ego and releasing an album every year, sometimes better and sometimes worse,' says Maciej Sondij, an ex-architect who runs Winnica Dom Bliskowice with his uncle, Lech Mill.

The estate started life in spring 2009, when the first vines were planted on the gentle inclines surrounding the villages of Bliskowice and Popów in the Wisła valley some two-and-a-half hours' drive south of Warsaw. They had plumped for one of Poland's best terroirs: the sunny, southwest-facing chalky-limestone slopes are peppered with ammonite fossils, with the Wisła river acting much like a natural air conditioner to mitigate the worst of the winter chills.

'Dom' means house in Polish and, truly, Bliskowice represents a homecoming for the country's top-quality wines, which you can spot on brilliant lists at the likes of Kol, Santiago Lastra's killer Mexican restaurant in Marylebone, London.

Maciej has many strings to his bow, as a co-owner of Wino Blisko, an artisanal importer focusing on Burgundy and organic wines, as well as the co-owner of Dyletanci ('dilettantes' in English), a chic neo-bistro in Warsaw listed in 2023's Michelin Guide with a gargantuan 1,500 wines on the list. The kitchen is headed up by chef Rafał Hreczaniuk who, like Maciej, studied design at college and grew up listening to punk.

'Being an importer is like being a rock star's agent. Mostly great, talented, unpredictable. You have to love it to do it,' Maciej says. 'Being a restaurateur gives you the big picture on what it's all about.'

The birth of his daughter was the catalyst he needed to quit his high-flying architectural job. 'I don't regret it. In the corporate world, time was going very fast. In ten years I designed

60 shopping malls, and now I can't stand them. When I started winemaking, I spent the whole year watching how the vines change; how slow life can be,' he muses.

At Bliskowice, the cellar is equipped with a tiptop kit, including casks from the best Burgundy domaines. Winemaking is a collaboration between Maciej and Lech, an oenologist and also an architect by training, with Maciej acting as a consultant and leading their direction towards low-intervention, biodynamic and macerated styles. 'It's a family business, with one non-family shareholder. We do everything by hand,' says Maciej. 'At the beginning, we started with very small, diversified plots.'

Many of the labels are designed by young Polish artists, including a galactic-inspired artwork by Aga Głód for Dzik ('wild boar'), an orange wine with a heady nose of candied apricots and jasmine tea. Maciej's partner, Ewelina, paints a vivid egg-yolk yellow 'J' on every bottle of the skin-contact Johanniter Ultra, our favourite of Dom Bliskowice's wines from Johanniter vines, a German crossing created in 1968 between Riesling and Seyve-Villard x Ruländer x Gutedel. Spontaneously fermented with indigenous yeasts and six-month ageing on lees, the wine is an earthy, herbaceous triumph with complex aromas of rosemary and vermouth leaf.

'Instead of convincing the domestic market, I started to travel with my wines and it was the best decision I could have made. The reception, firstly at Raw Wine in Vienna, was fantastic,' recalls Maciej, tattoos snaking up his forearms. 'I knew that I had no time to waste. It's either now or never. I believed in the product. I know it's good. I know the place. I know vines. I know the winery. I had to make the right people drink it.' His next mission is to change the minds of those closer to home. 'Now we have to convince Polish customers that natural wines don't have to be fizzy, funky or stinky.'

WORD FROM THE WINEMAKER

Which local restaurant represents Małopolski Przełom Wisły?

Maćkowa Chata in Janowiec, for regional home-style food [think soups; handmade pasta with mushroom sauce; duck]. Make a reservation if you're visiting on the weekend.

Where to eat in Warsaw?

Restaurants with both interesting wine lists and menus in no particular order: Dyletanci, Źródło, Alewino and Bibenda. For quick, honest Japanese food, I go to Sato and Japonki.

And the best wine bars in Warsaw?

BRAĆ polskie wina (for a Polish wine list), Kontakt, Rausz, Winem Powiśle, Cheers! and Relaks. And of course, our place, Blisko Bar.

Good places to eat in Kazimierz Dolny?

Hamsa is the sister restaurant to Hamsa in Krakow, specializing in hummus, falafel and tagines, open exclusively Friday to Sunday. It's atmospheric, especially the garden. Trzeci Księżyc ('three moons') is a bistro/bar overlooking the market square [the blood sausage is popular].

What is the best Polish comfort food?

Blueberry-filled *pierogi*, the ultimate summer food, which arouses memories of lazy holidays. They are filled with fresh wild blueberries, which are more tart and deep in flavour and colour, barely sweetened with sugar, topped with fatty sour cream. Purple stains on the face and shirt are unavoidable. Homemade is best.

What's your favourite Polish proverb?

Mądry Polak po szkodzie, 'a Pole is wise after the damage is done'. A sixteenth-century phrase referenced in a poem by Jan Kochanowski.

PORTUGAL

The Portuguese love wine. They consume more *vinho* per capita than any other country. But beyond port and Madeira, the famous fortified wines, and the groovy labels of Chin Chin-branded Vinho Verde, Portugal's wines don't tend to get much of a look-in in other parts of the world.

Vines are grown in almost every corner of the country. Production has long centred on cooperatives and big companies content to make somewhat unexciting wines. The vigneron style of making terroir wines is still relatively new in Portugal. That said, the country has more or less swerved the global trend for pulling out autochthonous varietals (of which it has more than 250) and replanting with Cab Sauv and Chardonnay en masse.

First, let's talk about port. A 1703 agreement between England and Portugal called the Methuen Treaty – based on trading English wool and Portuguese wine – made port a household name in Britain. It's also the reason why many established port shipping companies (think Cockburn's, Sandeman, Taylor's) have names that are so distinctly un-Portuguese.

Port starts life like any other wine, but the addition of a distilled grape spirit puts the brakes on fermentation: this fortifies the wine and means that some of the grapes' sugar is left unfermented. Initially this was done to stop it from spoiling during its long ocean-faring journeys. Port can be made from more than 100 varieties grown exclusively on the UNESCO-protected narrow stone terraces in the Douro Valley, in northern Portugal, then shipped downriver to Porto to be cellared. Ageing is super important to port: those big flavours need to be integrated and rounded out. Ruby is the younger, fruitier stuff, bottled after 1–3 years in the barrel; proper aged tawny port develops a deep amber colour from 10, 20, 30 or even 40 years in the barrel before bottling. Red ports are best enjoyed with salty blue cheese like Stilton. Tawny is ideal at cellar temperature alongside cheese, nuts or blood sausage. White ports are delicious on baking-hot days served long over ice and tonic (try Quinta de la Rosa for a tasty, unfussy white port).

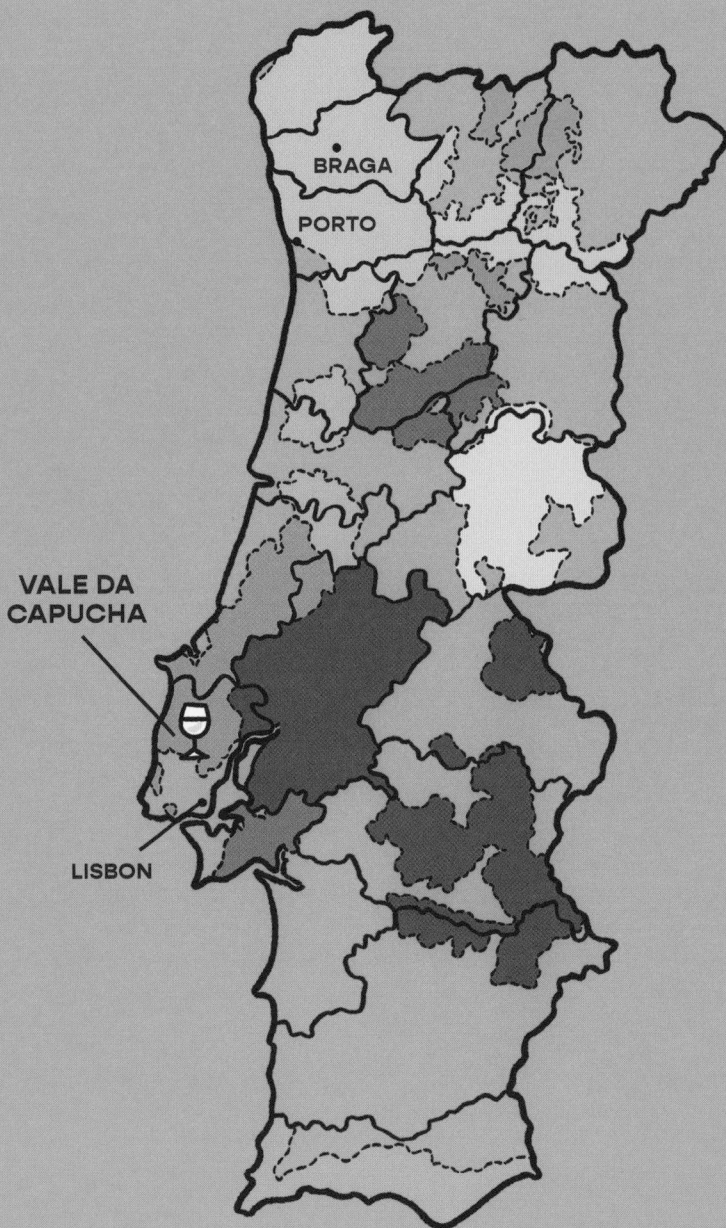

223

Before we move on we have to mention Dirk van der Niepoort, the fifth-generation scion of a Dutch port family and an icon among many winemakers. HQ for Niepoort Vinhos is Quinta do Nápoles in Douro. In the 1990s, Dirk pioneered the production of unfortified table wines in the Douro. And that less extracted, fresh yet finessed style that epitomizes modern-day wines? Dirk was doing it earlier, and better, than pretty much anybody else in Portugal. The maverick winemaker now makes gorgeous wines in Dão, Bairrada and beyond, balancing the threads of winemaking tradition, revolution and mischief. In his own words: 'I make what I want. Then I try to explain it to people.'

Back to fortified wine. Long-lived Madeira comes from vines grown on the volcanic soils of the island of the same name, about 520km (323 miles) west of Morocco. It's not just for cooking. The wines cover the spectrum of dry to rich, meaning the right bottle can pair with anything from caviar to chocolate. There's a lot of bog-standard Madeira out there but the best houses are Barbeito, H. M. Borges, Justino's and Pereira D'Oliveira.

A WHIRLWIND TOUR OF PORTUGAL'S WINE REGIONS

Portugal has 14 main wine-growing regions (IGPs), with 32 DOCs (Denominação de Origem Controlada). Generally speaking, the north is best known for its crisp, light whites. The reds vary a lot but those produced closer to the coast in the west will be fresher, while bigger, bolder reds are crafted inland towards Spain. Here's a dip into our favourite regions (from north to south) and some of the producers putting these regions on the map.

Vinho Verde
First things first: this is not a grape nor a blend but a rainy region in Portugal's north-west. Vinho Verde literally translates as 'green wine' – 'green' here meaning young: the fun, fizzy, inexpensive (usually) white wines bottled within six months and designed to be drunk ASAP, with a hint of spritz thanks to carbon dioxide from fermentation that's been captured in the bottle. These are fresh, thirst-quenching wines packed with green apples and lemon zest that work wonderfully with salads and shellfish. There's a more serious side to Vinho Verde though, with aromatic still white wines from the Loureiro grape.
Producers to look for: Adega de Monção, Aphros, Márcio Lopes, Anselmo Mendes, Quinta de Azevedo, Quinta do Montinho and Soalheiro.

Douro
The steeply sculpted, sun-baked granite and slate ridges hugging the curves of the Douro River on its way to the Atlantic are best known for port, but today production is roughly split between fortified and still wines, both white and red. The reds are typically succulent and structured with notes of plum and fig. Visiting? Note there will be super-windy mountain roads. Check out douroboys.com for intel and tips if you plan to stop by some of the best-known *quintas* (estates).
Producers to look for (still wines): Niepoort, Tecedeiras. The great port houses are Dow's, Graham's, Niepoort, Sandeman, Taylor's, Warre's, Casa Ferreirnha, Quinta de la Rosa and Quinta do Poeria.

Dão
There's a lot of attention on the vineyards scattered among Dão's cool, pine-clad mountains. For decades it was known for bulk production of over-extracted, super-dry, needlessly aged wines. Today's most exciting producers are crafting fresh, lifted examples on its granite and schist-rich soils, making the most of Dão's altitude and climate, and

working with indigenous varieties like the excellent Encruzado, a white grape with lemony floral flavours, and the fine red Touriga Nacional.

Producers to look for: Casa de Mouraz, António Madeira, Magnum Vinhos, Quinta da Lomba (Niepoort) and Alvaro Castro.

Bairrada

Some superb wines are made in the moderate, misty climes of Bairrada, an inland region with a maritime influence, turning out more than half of Portugal's sparkling wines. The best ones have an oceanic, oyster shell-like minerality from the Atlantic (a mean match for the gastronomic speciality of *leitão à Bairrada*, suckling pig). Careful handling of Bairrada's favourite red grape, Baga, by modern winemakers such as Luis Pato, has changed this stern, tannic red to an easy-drinking elegant wine with heady notes of frankincense.

Producers to look for: Bussaco, Gonçalves Faria (Niepoort), Filipa Pato (daughter of OG Baga rebel Luis Pato), Quinta de Baixo (Niepoort), Triangle Wines and Vadio Wines.

Lisboa

During much of the twentieth century the narrow coastal zone north of the Portuguese capital churned out masses of cheap table wines, often labelled with the names of its nine DOC sub-regions (Encostas d'Aire, Óbidos, Lourinhã, Alenquer, Torres Vedras, Arruda, Bucelas, Colares and Carcavelos). Times have changed and we think Lisboa's super-varied wines are the most exciting in Portugal right now: the Atlantic's strong, cooling breezes result in fresh, vibrant wines made close to the windswept coast (a surfing heaven); further inland, the vines grown in a more protected Mediterranean climate achieve richer, deeper styles. There's a brilliant balance between affordable quaffing bottles and quality stuff to be savoured. If you're visiting Lisbon, definitely squeeze in a trip to visit one of the dynamic wineries as well as making a reservation at Ramiro, Bert's favourite seafood restaurant in the world.

Producers to look for: Adega Regional de Colares, Baías e Enseadas, Vale da Capucha (see pages 228–30), Viúva Gomes, Adega Viuva Gomes and João Jacinto.

Tejo

Known as Ribatejo until 2009, Tejo lies just inland of Lisbon, named after the massive River Tejo (Tagus) that cuts it in half. This is lush, largely flat farm country dotted with Templar castles. Tejo produces an abundance of corn, rice, wheat, olives, tomatoes and Branco (white) melons. The region's wines are easy-drinking, amazing value and an ideal starting point.

Producers to look for: João M Barbosa, Ode and Quinta da Lagoalva.

Alentejo

The Phoenicians brought viticulture to this big, sunny southern region. Expect a chilled-out atmos, with uncrowded beaches, undulating plains and golden hills covered in cork oaks and endless wheat fields (it's nicknamed the breadbasket of Portugal for a reason). Red wines make up the lion's share of grape production, mainly full-bodied, complex wines with generous fruit (great value too). Alentejo's whites range from medium-bodied zingers to fuller-bodied gastronomic wines like Chardonnay.

Producers to look for: Dominó, Fitapreta Vinhos, Reynolds and Tapada de Coelheiros.

Açores (Azores)

The vibe on the Azores – a string of nine volcanic islands – is like being plonked on a fishing boat in the middle of the Atlantic Ocean. Pico, the second largest island, has the most established wine scene. Its lava soil vineyards are like something from outer space – surrounded by dry-stone walls made from black basalt to protect them from the extreme winds and salt spray. The crazy conditions result in one-of-a-kind wines, including fantastic mineral-driven still whites.

Producers to look for: Adega do Vulcão, Azores Wine Company and Pico Wines.

Pedro Marques
Vale da Capucha

Zip in the car 45 minutes north-west of Lisbon and you'll arrive at Vale da Capucha, a family-run wine estate in Carvalhal, within the Torres Vedras DOC. The vineyards here are tempered by the fierce, salty winds from the Atlantic Ocean (less than 10 km/6 miles away) and lie on a Kimmeridgian limestone faultline – the same kind of fossil-brimming soils interwoven with layers of marl that make up the best sites in Chablis in France.

'Our great-grandfather started a bulk wine business here,' says Pedro, a fifth-generation winemaker; he grew up in Lisbon, but was always in close contact with vines and barrels and warehouses in the countryside. 'All the wines were sold to the local *taberna*, or bistros, that were really popular 150 years ago.'

Armed with experience gleaned all over Portugal and overseas (Etude in Napa, USA, and Framingham in Marlborough, New Zealand) and a degree in Agricultural Engineering from Lisbon's School of Agronomy, in 2006 Pedro set about replanting his family's 13 hectares (32 acres) with native white grape varieties: Arinto and Fernão Pires plus some Alvarinho, Gouveio, Viosinho and Antão Vaz. During the 1940s and 1950s, almost all of the old indigenous vines in the area were grubbed up to make way for high-yielding vineyards producing inexpensive *vinho de mesa* ('table wine'), and the intricacies of pre-Second World War winemaking knowledge were lost.

Pedro's organic, artisanal style of working is still in its infancy in Portugal. 'Vale da Capucha is pretty much a domaine made from scratch,' he says. 'Even among our neighbours, there was no one we could speak with and try to understand [the history of] viticulture and winemaking here.'

If you visit, do not miss the bountiful, seasonal farm-to-table spreads put on by the Marques family – 'sometimes luxurious, sometimes super simple; it depends what we get' – they produce beautiful fruit and vegetables and high-quality meat from a small army of ducks, chicken, geese, rabbits, sheep and pigs.

Originally, Pedro had ambitions to become a medical doctor but that didn't quite work out. 'I was very happy with option two, winemaking,' he admits, but he's still a science nerd at heart. 'The conduction of fermentations is something that is exciting,' Pedro says with a wide smile. 'And understanding what a microbe needs, seeing how the actions that we take benefit its work... I'm that kind of geek.' He cites the wines of Loire, Jura and Savoie as his stylistic inspirations – 'places where you can get really deep fruit and rich wines without being flabby. They have an energy in the palate. These are the wines I love to drink and try to make.'

Not content just with Vale da Capucha (which is managed jointly with his brother, Manuel, and his parents), Pedro started another domaine with his wife, Sonia, a former psychologist. She went to wine school, became a WSET teacher and worked in enotourism at a big wine company. 'Now she's in love with the vineyard,' says Pedro. 'We have a small project working with very old vines in tiny parcels that are 50 to 80 years old: Fernão Pires and other varieties.' The couple have called it Las Vedras, a play on words in Portuguese. 'The DOC here is Torres Vedras, old towers. Vedras means old in ancient Portuguese, so Las Vedras is "the oldies".' The fact that it sounds a bit like Las Vegas is not accidental either. 'Our winery building is more than 100 years old, but there was a period when it was a dancing nightclub, if you know what I mean,' he says. The first wines were released in 2019.

The four concrete tanks in his winery come from France, inspired by the methods in Beaujolais, as advised by his good pal Éric Texier, a winemaker (and ex-nuclear engineer) in the Côtes du Rhône. Vinification is done with just a touch of sulphur, otherwise accepting the grapes as they are. This means Pedro's wines are sometimes 13 to 14 per cent ABV, rather than following the zeitgeist for lower-alcohol wines. 'I think as a winemaker you should not go against the essence of each variety. The philosophy here is to retain the fruit, the essence of each grape, in connection with soil and climate,' he says.

Pedro's research also took him to the Mosel, where he met the German winemaker Jan Klein of Staffelter Hof (see pages 137–40) in the mid-2010s. 'When you're a winemaker, you're also an explorer. If you want to see what you can do you need to see other people's realities. I always enjoyed Rieslings and I wanted to understand why the wines were sometimes so steely and mineral and austere. I stayed at Jan's place and we've been friends ever since. Jan came to Portugal. I sent grafts of Arinto and Fernão Pires and now he makes a wine with them – PortuGeezer.'

WORD FROM THE WINEMAKER

What's the best thing about make wine in your region?

It's the centre of the world! Good terroirs and a good climate. Close to the beach and to Lisbon too.

Best local restaurants for authentic regional bites?

Xico Faxuxa at Quinta de Fez [poolside spot serving comforting classics]; O Santinhos [traditional roadside restaurant for generous portions]; Ave Dourada [grilled seafood and meat dishes].

What's your favourite local bar?

ArdeBar on Praia de Santa Cruz (beach).

Your go-to restaurants in Lisbon?

Antiga Camponesa [riffs on Portuguese favourites in a rotating seasonal menu]; Essencial [contemporary cuisine in an intimate, pared-back space]; Prado [farm-to-table food in a former fish factory]; Chez Chouett [French-Portuguese bistro vibes].

What are the best bars in Lisbon?

Senhor Uva [natural wines and creative veg-heavy foods] and Tati.

Any insider tips for Lisbon?

Dinosaur footprints in Lourinhã!

Local sports teams to look out for?

Agronomia Rugby: I played for them as a student.

Who's your winery mascot?

Pinga and Arinto, my dogs, and Faisca the horse.

What's your favourite dish to make to pair with Lisbon wines?

Definitely *cataplana* (fish stew) from the catch of the day!

SOUTH AFRICA

Bert snuck in a jam-packed January visit to South Africa just before the world was plunged into the Covid-19 pandemic in 2020. Kicking off in Cape Town, he made his way through the usual (winemaking) suspects: Elgin, Walker Bay, Swartland and Stellenbosch, then on to an ultra-scenic road trip along the 300-km (185-mile) long Garden Route on the south-eastern coast to Knysna, a beautiful town that is a seafood stop of dreams. January really is the best time to swap the worst of mid-winter in Europe for summer in the southern hemisphere. There's only a two-hour time difference between the UK and South Africa at that time of year, so jet lag isn't an issue; once you get over the twelve-hour flight, you're set.

The gastronomic scene in Cape Town thrums with energy. Fun wine bars to check out include Publik and Leo's. The best meal Bert had was at The Pot Luck Club, a cool, adults-only, small plates restaurant with a super wine list and 360-degree view of the ocean, mountain and city. And then there's Emazulwini, chef Mmabatho Molefe's exciting spot at the Maker's Landing on the docks at the V&A Waterfront, which showcases Zulu and Nguni cuisine with a contemporary aplomb.

Jan van Riebeeck, a Dutch official, was the first to plant, grow, harvest and bottle wine in South Africa in the 1600s. This wine was produced for Dutch East India Company sailors, to be drunk on long trips to stave off scurvy. Coastal-influenced vineyards sprang up around the trading port of Cape Town in the Western Cape, including Constantia, Paarl and Stellenbosch. Over the following years, waves of French Huguenot immigrants left their mark, too, with their European vines and know-how.

Some of the early grape varieties brought over include Chenin Blanc (a versatile white originally from the Loire Valley), Sémillon (a golden grape from Bordeaux), Palomino (Spain's sherry grape) and various types of Muscat. A dessert wine called Vin de Constance, made just south of Cape Town in Constantia, became so popular throughout the eighteenth and nineteenth centuries that Charles Dickens and Jane Austen both wrote about it.

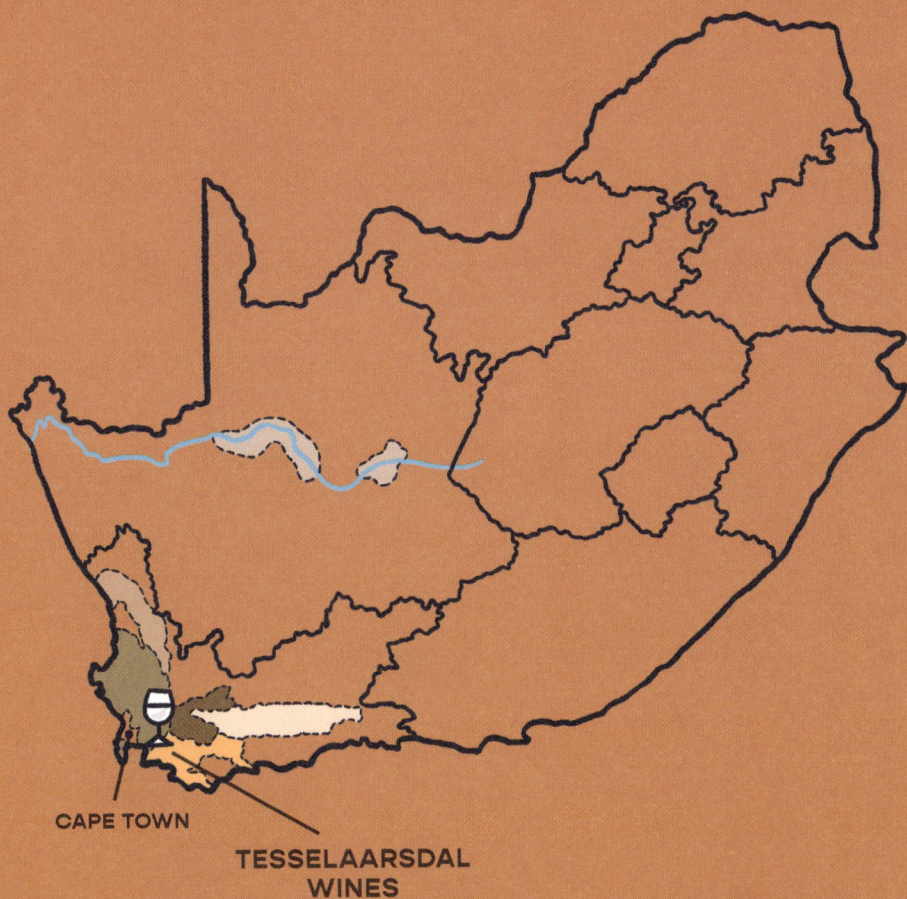

CAPE TOWN

TESSELAARSDAL
WINES

NOTES OF

BAKED FIGS

AND

BLACK CHERRY JAM

Despite its early start, the South African wine industry endured fitful stops and starts, held back by grapevine disease and the isolation of the apartheid years. It also didn't help that the state-controlled winemaking co-op focused production towards quantity over quality. After the mid-1990s, things started shifting into gear again once the export markets reopened. Boom times then followed.

We can't talk about South African wine without mentioning Pinotage, a hybrid grape with a seriously bad rep. Pinotage was invented at Stellenbosch University in 1925. At the time, Cinsault was known as Hermitage in South Africa, hence the Pinot Noir x Cinsault crossing was named Pinot-Age. The poor grape – South Africa's wine poster child – was a victim of its own success. As it was easy to grow, so many producers took advantage of its high yields to make cheap, crappy wine. When the 1990s rolled around, it had fallen massively out of fashion. Lots of the vines have since been grubbed up, which is a shame because in safe hands Pinotage can result in some wonderful wines with elan, more on a par with Beaujolais. Think notes of baked figs and black cherry jam with ripe tannins, which are pairing perfection alongside a *braai* – the South African equivalent of a barbecue. The first one to wow Bert was the Hell Yeah! Pinotage made by Tremayne Smith at Blacksmith Wines. Bernhard Bredell's version at Scions of Sinai should be on your list too.

Perhaps more than anywhere else we've visited, there's a culture of winemakers in South Africa helping each other out. It's refreshing and makes a lot of sense given the country's recent struggles with strict Covid lockdowns, alcohol bans and escalating daily power cuts. There's a new wave of winemakers inspired and encouraged by legends like AA Badenhorst, Sadie Family Wines and Hamilton Russell. The larger estates always seem keen to support the next generation of winemakers for the greater good of the country's industry.

Bert was crashing in the spare room of Samantha Suddons in Swartland, the VineVenom winemaker producing funky, non-vintage, skin-contact wines under the Terracura label, when he popped in completely unannounced at Thelema Mountain Vineyards. An epic vineyard in Stellenbosch, known for making bold reds in a traditional way, Thelema's wines are really special, especially the Merlot, Syrah (aka Shiraz) and Cabernet Sauvignon. Thomas Webb, the director of Thelema, pulled out a bottle of 1993 – rare vintages are like crack to wine nerds – and said please pass on my regards to your hosts. That evening, Bert and the Terracura crew enjoyed the gift with some barbecued boerewors (spicy spiral sausage). Lekker!

SWARTLAND

Bert is crazy about the Syrah and Chenin Blanc made in his favourite South African wine region, Swartland, just 40km (25 miles) north of Cape Town. The climate is pretty much Mediterranean: warm and dry, with cool nights and hot summers. Swartland is a region chock-a-block with wall-to-wall innovative producers. If you can get your hands on them, Sadie Family Wines use a lot of weird and wonderful grapes; plenty of old, bush-vine stuff and even some Portuguese varietals. Every wine Eben Sadie makes is exceptional. Check out the entry range from AA Badenhorst, Securers. It's an excellent springboard to Swartland by Adi Badenhorst, then crank your way up to his single vineyard series and finish off with a drop of his mezcal-style agave spirit, called 4th Rabbit. He also makes delicious vermouth using local botanicals, called Caperitif, a revival of a long-lost fortified wine last made over a century ago.

Producers to look for include Mullineux, The Sadie Family, Porseleinberg, Swerwer Wines by JC Wickens, Bryan MacRobert Wines, JH Meyer Wines (and Johan's collaboration with Indigo Wines, Mother Rock – Victoria's favourite), Blank Bottle, City on a Hill and AA Badenhorst.

ELGIN

South Africa's hippest winegrowing region near Cape Agulhas, Elgin is on the country's southernmost tip and is home to some of the coolest wines Bert tasted on his 2020 trip. Elgin's lean, cool-climate Chardonnays are worth shouting about. It's quite out of the way and better known for growing apples, so there's not heaps going on in this up-and-coming area yet. A lot of the wineries based out here aren't full time, but many from around the Cape source fruit from the region's vineyards. If you have a chance, drop in to Paserene's tasting room between Franschhoek and Stellenbosch, owned by music-loving Martin Smith and Ndabe Mareda. Bert had a blast when Martin hosted him, and the Elgin vintage Chardonnays really stole the show.

Producers to look for include Paserene, Richard Kershaw and Saurwein.

HEMEL-EN-AARDE

The name of this storybook valley in Afrikaans translates to 'heaven on earth', and yes, it really is that beautiful in real life. Hemel-en-Aarde is an exciting sub-region, part of Walker Bay on the rugged southern coast, stretching inland from Hermanus, one of the world's best whale-watching spots. The winds really pick up here, cooling the vineyards to keep the wines elegant and pure, but that also means the ocean can get really choppy. The Pinot Noir and Chardonnay produced here are considered South Africa's answer to Burgundy.

Producers to look for include Yo El Rey Wines, Hamilton Russell, Storm, Restless River, Wild Air, Lelie van Saron, Saurwein and Tesselaarsdal Wines.

STELLENBOSCH

The Cape's best-known fine wine district is Stellenbosch, famous for producing Bordeaux-style blends. Red grapes like Cabernet Sauvignon reign supreme here, as well as Merlot and Syrah, made in a diverse, Mediterranean-like climate tempered to the south by cooling, oceanic winds. The university town of Stellenbosch itself is very pretty, with whitewashed buildings and a botanical garden, but the undulating scenery beyond is even more so. Gentle rolling hills give way to jagged peaks in the distance and, depending on where you are, the complex soils are a meld of granite, shale and sandstone. Expect lots of classic wines and plenty of glossy options for bougie drinking and dining, the Postcard Café at the Stark-Condé winery has a tasting room on an island, for instance.

If you fancy some local fizz, Stellenbosch is a good spot to sample it. MCC (Méthode Cap Classique) is the county's very own Champagne-method sparkling wine. Bert had a languorous lunch in the rose garden at Le Lude in the Franschhoek Valley, not far from Stellenbosch, and can recommend pairing their Blanc de Noir with the homemade tartare.

Producers to look for include Boekenhoutskloof, Le Lude, Damascene, Thelema Mountain Vineyards, De Toren and Reyneke.

THE COMPLEX SOILS ARE A MELD OF —

GRANITE, SHALE & SANDSTONE

Berene Sauls
Tesselaarsdal Wines

In a tiny farming village called Tesselaarsdal, not far from Hemel-en-Aarde Ridge, Berene Sauls' ancestors were bequeathed land in the Tesselaarsdal valley by a former Dutch East India Company soldier, Johannes Tesselaar, in the early nineteenth century.

A direct descendant of freed slaves, Berene says 'I named my wine Tesselaarsdal after my hometown, to honour that legacy.' Berene is a long-time employee of Hamilton Russell, perhaps the most renowned estate in the Hemel-en-Aarde Valley. It's run by second-generation owner Anthony Hamilton Russell and his wife Olive. Bert first met this lovely pair while hosting a tasting and masterclass for the estate in 2017 at The Mandrake Hotel in London's Fitzrovia.

'I came to work at Hamilton Russell vineyards in 2001 as a red-cheeked 19-year-old au pair to Anthony's four beautiful daughters,' Berene explains. 'About a month into it, Anthony steered me into the wine business side of things. He always said I would have been wasted in the house.'

Berene is electric. Insatiably curious, optimistic and driven, she has worked every imaginable role and department at Hamilton Russell, from the cellar to marketing manager and import/export logistics, gradually gleaning an understanding of fine wine (something she had zero clue about when she started out). 'I must admit, if I do something, I do it really well. When I came in, a bottle of Hamilton Russell was the most expensive wine in Hemel-en-Aarde – that was intriguing to me; why would people pay so much for a bottle of wine? After years of Anthony indoctrinating me with Pinot Noir and Chardonnay, at the end of 2014 he said, "Look Berene, you've got no place to grow. Why don't you produce a barrel of wine in our cellar with winemaker Emul Ross?"'

Berene was to source her own grapes, but Anthony gave her the startup costs and let her use a building on the estate for her first experiments. She fixed a long-term contract with Babylon Vineyards, paying extra to secure the estate's best fruit, and 2015 became her maiden vintage, made under Emul's guidance. In typically Berene fashion, it was a hit.

South African Master of Wine Greg Sherwood dubbed Tesselaarsdal 'the next South African Pinot Noir icon'. Berene scooped an armful of awards and her initial 200 cases sold out almost instantly. Soon after her wines were stocked across some of South Africa's best high-end restaurants and wine boutiques, while in London they're on the wine list at places like the Ledbury restaurant and the Hedonism bottle shop. 'My winemaking style is really reflective of what the Hemel-en-Aarde Ridge is: straightforward, minimal intervention, with a pristine fruit profile,' Berene says.

Bert first came across Berene's wines when Damon Quinlan of Swig Wines – her UK importer – sent over a sample to try. Once Bert had worked through his tasting pile and got to Berene's 2021 Pinot Noir Tesselaarsdal, he was met with sour cherries, wild strawberries and a zippy freshness that echoed the rugged coastline of the beautiful place. Immediately, he got his phone out to make an order, but he wasn't fast enough. It was all gone.

The label shows a classic Tesselaarsdal village scene, complete with church, slender cow and pecking hens. 'The two little fingers walking over the mountain are my mum and grandma, off to trade with Stanford, another winemaking area,' Berene says. A German surname, the neck label is a nod to the Sauls' family crest with an updated helmet adorned with ostrich feathers and baby blue crane heads, the national bird of South Africa.

At the end of 2019, Berene committed what her accountant describes as 'business suicide' by clearing out her business bank account to buy a 16-hectare (39-acre) property in Tesselaarsdal in order to plant vines and erect a cellar close to her parents' home, where she grew up. Here, she hosts appointment-only tastings, catered by her dad (think waterblommetjie, a waterlily and lamb stew, or meat pies) who she's roped in to tend to her vines. A single mother of two boys, Berene cheerfully recounts myriad challenges on the site with a wide smile, including an arduous saga to source water via a borehole. She clearly cannot wait for the required seven years to be up until the first harvest of her initial hectare of Pinot Noir and Chardonnay respectively will be ready. 'You have to be a little mad to go back home and plant in Tesselaarsdal; it's a water-scarce region and is about 1.5°C warmer than the rest of the Hemel-en-Aarde Ridge. Maybe there's a reason why people raised livestock and farmed wheat here. It could be either the best or the worst Pinot ever.'

It's a passion project – Berene still works full time at Hamilton Russell – but more than that, it's a legacy for her sons. Her eldest, Darren, is following her into the wine world, with several harvests and a WSET (the popular qualification taken by drinks industry/enthusiasts) level three award already under his belt. 'Emul mentored Darren through 2023's harvest. Thank god I didn't have to do the foot stomping!' Berene laughs.

WORD FROM THE WINEMAKER

What is the most authentic local restaurant that represents your region?

I have three: The Restaurant at Newton Johnson, Creation Wines, and The Rock, New Harbour Hermanus. At The Rock, order the abalone starter (a sea snail sourced locally from an abalone farm) followed by either the crayfish main or the slow-braised lamb shank.

What favourite foods do you enjoy pairing with wines from your local region?

Here I also have a few: lamb chops cooked on the *braai*, oven-roasted leg of lamb with rosemary served on mushroom mashed potatoes, or waterblommetjie lamb stew with Pinot Noir. Seafood pasta or lean cuts of fish with Chardonnay.

Any insider tips for Hemel-en-Aarde?

Definitely any of our three beautiful beaches – Grotto, Onrus or Sandbaai – as well as the cliff path near the Old Harbour.

Which foods remind you of home?

Waterblommetjie lamb stew.

Who is your favourite South African chef?

Bertus Basson.

Which three things would you have on your dream braai?

T-bone steak (thick cut), boerewors (sausage) and skilpadjies (lamb's liver).

What's a local saying that you identify with?

'Get the job done.'

What is the best thing about making wine in your region?

The climate and setting, as well as the overall quality of grapes and wine found in this region. Plus the good fellowship among wine producers.

SPAIN

There are tons of viticultural happenings in *España* right now, and one of the best things about Spanish wine is that it is not yet as hyped (read: pricey) as the French and Italian stuff. Land here is relatively cheap and vines flourish, with many flat fertile spots resulting in huge yields, perfect for bulk winemaking. Indeed, Spain has more land under vine than any other country. However, the dominance of big winemaking co-ops has been a hindrance for its vinous image.

The Spanish stereotype is cheap and cheerful wines, not shy with alcohol levels and often featuring an unfashionable fondness for heavy oak. But there's so much more diversity in styles beyond those made in the top regions, Rioja and Ribera del Duero, within a vast range of areas and climates from mountainous to Mediterranean and maritime, not forgetting Spain's 48 inhabited islands. The lush, Atlantic Ocean-sprayed vineyards in green and pleasant Galicia are home to the Albariño and Godello grapes, which both make well-priced still whites with serious oomph. Then there are the low-yielding Malvasía Volcánica vines grown on Tenerife's black soils in the shadow of the country's tallest mountain, Teide, by winemakers such as Bodega Cohombrillo and Bodega Erupción, and the underrated sweet wines of Málaga – try Samuel Párraga's Dolce, a lush Moscatel, which Victoria first tasted at the excellent La Casa del Perro restaurant and wine shop in Málaga, run by Ana Vicaria and her partner, Fede Ayllón. Or make the foodie pilgrimage to wander the streets of San Sebastián for piles of *pintxos* alongside glasses of palate-cleansing Txakoli – a slightly effervescent white, usually made using the indigenous Hondarrabi Zuri grape variety from the Basque country.

The wine trade is currently in the grip of the Spanish New Wave movement, a new generation of vignerons and bodegas going back to traditional methods, embracing neglected varieties and making fiercely individualistic wines. They've turned their back on mass production and the aggressive use of oak, instead working with forgotten vineyards, in old subregions and off-piste terroirs. Some favourites include Daniel Landi (Castilla y León), Fernando García (Sierra de Gredos), Jorge Monzón (Ribera del Duero), Envínate (various regions including Ribeira Sacra, the Canary Islands and Castile-La Mancha), Dominik Huber (Priorat), Jose Gil (Rioja) and Jaunjo Tallaetxe (Basque Country).

245

RIOJA

ZARAGOZA

LEÓN

MADRID

BARCELONA

SEVILLE

ALICANTE

CÁDIZ

MÁLAGA

EQUIPO
NAVAZOS

CATALONIA

Hit rewind to Catalonia's pro-independence riots of late 2019. An inopportune moment for Bert and Beth, his partner, to be enjoying a mid-October getaway. Things had turned violent. Spanish flags on fire. First skirmishes. The plan had been to hit some favourite eating and drinking haunts in Catalonia, starting in the pretty riverside city, Girona. To name a few, Plaça del Vi, Brots de Vi, Safo Bar and La Garrina (always finishing a meal with a glass of Ratafía, the typical digestif from the area). Instead, they were met with a mess of burnt-out cars. They dodged the riots by moving further down the coast, making the prerequisite stop in Figueres to see the Salvador Dalí museum and to lunch at Integral Figueres for a veg-heavy spread. Next on the list was the seaside town of Cunit for a visit to L'Arrosseria,

the restaurant by rice-obsessed chef Andreu Ruiz. Besides the selection of *arroces marineros* (seafood rice), his *fideuá* (a broken noodle dish cooked with seafood) is magnificent, as is the extensive wine list.

Then onwards to Barcelona, where more riots broke out and all reservations had to be cancelled, including one at the go-to wine bar Can Cisa/Bar Brutal in the city's Ciutat Vella district. Winemaker Pepe Raventós, ever the gent, happened to be away but generously offered up his country bolthole amid the vines in the heart of Cava country in Penedès, Catalonia's largest and best known wine region to the southwest of Barcelona, as a refuge from the eruptions on the city streets. He added 'help yourself' to the wine cave and fully stocked fridge. Beth fell in love with a cute pig in the field next door. An invite followed to come back to eat it.

Often seen as Champagne's poorer sibling, Cava (which means cave in Spanish) started out with good intentions to make quality sparkling wine using the aromatic Spanish white grapes Macabeo, Parellada and Xarel·lo. But it seems to have got lost along the way. Instead of celebrating their own uniqueness, producers compared themselves to Champagne while trying to compete with Prosecco on price, resulting in vast quantities of astronomically cheap, dull and manipulated wines.

But Cava has its mojo back. A group of Catalan producers became frustrated that their artisanal wines had been tarnished with this reputation. Six of them left the regulating body, Cava Denominación de Origen (DO), to become the founding members of the Corpinnat association. Since September 2017 they have been united by a set of shared values and rules to make serious wines, adhering to careful viticulture and minimum intervention, vinified on the premises, with extended ageing in bottle and a commitment to historic varieties.

One Corpinnat producer to know is Recaredo, which has been around since 1924. Their ageing cellars include a maze of winding caves, where some of Spain's longest-aged sparkling wines rest today. Absolutely everything in the cellar, including the riddling and disgorgement, is done by hand. A couple of bottles of 2005 were like eating the most delicious apple ever, baked with almonds and lemon zest, perfectly balanced, with plenty of acidity and toasty notes.

If you're big on low-intervention wine, Catalonia is ground zero in Spain. Beyond quality fizz in Penedès, seek out producers like Partida Creus, a winery founded by a Piedmontese architect couple dedicated to native northern Spanish varietals such as Garrut, Vinyater, Samsó and Queixal de Llop.

Catalonia's wine regions also encompass the southeast of the Pyrenees, where Raül Bobet of Castell d'Encús is making wonderful red and white still wines at an altitude of 800–1,230m (2,625–4,035 feet) above sea level, utilizing twelfth-century stone vats left by the first winegrowers in the area, Hospitaller monks of the Order of St. John. For local Pyrenean specialities, Raül recommends eating at Lo Quiosc, Casa Masové or Lo Paller del Coc. Then there's the ruggedly beautiful Priorat, known for its slate-rich llicorella soils, producing lusty rich reds, from Mas Martinet or Álvaro Palacios. The doughnut-like ring of land that encircles Priorat on all sides is the (less famous) wine region of Montsant; check out Celler Joan d'Anguera for some of the best examples of modern Spanish Garnacha around here.

RIOJA

This northeastern region is home to Spain's flagship reds, and Rioja's wines are some of the most glugged in the UK. Indeed, the distinctive yellow label of Campo Viejo's Rioja featured strongly around our respective university eras (at that point we considered it the height of sophistication) and we both still have a soft spot for the region's bottles. All Rioja wine comes from the Rioja *denominación de origen calificada* (DOCa) area, a 100km (62 miles) long and fairly narrow (40km/25 miles north to south) band of land, cut through from west to east by the Ebro river. Rioja is further split into three subregions: Rioja Alta, Rioja Alavesa and Rioja Oriental (formerly Rioja Baja).

Most of the DOCa falls within La Rioja province, which gets its name from the River Oja (Rio Oja in Spanish), but it partly strays into other provinces – Álava (thus Rioja Alavesa) in the Basque area to its north; Navarra to the northeast; and a small chunk of Burgos (part of Castilla y León). For authentic pronunciation, roll your tongue over the R and pronounce it phonetically like RRYOH-HAH (there's no harsh K in it).

The traditional way of labelling Rioja wine is by age of the maturation period in cask and bottle. A label lists how long the wine has spent in American oak from the youngest 'joven' styles through to crianza, reserva, and the oldest, gran reserva. But now it's permitted to reference single vineyards, as they do in Burgundy. There are no crus, but that will be the next evolution for the area.

Big bodegas with enormous productions dominate. These are impressive to see and will certainly have the facility to host tastings at the cellar door. For an idea of scale, the 15 largest bodegas account for 85 per cent of the total production from the whole region. As always, expect a more personal but less slick experience if you book in for a tasting somewhere smaller-scale and independent. Some of our favourite wineries to seek out are Olivier Rivière, Bodegas Moraza, Bodegas Urbina, Gran Cerdo, Remelluri, Jose Gil and Dominio del Carabo.

The region is the spiritual home of Tempranillo, a deep-coloured variety that accounts for about three quarters of all grapes grown in the appellation. Then there's the late-ripening Garnacha, once Spain's most-planted red grape. This is often mistaken for a French variety, where it goes by Grenache, and makes up a large part of the wines made in the Rhône Villages and Châteauneuf-du-Pape. In Rioja, Tempranillo and Garnacha are often blended to build complexity; the weightier Garnacha offers baked plum, dried blood orange and cooking spices, while Tempranillo adds notes of fig and cherry.

You'll find Rioja's oldest wineries in **Rioja Alta**, in the far west. Many of the vineyards here are planted at altitude on a varied mosaic of soils in an Atlantic-influenced climate. One favourite is Bodegas R. López de Heredia (LDH), a winery where nothing is rushed. A tour will demonstrate the beautiful old presses and casks still in use; much

like the traditional labels, it seems as if little has changed since it was set up in 1877. The focus here is on slow, gentle development – LDH releases its wines only when they deem them aged enough. For instance, the entry wine, Viña Cubillo Crianza, is eight years old, way more than the legal requirement of six months for a crianza. LDH's most-loved wines come from their largest vineyard, Tondonia, while the Viña Gravonia Blanco is made from Viura (a floral white known as Macabeo in France), which is best decanted to make the most of its depth and potential. The holy grail is the Tondonia Rosado, still the best pink wine Bert has ever tasted. He has no idea how you pack in so much crazy complexity – savoury yet sweet berry flavours and ultra-refreshing. Over the road in Haro, the capital of the subregion, you'll find Bodegas La Rioja Alta, which is almost as old as LDH (1890). When Bert last visited on his birthday, they served him a classic Riojan supper of tender new season lamb chops cooked over vine shoots, paired with a 1988 birth year bottle of Rioja Alta, still fresh with plenty of vibrant fruit.

The northernmost subregion, **Rioja Alavesa**, is known for producing lifted (fresher, more acidic) wines with a mouth-watering acidity. Many vineyards are grown on dramatic clay-limestone terraces with a stronger influence from the Atlantic Ocean. On one visit to the vineyards of Alavesa, just as golden hour approached, clouds started to form around the Cantabrian peaks and slid down the mountains like an avalanche as the sun was setting – the windows shook as the cloud passed, with an accompanying blast of cool air. This misty mountain air is the magic to this subregion, stopping the vines from too-speedy ripening.

Rioja Oriental in the east is responsible for 40 per cent of Rioja's vinous output. Soils are varied, but more commonly feature alluvial deposits and ferrous clay, thanks to several rivers, and the area experiences hotter, more Mediterranean climes. Oriental's wines were long seen as inferior to those from Alavesa and Alta; the region's old name, Baja, is a reference to the low altitude of its river plains where you'll find the bulk wineries. However, the wines produced in Oriental's cooler, mountainous zones by enterprising New Wave makers such as Javier Arizcuren (Bodega Arizcuren) and sisters Clara and Patricia Espinosa (of Señorío de Librares) have nothing in common with mass-produced plonk.

JEREZ

Of all the world's wines, sherry remains the most misunderstood and undervalued. If you believe the trade press, this fortified wine has been on the cusp of a renaissance for the best part of a decade. Out on the restaurant floor it's been a lot tougher to convince guests to sing from the same hymn sheet. The problem is that many Brits associate sherry with cheap cream sherries – the blended, sweetened stuff of 1970s dinner parties (and the favoured bev of Richard Griffiths' melodramatic Uncle Monty in the 1987 cult film *Withnail and I*), which you might have seen at the back of your great-aunt's cocktail cabinet, crusted around the lid and with that blue label.

If you shudder at the thought of sherry, we implore you to give it another go.

Once you taste the good stuff and find one you like, we hope you'll agree it's a fine wine with plenty of character, complexity and balance. Why is it so cheap? Aside from shrivelling demand, sherry is often non-vintage, in other words blended from many different vintages and plots, which increases the consistency and lowers the price.

To be called a sherry, this kind of wine has to be made in the Sherry Triangle, an area in the province of Cádiz in southwestern Spain, between the three towns of Jerez, Sanlúcar de Barrameda and El Puerto de Santa María. It's also the seat of Spain's wine history, when the Phoenicians founded the city of Gadir (now Cádiz) around 1100 BCE. This is southern Andalusia – one of the world's hottest fine-wine zones – where the grapes (almost always the Palomino Fino variety) are grown on a special, almost-white *albariza* soil. It is full of chalk and acts like a sponge, retaining rainwater during the long, scorching summers.

Some producers shaking up the sherry world include Fernado Angulo, Willy Pérez and Ramiro Ibáñez, Forlong, and Alejandro Muchada. Genre-busting makers are also experimenting with alternative styles; for instance, Fernando Angulo's ancestral sparklers in Sanlúcar de Barrameda, and the still whites made from Palomino grapes by Muchada-Léclapart – a collaboration between the top Champagne grower David Léclapart and Andalusian native, Alejandro Muchada – wines marrying the soul of sherry with the precision of Champagne.

Sherry offers a vast, versatile and nuanced range of options ranging from bone dry, refreshing styles to velvety and treacle-like. In a nutshell, the finished sherry will depend on whether it has been aged biologically (under a layer of *flor* yeast) or oxidatively, or a combination of the two. Biologically aged sherries will be a lighter tipple which, like a regular table wine, won't keep for more than a few days, while the oxidative styles are richer, more robust and can be kept open for longer. Almost without fail Bert puts a tiptop (but remarkably good value) Manzanilla from La Guita by the glass on his wine lists. It's partly oxidized, so it can be kept open for a while. The first thing that hits you is the texture like juicy green olives. Then there's the crispiness of a green apple and a cobnut skin finish.

SHERRY STYLES

Fino and Manzanilla
Any sherry journey should start here. Lively and lemony in taste and colour, these are two similar beginner-friendly dry styles, hovering at about 15 per cent alcohol, making the quintessential aperitif (best served chilled) or best friend to bowls of olives, the soft crunch of golden Marcona almonds and delicate seafood. Fish and chips also pair well. Fino is produced in Jerez, while Manzanilla is made about half an hour's drive away near the Atlantic coast, in Sanlúcar de Barrameda. It's like an intense local football rivalry, so when you visit, drink according to where you are (if you want to make friends, that is).

Amontillado
This starts life as a fino, but with an extended ageing, which helps to unlock some complex flavours. Generally dry, these wines are aged between four and six years and will have a slightly higher ABV than a fino. Amontillados are brilliant paired with food. Our favourite is with garlicky roast chicken or Iberian ham.

Oloroso
Dark and dense with wonderful earthy flavours and baked walnuts on the palate. Oloroso will cut through fatty and rich foods. Try it with some nutty aged Spanish cheese, like the local Payoyo.

Palo Cortado
Lesser spotted, the sherry geek's drink of choice. The flavours are deep and interesting, with dried orange zest and intense almond flavours. This is great after a meal as a digestif. A rare sherry combining the best bits of amontillado with the more oxidized notes of oloroso.

Pedro Ximénez
The name of both a grape and style, this is a mahogany-brown, viscous wine that's among the sweetest in the world. The flavour concentration is off the scale, like someone has blended up a smoothie out of a boozy Christmas pudding. We love it! Drinking PX can seem pretty intimidating – but pour it over a couple of scoops of vanilla gelato and you have the world's best rum and raisin ice cream.

Jesús Barquín and Eduardo Odeja
Equipo Navazos

In less than two decades, Equipo Navazos has become the last word in pure, unblended sherry. It's led by crack team Jesús Barquín (a charismatic professor of criminal law at the University of Granada) and Jerez-born Eduardo Odeja, who has more than 40 sherry harvests under his belt. Wine writers have heralded Jesús as the saviour of sherry, but he's an atheist fiercely on the side of Darwin, who dubs biodynamics 'mumbo jumbo'. Eduardo, meanwhile, compares his role to making wine in Jerez to shepherding. 'More than creating the thing we have been driving, managing it – and trying not to spoil it,' he says.

'We are science people and we believe in what can be proved,' Jesús effuses. 'Darwin is the triumph and hero of rationality; if we talk about it like a football game, we are on the side of Darwin and not on the side of people like Steiner [the pioneer of biodynamics]. Wine writers are too obsequious on this topic; I always disagree with Jancis Robinson on this.'

The pair's friendship blossomed in 2003, when Eduardo was hosting a tasting at a Fenavin wine fair in Ciudad Real, central Spain. 'At the end of the event we got talking about wines, whisky and sherry, and agreed that Jesús would come to Jerez to visit me,' recalls Eduardo, who at that point was the technical director of sherry bodegas La Guita and Valdespino.

Things snowballed after a visit to a winery, Bodega Sanchez Ayala, a little up the coast from Jerez. 'In December 2005 we found a special, old *amontillado* [cask] that was untouched for 20 years, which became the beginning of Equipo Navazos,' Eduardo says. 'We started, inspired by the independent bottlers in Scotland. It's a coincidence that both Eduardo and I are strong whisky lovers. We decided to bottle a small release for ourselves and our friends.'

Equipo Navazos called this first run of 600 bottles La Bota de Amontillado No.1, after Edgar Allan Poe's short story of the same name: *The Cask of Amontillado*. 'It's a story of vengeance and terror written almost 200 years ago,' says Jesús, a culinary critic and prolific author on many subjects beyond wine. 'None of the characters were Spaniards, but it shows how relevant these wines have been to history. We also wanted to communicate that it was a wine bottled straight from the cask; that it was a real sherry.'

Equipo Navazos does not produce grapes in-house but through cultivating close, long-standing relationships with producers and vineyards across Andalusia. It has become a micro-négociant; something Jesús describes as 'the outcome of many years of friendship and mutual trust – we don't have contracts'.

Since setting up in 2007, the team of collaborators has grown into a consortium of 30 or so sherry nerds and partners dotted across the globe. Initially, bottlings were distributed privately, but the distinctive wines garnered such a following that Equipo Navazos evolved naturally into a small commercial enterprise. Admittedly, for sherry, their bottles are relatively spenny (from £30ish up to the hundreds), but anyone who's tried them will confirm Equipo Navazos makes magnificent, complex and concentrated stuff.

The focus remains on super-artisanal, singular wines from *soleras* and individual casks, but the series of La Bota wines has proliferated, with limited bottlings released in consecutively dated and numbered editions, as well as spin-offs made in collaboration with other great minds such as Dirk Niepoort, the latter resulting in a deliciously saline, still wine made from wild-fermented Palomino Fino that tastes a bit like something that might come out of Jura. There's another partnership with Colet, the sparkling wine producer in Penedès, making use of the structural similarities between Champagne and biologically aged sherry: 'vineyards grown on white chalky soils, the relatively neutral character of the base wines,' Jesús says.

I Think Manzanilla is an homage to Darwin, named after one of Jesús's many visits to the law faculty at Cambridge University; the library houses Darwin's famous notebook with a drawing of a tree of life and scrawled and above it, 'I think'. We're betting the name is also a prod at proponents of biodynamics. The wine is such a pure expression of manzanilla: delicate on first taste, then developing with a wonderful sea breeze and almond skin complexity. It continues blooming on the palate for ages and, although Bert has tasted it hundreds of times, every time he does he has the same reaction: wow!

Some say mixing sherry into a cocktail is blasphemy. Jesús says otherwise. 'It's an excellent mixer. In summer, in a fridge by the swimming pool I have a bottle of very old amontillado and I mix it with the equivalent of Sprite or sparkling water with ice.' Eduardo also enjoys one of our favourite summer drinks: 50ml (2fl oz) of Fino or Manzanilla over ice with 100ml (31/2fl oz) of tonic water. This is lower in alcohol than a G&T and way more refreshing.

WORD FROM THE WINEMAKER

Which wineries and locations have you previously made wine at?

I worked for 17 years for Croft and 23 years for José Estévez (Valdespino and La Guita).

What is the most authentic local restaurant that represents your region?

It's difficult to choose only one. I really enjoy Mantúa, La Carboná and La Marea in Jerez. And Casa Bigote and Taberna El Loli in Sanlúcar.

Do you have any other insider tips for your region?

I like to walk through the centre of Jerez. In Sanlúcar, I like everything close to the mouth of the Guadalquivir river. Around Jerez (northwest) and on the road to Sanlúcar, you can see some beautiful vineyards.

Any favourite bars in Jerez?

La Moderna and Albalá.

And your favourite bars in Sanlúcar de Barrameda?

Taberna der Guerrita and Los Caracoles.

Local sports teams to look out for?

The best football team in the region is Cádiz C.F.

What's the best thing about making wine in your region?

Being able to walk through the vineyards and enjoy its landscape and be in the winery tasting wines and enjoying its quality and diversity.

Are there any local artists that have inspired you?

Not so much as an inspiration, but hearing flamenco in the voice of La Macanita makes me feel Jerez in the same way as when I drink sherry.

USA

The North American wine scene has long been dominated by the Golden State of California, which, thanks to its exceptionally wide range of climates and a reputation founded on the worldwide fame of Napa and Sonoma, accounts for more than 80 per cent of the country's overall production. That's a lot of wine, given the USA is the globe's fourth biggest producer after Italy, France and Spain.

In Napa, small producers shaking things up include Matthiasson Wines, whose lively, creative wines are made via organic regenerative practices using off-piste varieties such as Ribolla Gialla, an ancient white grape rarely found outside of the Friuli-Venezia Giulia region in northeast Italy. Yet there's much more to explore beyond California. These days, as the modern palate is leaning towards cool-climate wines, New York State's aromatic Rieslings are challenging the Golden State's crown, while in the Pacific Northwest, we love Oregon's elegant Pinot Noirs and Washington State's bold, structured reds. Up-and-coming producers are pushing boundaries in New England's Vermont and across the wildly diverse topography of the Southwestern states, including Texas, Colorado and Arizona.

From the sixteenth century onwards, successive waves of European colonisers brought *Vitis vinifera* across the Atlantic with them, originally for use as a sacramental wine to celebrate Mass, and by the eighteenth century, winemaking in California was flourishing until Prohibition (the nationwide ban on the sale and import of alcoholic beverages between 1920 and 1933) put the brakes on things. It would take more than a half century for Cali's winemaking volumes to recover to their heady pre-Prohibition levels. In a Parisian hotel in 1976, a blind tasting event dubbed the Judgment of Paris changed everything for American wines, when California's winemakers scooped first place in both the red and white categories: a 1973 Stag's Leap Cabernet Sauvignon beat Bordeaux's best, including a 1970 wine from the centuries-old Château Mouton-Rothschild estate, while a 1973 Chardonnay from Napa Valley's Chateau Montelena pipped top white winemakers from Burgundy to the post. This shock win first propelled Napa to the world stage, proving American wines could rival the Old World establishment.

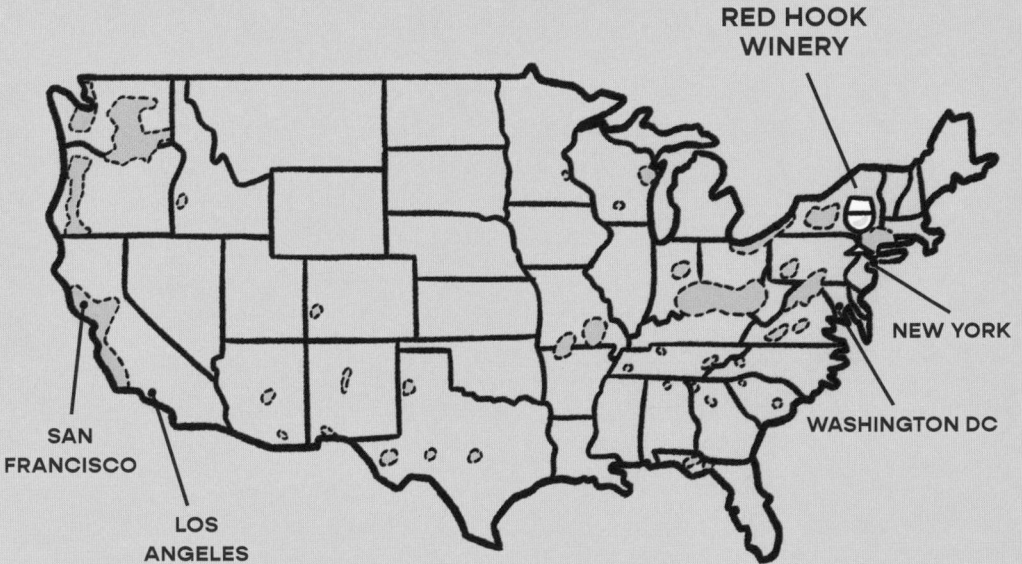

RED HOOK
WINERY

NEW YORK

WASHINGTON DC

SAN
FRANCISCO

LOS
ANGELES

GO-TO US PRODUCERS

Ridge Vineyards – Santa Cruz
Mountains
Heitz Cellar – Napa Valley
Kistler – Sonoma Coast
Sine Qua Non – Central Coast

Kelley Fox Wines – Willamette Valley
Brick House – Willamette Valley
Arnot-Roberts – Sonoma County
Littorai – Sonoma Coast
Abe Schoener – Various

NEW YORK STATE

This state's fertile glacial soils include more than 470 wineries within 11 American Viticultural Areas (AVAs) – the US's answer to European controlled appellations of origin such as France's Appellation d'Origine Contrôlée (AOC), although in the US they're concerned only with a specified area's geographical boundaries. New York's AVAs include Finger Lakes, which has cemented a rep as a leading cool-climate wine region in the United States for its Rieslings and Cabernet Francs; Lake Erie; Niagara Escarpment by the Canadian border; the Hudson River Region; and Long Island.

Cross the Brooklyn Bridge from Manhattan and you're on Long Island, though it must be said that you won't find vineyards in the New York City boroughs of Brooklyn and Queens at the western end of the island. Another

115km (70 miles) will bring you to the town of Riverhead where Long Island splits into two forks, separated by the Great Peconic Bay. Turn right and you'll end up in the Hamptons, a slice of Gatsby glitz where moneyed New Yorkers own multi-million dollar clapboarded second homes. Take a left and you'll end up in the North Fork, a neighbourhood historically filled with market gardens and, these days, more than 60 wineries. NoFo (as it is known by the laidback locals) is peppered with vintage stores, cool cafés and restaurants serving up the catch of the day.

The North Fork's wine-producing history dates back to 1973, when Alex and Louisa Hargrave founded the first commercial vineyard and winery here. Back then, Long Island's focus was on growing Bordeaux varieties (given it is on a similar latitude). Now, North Fork's wines are developing their own identity and we think it's fast becoming the most exciting wine region in the USA. The principal challenge to wine-growing here is humidity, but the coastal winds keep the freshness within the wines.

More than 8 million New Yorkers are sardined into the state's five boroughs.

For anyone visiting the city, scouting out the best bagels, pizza slices, pastrami and pretzels is a prerequisite, but we'd urge you not to miss the state's vibrant wines, many of which aren't available outside of the New York area. Some of our favourite Long Island producers are Bedell, Channing Daughters and Lenz.

Christopher Nicolson
Red Hook Winery

Stepping off the ferry at Red Hook in South Brooklyn feels like walking onto a film set. It's a neighbourhood with a bohemian small-town feel unlike any other in New York, punctuated with indie businesses like Defonte's Sandwich Shop (opened in 1922), OurHaus (a fun-loving restaurant run by an ex-dominatrix) and Red Hook Winery, housed in a converted waterfront warehouse on Pier 41, right across the bay from the Statue of Liberty, Governors Island and the New Jersey shore.

The urban winery is the brainchild of Mark Snyder, a musician who has worked as a rig designer for Billy Joel and Peter Frampton, with the aim of making the most of North Fork's underappreciated grapes. Up front, there's a retail tasting room (where you can get wine and nibbles) with barrels and vats at the back, plus outdoor seating for warm-weather drinking beside lapping waves. It's a stellar place to head for some respite from the city's sweltering summers and frenetic pace.

When we meet Christopher, a commercial fisherman and the eloquent head winemaker here since Red Hook's opening in 2008, he's whistling sea shanties to himself as he tends to his barrels. He's been aboard boats since babyhood: his mother is indigenous Alaskan and his family has been fishing there [in Alaska] for more than 200 years. Every summer, during June and July, he goes out catching wild sockeye salmon in the Kvichak area of Bristol Bay, Alaska, for the family biz (Iliamna Fish Co.) and sells their annual haul to the likes of Dan Barber (of Netflix *Chef's Table* fame).

For the rest of the year, he works at Red Hook alongside two Napa Valley consultant winemakers with a cult-like following: Abe Schoener, a former classics professor with whom Christopher bottled one of his first wines around the turn of the millennium, and Robert Foley, nicknamed 'The God of Cabernet'. Christopher also trained at Selvapiana in Italy's Chianti Rufina and at Littorai in northern California.

He is friendly with all the growers – around 90 per cent of their grapes are sourced from five vineyards within about 16km (10 miles) of each other in the North Fork, and the rest come from the Finger Lakes. 'At their best, the wines of the North Fork should have some kind of maritime character, something oceanic, something saline, because the farming is so dominated by the sea,' Christopher says. 'It was our hope, when we started to bring a fresh winemaking perspective to this region, to make it be more like itself and not ape somewhere else.'

And we can confirm, whatever he's doing, it's working. Devoted and dreamy, Christopher exudes a frank kindheartedness with a touch of Jeff Goldblum-esque eccentricity which has helped to turn Red Hook Winery into a magnet for New York State wine production.

He's experimenting with grapes like Nebbiolo – using a long, slow, gentle maturation to produce a bright, tannic, 'fasten your seatbelts' kind of wine – and 2019's Lot 10 Vineyard Riesling, which is aged for 23 months before release. Even after this extended ageing period it's so fresh and zippy that it tastes like it was bottled yesterday (in a good way). Refined and elegant, it has a mineral finish with notes of white nectarine and lime zest.

Christopher was raised in Montana and like his wife, Emily, an Italian-American from Philadelphia, is a music obsessive. 'My patient bride and I are both super-nerdy people. We cook a lot. Because of fishing, we're pretty tied into farmers' market culture and foraging.' He also does a little bit of fish-curing in the winery. 'There's a whole lox culture in New York,' he says.

Despite his sea captain energy, Christopher loves New York. 'I do like the city, maybe because I get to spend the summers in the bush. Like London, it's wonderful to have all these different people in one place. I guess it makes you appreciate both the country and the city more in both cases,' he says, and as we leave, he lets us in on his boating fantasy for New York life. 'I've been wanting to get a little Zodiac, like Jacques Cousteau, to zip across the bay.'

WORD FROM THE WINEMAKER

Which restaurants would you visit if you were celebrating?

Blue Hill at Stone Barns, Dan Barber's farm-to-table restaurant in Tarrytown, and Noodle Pudding, a cash-only, no-reservations Italian restaurant in Brooklyn Heights.

Any other New York restaurants you rate?

Justine's on Hudson in West Village. Chef Jeanne Jordan is doing really cool Filipina interpretations of European dishes.

Where would you go for New York classics?

Pizza: Luigi's in Brooklyn. Hot dogs: Grey's Papaya in Manhattan. Bagels: Bagel Hole in Brooklyn. And pretzels: Center City Pretzel in Philadelphia.

Where do you go for a late-night drink?

Brooklyn Inn on Hoyt Street.

Best farmers' market in New York?

We regularly visit the Greenmarket (NYC has a city-sponsored farmers' market organization, called the Greenmarket, which assures locality and specificity of the produce on offer – it's an important support system for New York state-based farming, animal husbandry, and food production). Our local Greenmarket is at Grand Army Plaza in Brooklyn. We also visit the Greenmarket in Williamsburg. In addition (it's a standalone farm) we visit HOG Farm with regularity in Brookhaven on Long Island.

Good strolls in New York?	Prospect Park in Brooklyn, or walking along the harbour in Red Hook.
What's on the winery playlist?	We are music nerds here, so the music is varied and wide-ranging. Lots of jazz (Nina Simone and Hank Mobley and Makaya McCraven), lots of choral (John Tavener and Robert White), rock and roll (Hawkwind and Ron Gallo), deep soul (Numero Group records), gospel (old school Sensational Nightingales) and lots of reggae (Marcia Griffiths and Horace Andy).
Any favourite recipes for the fish you catch?	Freshly caught (or properly flash-frozen) wild Alaskan sockeye salmon from Bristol Bay, seasoned liberally with salt, tamari, finely pounded dry chillies, a scant sprinkling of demerara sugar, and an extremely thin coating of butter and then carefully cooked to 49°C (120°F). Serve hot or at room temperature. Drink with well-chilled (but not TOO cold) manzanilla sherry.

WALES

We've dedicated a chapter to Wales and its wines, rather than simply lumping it under the umbrella with England. This beautiful nation might be small but it packs a punch. Laden with the lore of dragons, Wales has an almost indecent share of jaw-dropping scenery to explore, from the dramatic peaks of its three glorious National Parks and seal-spotting along almost endless coastal walks to a string of fairytale waterfalls in the south-western bit of the Brecon Beacons.

Wine in Wales has had various fits and starts: Suetonius Paulinus, the Roman governor who defeated Boudicca, is thought to have planted vines to the east of modern-day Cardiff in around 70 CE, and in the late nineteenth and early twentieth century wines were produced at Castell Coch, north of Cardiff. Today, there are 70 hectares (173 acres) under vine across Wales, and more than 30 commercial vineyards; among the oldest of these are Parva Farm, Tintern, now in the care of Dave Morris of Mountain People Wine (see pages 270–72), and Glyndwr Vineyard in Cowbridge, both planted in the late 1970s. Other brilliant Welsh producers include Ancre Hill near Monmouth; The Dell in Raglan, Monmouthshire; Montgomery Vineyard, near the small town of Montgomery; and Whinyard Rocks near Presteigne, in Powys. We're predicting big things from the Welsh wine industry in the coming years: *iechyd da!* (Cheers!)

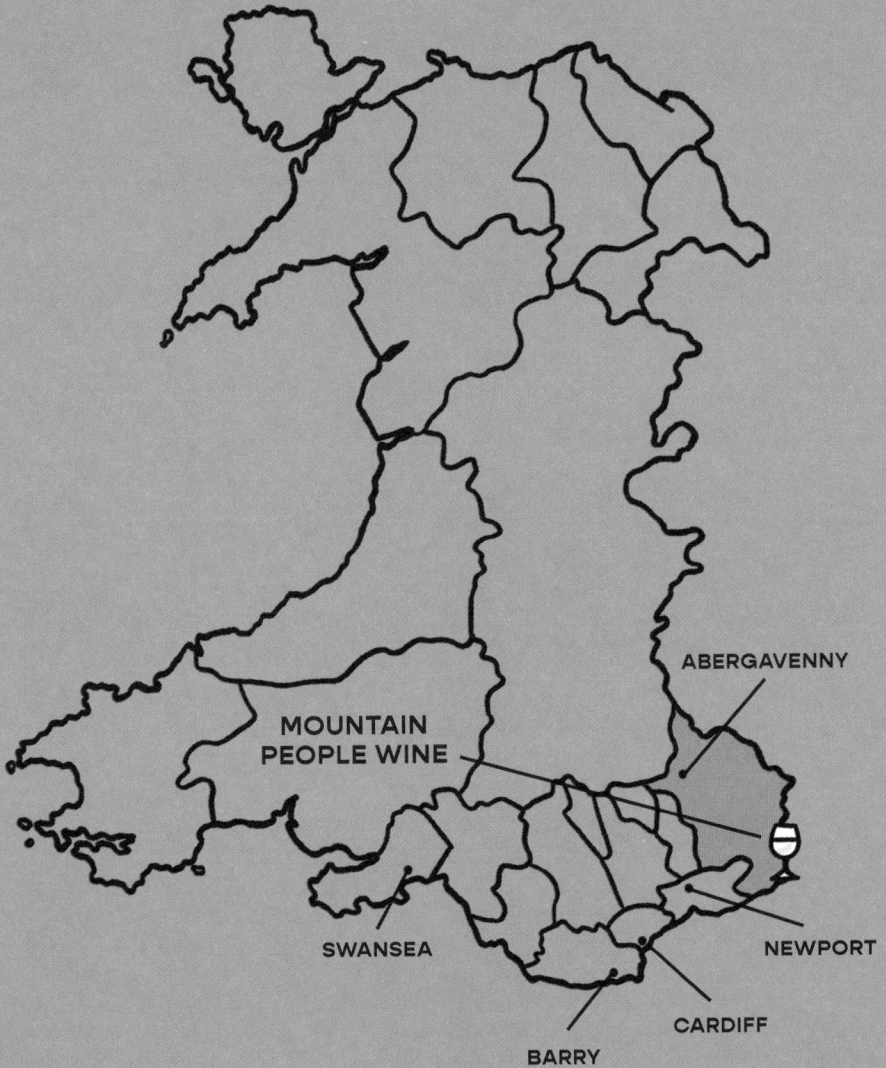

→ THE DRIVE ACROSS THE SEVERN BRIDGE IS THE MOST ↓ DRAMATIC WAY TO MAKE AN ENTRANCE

MONMOUTHSHIRE

Nicknamed the food capital of Wales, Monmouthshire is a lush border county in the south-east, nestled between the Brecon Beacons National Park and the Wye Valley Area of Outstanding Natural Beauty. It's also a hub for wine tourism as Wales's most-planted county for vines. It's easy to get to from Cardiff, Bristol or London, although we can confirm the drive across the Severn Bridge from England is the most dramatic way to make an entrance.

Several rivers snake through the county (including the Wye, Usk and Monnow) and its best-known towns include Monmouth (ex-raver Bez from the Happy Mondays lives nearby); Chepstow, home to the oldest stone castle in Britain; and Abergavenny, which hosts one of the UK's best and biggest food festivals every September.

Feast on exquisite local rhubarb and asparagus, and sup on Hive Mind's smoked honey porter and mead, or stellar single-variety vintage ciders at Apple County Cider Co. Near Monmouth, beautiful Tintern in the Wye Valley and its ruined Cistercian abbey has long been a magnet for poets and artists, from Wordsworth and J. M. W. Turner to Lord Tennyson.

Wales is notorious for its heavy rain, but the climate in Monmouthshire is drier and warmer courtesy of the rain shadow created by the Black Mountains and Brecon Beacons. When you arrive in the Wye Valley, you'll notice the region resembles a medley of the Mosel in Germany, with its winding river, and the verdant hills of Chablis in France. It's these steep slopes that help vines soak up the sunshine and achieve ripeness.

David Morris
Mountain People Wine
(Gwin Pobl Y Mynydd)

David Morris keeps a low profile. When we spoke to him he didn't even have a website or Instagram, but we think he's making the best wines in Wales right now.

A curly-locked trailblazer in Wales's burgeoning natural wine movement, David played a fundamental part in setting up Ancre Hill, his family's 12-hectare (30-acre) estate in Monmouthshire where he worked for nearly a decade implementing biodynamic practices. His winemaking CV stretches back to 2006 with stints at Sussex fizz giant Nyetimber; Millton in Gisborne, New Zealand's first organic wine estate; and Domaine Le Soula, biodynamic high-altitude vineyards in the foothills of the Pyrenees in southern France.

David has been doing his own thing since 2019 with his solo project, Mountain People, named after a 1997 song of the same name by the Cardiff band, Super Furry Animals. The words struck a chord with him (*They don't care about | You and me | Obviously | No not us | We're the mountain people*) and David chose the name to serve as a reminder not to neglect his wines nor indeed Wales.

Mountain People's logo, a riff on Joy Division's iconic *Unknown Pleasures* album cover, traces the topography of the Wye Valley, and was designed by his brother-in-law, Jon Peeler, a talented tattoo artist.

David has been tending a one-hectare (2.5-acre) vineyard at Parva Farm in Tintern on a steep, south-facing slope 100m (330 feet) above the River Wye. It's a special pocket that receives even less rain than the Monmouthshire average. It's still early days for the multi-varietal site: in 2020 and 2021 David produced two cuvées, both with his signature light-footed, punkish spirit. The first is a field-blend rosé comprising eight varieties, at around 8 or 9 per cent ABV. The second, St Jude, a Pinot Noir-heavy blend that's the best UK-made still red we've ever tasted, is named in honour of David's dear mate and colleague, Mickey Jude. 'St Jude is the patron saint of lost causes, which has always been a running joke between us,' he says. After Mickey fell ill for a spell, David adds: 'I don't know what I'd do if I lost him and I wanted to show how appreciative of him I am.'

Making wines this good in Monmouthshire's climate is a tough task and David isn't just after a quick quid. His philosophy is 'doing more work on less land'. Climatic constraints mean he'll ultimately produce less fruit on the site, but the quality shows in the glass: it's important work that many other wineries in England and Wales aren't brave enough to do.

Welsh wine has 'so much potential', David says, admitting that the country's viticultural evolution has been 'slow' and he misses being part of a thronging wine community (as he was in France) where you could constantly taste, share ideas and also compete with your neighbours. His local(ish) favourite producers include Mark and Laura Smith from Black Mountain vineyard in Herefordshire, on the other side of the Brecon Beacons, adding that the West Country low-interventionist winemakers Daniel and Nicola Ham at Offbeat 'are knocking out some really good wine'.

David also set up Wales's first contract winemaking cellar, where he produces not only his own wines, but wines for other Welsh vineyards. His methods for fermentation and ageing include oak barrels and Spanish *tinajas* (amphoras), resulting in collaborations with the likes of Hebron Vineyard, a regenerative producer in Carmarthenshire. He sees this side hustle as a self-fulfilling prophecy, viewing contract winemaking as a way to encourage a greater number of top-quality producers locally. 'If I've had a hand in that, then it creates a scene rather than just one person doing something,' David says.

'I'm just making a drink at the end of the day. So long as it tastes good, the parameters are what they are, the fruit comes in, and it is what it is,' he says with trademark modesty. 'The dream would be to have four hectares (10 acres) spread out over four or five different sites all along the Wye Valley, set up like a proper little domaine. It spreads the risk; you can have different varieties in different microclimates. I'll carry on doing what I'm doing until I physically can't anymore – or until the kids intervene.'

WORD FROM THE WINEMAKER

A local restaurant you'd visit if you were celebrating?

The Walnut Tree in Llanddewi Skirrid near Abergavenny sits on the edge of the Brecon Beacons. It has a Michelin star and Shaun Hill shaking the pans.

What's the most authentic local restaurant?

The Bear Hotel in Crickhowell; my grandpa's favourite drinking den. It hasn't changed in 30 years!

What are the top pubs in Monmouthshire?

We like the Lion Inn in Trellech. The Black Bear Inn near Usk is an awesome little pub run by chef-landlord Joshua Byrne (who used to do the cooking at Poco in Bristol) and his wife Hannah. [Victoria rates the whipped cod's roe and potato skins here.]

Your favourite local bars?

Ye Old Ferrie Inn in Symonds Yat for a beer, or Chester's for wine in Abergavenny.

What's on the winery playlist?

The latest vintage was all about Pavement [a Californian indie rock band fronted by Stephen Malkmus].

Which foods pair well with Mountain People wines?

You can't go wrong with mackerel or *sewin* (sea trout) with Welsh wines. And I love taking all day to cook a Sunday roast with a bottle beside me.

Where's the best place to buy local Welsh lamb for a Sunday roast?

Kiloran Buckler in the Llanthony Valley.

Who's your winery mascot?

Seefa, our dog. She has a habit of barking at the hose.

Any insider tips for your region?

Late winter, walking to the top of the Kymin. Or cycling with the whole family to our favourite swimming spot on the River Monnow. Wouldn't be our favourite for long if I told you where it is though.

Darren Smith

In this book we've intentionally chosen to focus on a solid number of outsiders, career swappers and folks with unconventional routes into wine, but Darren's move towards nomadic winemaking resonated with us so much that we decided to dedicate an entire chapter to him. Some winemakers simply prefer not to be bound to a single place.

Hailing from a teetotal household on a council estate in a post-industrial West Yorkshire town, Darren has made wine everywhere from Chile to the Canary Islands, Georgia to Germany and Peru. He only started drinking the stuff when he moved to Oxford for a theology degree in 1999, always opting to pick up a corner shop bottle over anything else.

Read any big estate's biography and you'll notice there'll be much mention of 'winemaking in the blood'. As in any other agricultural sphere, the importance of inheritance, land and clandestine knowledge passed along generations in this industry can't be underplayed, which makes experiences like Darren's all the more impressive.

'I was on the path to a journalism career and I quit abruptly to work as a chef in a Cotswoldy gastropub in Oxfordshire,' he says. 'To save money they made me head chef after six months – I was really in over my head.' Next came immersion into the wine side of things, through tastings with suppliers and, on days off, sampling glasses from his local, Summertown Wine Bar.

'I didn't grow up with wine, but it became like a disease,' Darren says. Within 18 months this bug had bloomed into a fully fledged obsession. He started wine writing ('I was blagging it at first') alongside casual shifts at The Sampler (a north London wine shop with a rotating roster of 80 different bottles) as well as traversing Europe via spells as a grape-picking volunteer.

Darren's nomadic winemaking journey kicked off in 2018, during an internship with Dirk Niepoort (a name mentioned repeatedly throughout this book), the charismatic Portuguese winemaker who knows talent when he sees it. Darren was ensconced for harvest in the Douro Valley. 'Over lunch, I mentioned that I wanted to start this project making wine in different countries,' he recalls. 'I asked, can you help me look into where to buy grapes, maybe next year? And Dirk is one of those unusual characters who'll make things happen.'

Cue the big turning point. 'Why wait?' said Dirk, and told Darren to pack his things. Sergio Silva, a winemaker from Barriada, came to collect him and that was it – Dirk gave Darren access to his best fruit, plus all the help and encouragement he needed. The resulting wine he and Sergio made together was from a native Portuguese red called Baga. On his first attempt, Darren whips this deep and dark Baga grape into an elegant, drinkable bottle – plenty of rose petals on the nose and deep red fruits that are cut with a fine limestone edge.

In typically self-deprecating Yorkshire style he calls himself lazy and disorganized – which is entirely untrue. He's christened the project The Finest Wines Available to Humanity, or TFWATH for short. The line is not some egoistical declaration; it's taken from his favourite film, *Withnail and I*, Bruce Robinson's 1987 booze-soaked comedy starring Richard E. Grant. 'I can pretty much quote it verbatim. It's a very long-winded name, which goes against all the rules of business. But I don't want to do something neat and salesy. I'm lumbered with it now.'

Since then Darren has been addicted to learning the ins and outs of winemaking, doubling up on back-to-back harvests each year (bar a pandemic blip) – one in the northern hemisphere and another in the south, where the seasons are reversed. The winemakers he collaborates with are those who practise as little intervention as possible, whose wines are defined by the quality of the grapes, in turn defined by the integrity of the farming. You can expect niche wines, diverse stories and old grapes from Darren, many of which are new to a UK audience. In each instance his aim is to shout about underdog varieties from regions and terroirs off the beaten track. 'I trust the people that I work with to look after my wines as if they were their own,' he adds.

Darren is based in London between harvests and does all the importing and selling himself. He continues to write about wine (beautifully, we might add), also running a market stall in Walthamstow, east London, where Victoria initially discovered TFWATH, and wholesaling to restaurants and shops, where he first met Bert at Bottles 'n' Jars (now Classic Car Bar), in Highgate, north London.

Spain has ended up being a sort of axis for a lot of the action, including La Palma (he learned from the excellent Victoria Torres Pecis), Murcia and Andalusia. Darren's 2022 collaboration with Raúl Moreno Yagüe in Jerez is an unfortified Palomino – the white grape usually used to make sherry – which makes a dependable partner to fatty Iberico pork. Darren and Raúl make a formidable pairing too, given Raúl's background as not only a winemaker (of Domaine Dujac in Burgundy) but master of viticulture and wine science, former sommelier and ex-Marco Pierre White chef. The Palomino grapes were handpicked, foot-stomped and fermented on the skins for ten days, followed by seven months in old chestnut Amontillado casks. The resultant wine is raw and beautiful, with bruised apple notes, bay and a wonderful salinity. (Read more about Jerez on pages 251–52.)

With each new release you can taste Darren growing in confidence and clarity. 'It's fun, exciting and interesting because you don't know what you're getting into when you start – it's almost like being on the hoof when you're working,' he says. 'Some places I go to, particularly in the South American regions, it's a basic, rudimentary setup.'

Few know that Peru was once the biggest wine exporter in South America. Here Darren has made a Quebranta – a pink-skinned, uniquely Peruvian crossing of Negra Criolla (Chile's País) and Mollar (Negramoll from the Canary Islands) – in collaboration with Pepe Moquillaza. Pepe, Darren says, is a 'force of nature', and a bit of a local legend. Besides wine he also makes pisco, a type of grape brandy, that's so good you'll find it on the lists at triple Michelin starred Celler de Can Roca in Girona. The stops on Pepe and Darren's culinary jaunt around the capital Lima are detailed on page 280.

Darren notes that winemaking culture in southern Chile, around Itata and Bío-Bío, 'is kinda comparable to Georgia.' 'You've got lots of people making wine on a small scale and with their own little plots of vines, which has existed without outside interference for centuries.' Meanwhile 2023's harvest in Bolivia, alongside British-Indian winemaker Nayan Gowda (see pages 58–61) and founder of Jardín Oculto, Maria Jose Granier, was dazzling: 'Pink, Grand Canyon-type valleys, with vineyards like little mini forests ... there are no trellis-trained vines, instead everything's growing up wild quince and pink peppercorn trees.'

He still hasn't bothered with formal oenology training, preferring to learn on the ground, fingers stained with grape juice, while roaming the world. 'I've been extraordinarily lucky so far to work with the people I've worked with, and to go to the places I've gone to, and to make the wines of a quality that I have so far,' Darren says. He has an ever-longer list of places he wants to visit and make wine in the future. We can't wait to taste what he comes up with next.

WORD FROM THE WINEMAKER

Your favourite BYOs in London?	Xi'an Impression (a tiny eatery opposite Arsenal Football Club's Emirates Stadium specializing in the biang biang noodles of Shaanxi province), Mangal 1 (a Turkish institution in Dalston) and the rotating chef pop-ups at Hackney Chinese Centre (such as Guan Cha's).
Which tracks are on repeat in the winery?	Depends on the winemaker I'm working with! They tend to dictate, which can be good, can be a nightmare (endless reggaeton in Itata got annoying; Toumani Diabaté in La Palma was lovely; Queen in Bolivia was somewhere in between).
The wineries or winemakers you've made wine with?	Niepoort (Bairrada), Roberto Henríquez (Bío-Bío), Victoria Torres (La Palma), Julia Casado (Murcia), Baia's Wine (Imereti), Ignacio Pino Román (Itata), Raúl Moreno (Jerez), Pepe Moquillaza (Ica).
Your favourite food memories from Bolivia?	Barbecuing *anticuchos* (spiced beef heart skewers) for the harvest team at Jardín Oculto in the Cinti Valley; eating a perfect bowl of *sopa de trigo* (wheat soup) in Camargo after a backbreaking day of climbing trees to harvest grapes in the *arbolitos* [traditional 'forest' vineyards in which grapevines are trained up trees] of Cinti. Chef Nayan's (Jardín Oculto winemaker Nayan Gowda) excellent southern fried chicken. Discovering that you could eat a huge plate of *arvejada* (a rice dish) for one dollar in the indoor market in Tarija.
Any restaurants in Tarija you'd recommend?	Casona del Molino in Tarija. If you like meat, you will not be disappointed. Beautiful terrace. Formidable buffet. Even more formidable barbecue set-up.

What are your favourite food memories from Chile?

All the cured meats at Taller Macera in Concepción; simple suppers of tinned mussels and tomato salad while looking after the ferments in a dirt-floor cellar in Tanahuillín, Bío-Bío, in 2019. Crazy seafood that I'd never seen before at Mar y Limón restaurant in Concepción (NB: I don't think I'll be eating *piure* [sea squirt] again).

Any bar and restaurant recommendations in Itata Valley?

Borra Bar in Guarilihue, Itata. This is the beating heart of south Chilean wine. During harvest all the winemakers pass through here and you can find all their wines on the shelves. The people who work here are just lovely.

And your favourite food memories from Peru?

Tasting menu at Central, Lima, paired with Pepe Moquillaza's wines (there was a fish dish with a soy-based sauce that was exquisite with Pepe's Quebrada de Ihuanco); the thrustingly brilliant tasting menu at Mérito in Lima; soulful Criolla [traditional food from the north] food at Awicha, Lima; *leche de tigre* [a spicy, citrus marinade used to flavour ceviche] everywhere.

Any bar and restaurant recommendations in Lima?

Mérito (brilliant, imaginative Peruvian–Venezuelan menu by former Central chef Juan Luis Martínez; great wines too), Juanito (beer and simple, irresistible ham sandwiches, timeless atmosphere, impromptu acoustic guitar jams, in Barranco, Lima); Central – visionary menu, somehow manages to encapsulate the disparate geography of Peru and its precious local ingredients; El Pan de la Chola – best pizza in Lima; Hass in Chincha – Peruvian/international food. Chilled venue, fantastic fish.

Which foods remind you of home?

Arvejada in Bolivia – it's basically rice, peas, egg and chips mixed together. Growing up where I did in Yorkshire, we had chips with everything.

What's the best thing about making wine in different locations?

Making friends in different places, being totally immersed in the age-old work of harvest and in the local culture of a place. Connecting people from the different places I've worked.

RESOURCES

WINEMAKERS

Armenia
Zorah Wines
zorahwines.com
info@zorahwines.com

Australia
Cullen Wines
cullenwines.com.au
tastingsandsales@cullenwines.com.au

Austria
Weingut Birgit Braunstein
weingut-braunstein.at
office@weingut-braunstein.at

Pittnauer
pittnauer.com
weingut@pittnauer.com

Belgium
Wijngaard Lijsternest
wijngaardlijsternest.be
servaas.blockeel@gmail.com

Bolivia
Jardín Oculto
jardinoculto.com
informaciones@jardinoculto.com

Canada
Bachelder
bachelderniagara.com
wine@bachelderniagara.com

England
London Cru
londoncru.co.uk
hello@londoncru.co.uk

Westwell Wines
westwellwines.com
cellardoor@westwellwines.com

Matt Gregory Wines
mattgregorywines.co.uk
matt@mattgregorywines.co.uk

France
Maison Jérôme Lefèvre
maisonjeromelefevre.com
hello@maisonjeromelefevre.com

Domaine Barmès-Buecher
barmes-buecher.com
info@barmes-buecher.com

Mark Haisma
markhaisma.co.uk
mail@markhaisma.com

Château Pesquié
chateaupesquie.com
contact@chateaupesquie.com

Georgia
Oda Family Marani
odawines.ge
oda.wines@gmail.com

My Wine Trail
mywinetrailmwt@gmail.com

Germany
Staffelter Hof
staffelter-hof.de
info@staffelter-hof.de

Greece
Iliana Malihin Winery
ilianamalichin@gmail.com

Italy
Azienda Agricola Lalù
info@lalu.wine

Tenuta di Valgiano
valgiano.it
info@valgiano.it

Tenuta di Carleone
john@thewinemakersclub.co.uk

Contrà Soarda
contrasoarda.it
info@contrasoarda.it

Frank Cornelissen Winery
frankcornelissen.it
info@frankcornelissen.it

Japan
Grace Wine
grace-wine.com
info@grace-wine.com

Luxembourg
Domaine L & R Kox
domainekox.lu
info@domainekox.lu

Poland
Winnica Silesian
winnicasilesian.pl
biuro@winnicasilesian.pl

Winnica Dom Bliskowice
dombliskowice.com
maciek@winoblisko.pl

Portugal
Vale da Capucha
info@valedacapucha.com

South africa
Tesselaarsdal Wines
tesselaarsdalwines.co.za
Info@tesselaarsdalwines.co.za

Spain
Equipo Navazos
equiponavazos.com
equipo@navazos.com

USA
Red Hook Winery
redhookwinery.com
manager@redhookwinery.com

Wales
Mountain People Wine (Gwin
Pobl Y Mynydd)
dh.morris@hotmail.com

Nomad
Darren Smith
tfwath.com
info@tfwath.com

STOCKISTS

All the wineries and
winemakers in this book
produce wine in small
quantities, but their bottles
are still widely available
on the shelves of the best
independent shops in the
world. For more information,
recommendations, or help
sourcing these wines, contact
Bert's bar and shop in Norfolk,
England – North Norfolk
Cellars (www.nnc.wine).

Here's a selection of our
favourite wine shops around
the world where you can also
find these wines. We've always
found the staff keen to share
winemakers' stories and offer
great recommendations.

Australia
Melbourne
*City Wine Shop – Euro-leaning,
classic and cutting edge.*
*Blackhearts & Sparrows –
Natural, funky, local-focused.*

*Prince Wine Store – Deep range,
strong on Aussie and Euro
bottles.*
Sydney
*P&V Flagship for natural, low-
intervention wines.*

China
Hong Kong
*Watson's Wine – Widespread but
offers depth in fine wine.*
*Altaya Wines – Burgundy and
Bordeaux specialist.*
*Ponti Wine Cellars – Great for
sourcing rare European wines.*

England
London
*Hedonism Wines – Luxe,
collector's dream, rare and
fine bottles.*
*Shrine to the Vine – Impeccable
taste from the team behind
the magazine and restaurants
Noble Rot.*
*Berry Bros. & Rudd – Oldest
wine shop in London, timeless
and top-tier.*

France
Paris
*La Dernière Goutte – Great for
natural wines and tastings.*
*Juveniles – Wine shop and bar
hybrid with rare bottles.*
*Legrand Filles et Fils – Historic
arcade location, old-school
excellence.*

Japan
Tokyo
*Hasegawa Saketen (Tokyo
Station) – Curated
international selection, great
sake too.*

*Enoteca – High-end, beautifully
displayed wines from around
the world.*
*Vinos Yamazaki – Deep cellar
with fine Bordeaux and
Burgundy.*

Scotland
Edinburgh
*Raeburn – Always dusty back
vintages and gems hidden
away.*

USA
New York
*Chambers Street Wines –
Benchmark for natural and
old-world wines.*
*Flatiron Wines & Spirits – Huge
selection, great Burgundy and
California lists.*
*Le Dû's Wines – French-focused
with a sommelier's curation.*
*Astor Wines & Spirits – Iconic
shop with breadth and
education focus.*
San Francisco
*K&L Wine Merchants – Iconic,
encyclopaedic range, sharp
pricing.*
*Ruby Wine – Neighbourhood
favourite for natural and
minimal-intervention wines.*
*Bi-Rite Market (Wine Dept.) –
Small but fiercely curated.*

INDEX

FURTHER READING

Some of the brilliant resources we've pored over during our research include:

jancisrobinson.com
noblerot.co.uk
decanter.com
chateaumonty.com
wineanorak.com
wineenthusiast.com
worldoffinewine.com
wordonthegrapevine.co.uk
falstaff.com
wideworldofwine.co

ACKNOWLEDGEMENTS

Thank you to everyone who made this book possible!

Holly Sharpe, John Baum, Adam Michocki, Eljesa Saciri, Lance Foyster, Claire Thevenot, Ovidiu Draghici, Madeleine Waters, Jeri Kimber-Ndiaye, Andrew Platt, Josh Dunning, Jo Lory, Benedict Butterworth, Damon Quinlan, Ioana Statescu, Claire Strickett, LV, Maka from My Wine Trail, Ben Llewelyn, Charlie Blightman, Angus Barnes, Kate McFruin, Ellen McNair, David Murphy, Neil Ridley, Rupert Taylor, Clare Double, Lisa Pendreigh, Carol Lewis, Lizzie Frainier, Hugh Graham, Melissa York, Lucy Smith, Alice Kennedy-Owen, Shamar Gunning, Daisy Gudmunsen, Grace O'Byrne and Rafi Latif.